THE THIRD
DEGREE
THE BRENDON BATSON AUTOBIOGRAPHY

First published in 2023 by Curtis Sport

ISBN: 978-1-7398342-4-1

Cover design & Production Editor: Aidy Hewlett

Design and production by Curtis Sport

CONTENTS
The Third Degree

CONTENTS
The Third Degree

FOREWORD
Sir Lenny Henry

1978. What a time it was to support West Bromwich Albion. They were such a good team.

We had Laurie Cunningham, of whom Ron Atkinson said: "That lad could run through snow and not leave a footprint." Then there was Cyrille Regis, who took on Manchester United, got down and dirty with them in the mud at Old Trafford, and disproved that whole thing of "they don't like the cold" and "they're a bit lazy" and all that rubbish. Nice one Cyrille.

And, of course, there was always Brendon.

Brendon. Brendon, the missing piece of the jigsaw puzzle.

Cyrille and Laurie could have taken on the First Division as McFadden and Whitehead - rocking afros, Afghan coats, Fedoras and singing Ain't No Stopping Us Now- but now we had a third member.

There was something about three young, handsome and fit men of colour that captured the fans' imagination. They were christened the Three Degrees, for obvious reasons – because there were three of them and they were black, just like the girl group. Mind you I've never understood this logic: I would have called them The Supremes, which seems more apt.

But never mind all that.

At the time there was the cat-calling, racism and on-pitch roughhousing. But when it came to football, they were given a platform

> **At the time there was the cat-calling, racism and on-pitch roughhousing. But when it came to football, they were given a platform on which to reign.**

on which to reign.

Brendon's reach as a footballing icon was always far and wide - he played at the highest level, was appointed deputy chief executive of the PFA (the Professional Footballers' Association, not the Parliament-Funkadelic Alumnus, obviously) and did so much for black sportsmen and women.

He has an OBE and an MBE for services to football and his campaigning against racism. Respect.

And just on a personal note of admiration: damn, Brendon, did you look good on the pitch with that Afro.

Mad respect on all levels to Brendon and all that he's done over his career.

Enjoy what you are about to read.

Brendon, I salute you!

Sir Lenny Henry

Armchair fan of the Three Degrees

INTRODUCTION
Brendon Batson OBE

Firstly, thank you for picking up this book. I hope you enjoy the coming insights into my family life and my footballing career.

I undertook this project at the promptings of my family. My children, Zoe and Jason, and my five grandchildren were the catalyst for this. I was telling them stories and both Zoe and Jason said I needed to record as much as possible on paper, so the grandchildren could read it.

My sister-in-law Cutie decided to do her father Cecil Kenrick's story – he passed away when he was 97 - and it turned out to be a wonderful account. I thought I knew my father-in-law, but I didn't know his background story. His book is called Humble Beginnings and told of the sacrifices his own mother made.

And that made me think that, yes, I really need to tell my story. A few of my peers had published their stories so I thought that maybe now was the time – now that I've gone past my 70th birthday – to finally tell you a little bit more about my life so maybe my grandchildren, their children and beyond can learn all about my story.

From my point of view, it's a reflective and, at times, an emotional piece about some of the challenges my family and I have faced from those beginnings to where we are now. This has been a great experience for me because, as I've gone along, I've learned new things about my family, my life, my career and even recalled some memories of my own self.

I've returned to places of happiness, anguish, joy and sorrow. I now realise how many people have helped me on my journey, how many people I've met who have shaped my life across the years. For instance, you'll find out about my wife's Auntie Maysie Samuel, who introduced me to the niece who was to one day become my wife. She was one of the most influential people in my life because of the chain of events that led to me not only meeting, but later marrying Cecily.

Forget my football achievements, that was the best decision of my life.

I have made some good friends over the years, while working alongside some of the greatest in my industry.

You'll learn about the influence and values of Bertie Mee and the wonderful people at Arsenal who set me on my way in my professional career. I head to Cambridge to continue my footballing education. I move to West Bromwich, playing alongside some of the best footballers in the country.

You will read about how I came to terms with my playing career ending earlier than I'd planned. I will touch upon some personal accounts that I have never shared before. It won't surprise you to know you will also read about some of the more uncomfortable moments in my life, when I was subjected to abuse because of my skin colour and the consequences of those horrible and hurtful remarks. You will also find out more about how some of my working and personal relationships were challenged over the years due to racism and discrimination.

I will give you an insight into myself as a person: the father, the granddad, the man who is immensely proud of the loving family that have supported me over the years.

I would like to thank all of those who helped bring this book to life, including author Chris Lepkowski who ghosted my words, the good people at Curtis Sport for bringing the book to fruition, and all the others who provided support, guidance, insight or simply jogged my memory about certain things.

Finally, I hope you find this book as enjoyable and fulfilling to read as it was for me when I explored and reflected on my own journey to where I am now.

Brendon Batson OBE, September 2023.

INTRODUCTION
Chris Lepkowski

I have known Brendon for the best part of 25 years, so to be given an opportunity to showcase his story was, and remains, a huge honour. I thought I knew Brendon, but it wasn't until we started the journey that I realised just how much more there was to his background and so many of the other milestones that helped shaped his life. It has been a privilege to work alongside Brendon on this project and I hope you, as a reader, get as much enjoyment from the subsequent chapters as I did in helping to deliver them.

I do have one further disclosure – there is part of this book that Brendon knew nothing about. I felt it would be fitting to gather a collection of tributes from some of Brendon's family, friends and former colleagues from across his career.

I would like to thank the following people for their personal comments about Brendon: Dan Ashworth, Alan Biley, Len Cantello, David Garrett, Charlie George, David Harrison, Lord Herman Ousley, Mark Palios, Bryan Robson OBE, Gordon Taylor OBE, Bob Wilson OBE, Henry Winter and Garth Wooldridge.

In addition, I extend further gratitude to Pamela Roberts for her hospitality and kindness; Geoff Snape of the WBA Former Players' Association for his guidance, support and contacts' book; Professor Diane Kemp of Birmingham City University and, of course, Sir Lenny Henry for his wonderful and amusing tribute to Brendon. On which note, I salute his management team for allowing us to use Jake Turney's Comic Relief photo. Brendon, I appreciate you lending me your scrapbook - some of which has been reproduced in the photo section.

I also thank Godfrey Batson, Diann Jacobs, Jason Batson and Zoe Batson for their lovely words, and to Curtis Sport for their patience and assistance in making this book possible. The front cover photo was produced by Monica Monje Fotografia Calpe. She can be found on Instagram @LiveLoveMiau.

Back to you Brendon...

Chris Lepkowski, ghostwriter of The Third Degree, September 2023

CHAPTER ONE
Welcome to the UK

"Maybe cricket is your game?"

Let me introduce myself. I was born Brendon Matthias Batson.

I was born in a place called Sauteurs in Grenada on February 6, 1953. My mum was Grenadian. She was a wonderful woman – someone I will tell you more about.

My family were actually Trinidadian. I've got an older brother and sister who were born in Trinidad. My father Lennox was Trinidadian. He and my mother Evelyn split before I was born and she went onto Grenada, so I never saw him during my time over there. Me? I consider myself Grenadian. And I was the baby of the family.

My earliest memories are of playing along Darvey Beach. I've always had a fondness for the sea and the coast. That's a strange thing to say perhaps given I was to spend so much of my life in the landlocked London and the West Midlands. But home has always been back home.

And I love my beaches. Grand Anse Beach in Grenada is one of the best 10 beaches in the world and I have so many happy memories of running along there. There was a big jetty along there and I can remember running off that jetty and jumping into my mum's arms. She would always collect me. I always felt safe with my mum and that was something that stayed with me forever. She was always there for us, even in deep water, when I often wondered how she was managing to stay afloat in what I assumed to be the deep ocean.

As I said, I have two siblings. Diann is five years older, Godfrey is four years older. As you can imagine, I would get away with murder as the youngest one. My brother was always tough. What would usually happen is that Godfrey would be tough, I would be crying about something or other, and then my mum would run in and would blame him. My first line of defence was to scream at the top of my voice and get my mother to come in to reprimand my brother. Godfrey, for that, I can only apologise.

My mother was the rock of our family. She was everything, she was my world.

Mum was also a nurse. She worked for a local hospital in the early 1960s. We had an uncle called Sinclair, who lived in Antigua. For a while my brother went across there to live with him and my auntie Pat. They had two children – Laurie and Sharon. Laurie was 6ft 6ins and Sharon was 6ft 1ins. We had height in that part of the family. I remember at one point we were split up, so my brother spent time there. My sister spent time with my mum's sister. We were scattered a lot during those early years, which was unsettling at times but also part of my life. I knew nothing else, so it seemed normal.

Six years went by unremarkably, although I did almost get run over by the local taxi driver. I went down the steps next to our house and ran out without looking. My mum just heard the brakes squeal and the taxi driver called Bruno – who I got to meet many years later – almost ran me over. My mum came down and gave me a right telling off and I skulked off back home with my tail between my legs. I could be quite injury prone as a kid and poor mum, who spent most of her working life tending to people, spent way too often in hospital because of our little accidents or my many scrapes. I even managed to break my collarbone falling off the roof when I was only about five-years-old. I'd clambered from a window onto the roof, managed to lose my footing and I actually fell down, literally on to one of my sister's friends. She broke my fall, but I still managed to break my collarbone. She was okay and I should be grateful she was there otherwise the consequences for me would have been far worse. Diann had a really bad fall from a tree and got speared by one of the branches, suffering an injury to her thigh. My brother Godfrey was involved in all sorts of things – he even put his foot through a glass door at our home in St George's. The hospital was like our second home at times. But I was by far the clumsy one.

Despite all of this, I had a happy boyhood. My mum was very much the centre of my universe. What transpired later on is that my name had not gone on my birth certificate. I remember many years later Cyrille (Regis) telling me that his name was actually Gilbert – his uncle had forgotten his name when he went to register the birth – and I too had problems, which I only realised when I needed to produce my birth certificate and realised my name was not on it! I had to go back for my birth certificate later on...a friend had to go to the church in Sauteurs where it was in the register and got a duplicate birth certificate for me.

My mum felt indebted to go back to Trinidad because there were job opportunities. You have to remember that my mum had split up from my father very early on. I got the story from my uncle Mike, who was married to my aunt Monica Batson. When I went back as a 17-year-old to Trinidad I stayed with them as they owned a small guesthouse in Maraval in Port of Spain. He was a great storyteller and he told me about the split. Apparently, the family were dead against the break-up of the relationship, but my father was a drunk. He was an accountant and apparently a brilliant bloke, but he had a habit and that was alcohol. My mum decided it wasn't a good environment to be in, so she decided to leave. She was heavily pregnant, and having to look after my brother and sister. She booked our passage on a rust bucket boat to Grenada, which was a world away from the cruise ships that you get these days. Uncle Mike offered to pay for a flight, but she refused it and insisted on going under her own steam. My uncle's abiding memory is my mum getting onto this boat with a huge belly and two children, one either side. As it transpired, the captain of the boat gave my mum his cabin. But that was my mum – she always put us first in all she did, even if that meant being apart from us at times or moving us from one place to another.

As for my father, I only remember meeting him twice and that was in Trinidad in the time before I moved to England. One was in extremely unpleasant circumstances, and the other time being when he promised to buy me a pair of trousers, but never did. I could smell the alcohol on his breath. You don't think of that being bad or unusual, but only later did I realise he had a habit. The other time there was almost a fight between him and my brother because he was drunk and being aggressive to my mum on the one occasion he came to visit. My brother and sister had memories of him and they had more to do with him later on a letter-exchanging basis. I didn't really have that. I remained a stranger to him, he was a stranger to me. That's fine. I considered mum to be my mum and dad.

Moving around was a big part of my early life. We moved to St Paul's, another part of Grenada, before moving onto the capital Saint George's. We lived on the corner of Tyrrel Street and Green Street. Whenever I go back there I always look it up to see the changes.

Those early years, I cannot remember the school I went to in St George's. My main memories were of running along Grand Anse beach and enjoying myself as any kid would. But there was nothing extraordinary. Mum was a nurse; she cared for people. That's how I remember her.

And then things changed. We had moved to Trinidad where my mum got a job on a ship and we were then billeted to a family called the Valentines, who had no children. That was a desperate time for us, especially myself – although I dare say we all struggled. I hated it. Mum was away on the boat while we were in Trinidad with this family. I was only about seven or eight-years-old. What made it worse and more horrible was that we lived near the docks and could hear the ships coming in. We would be waiting and waiting, hoping it would be mum's boat. It never was…until, one day, eventually it was!

Firstly, we were away from my mum, but also because of the way this family treated us. My mum would send us little gifts from the ship and they would practically ration them, like they were punishing us for the slightest thing. My mum always explained everything to us when we were little. She was honest, but protective when she needed to be. I would complain about everything, but I knew it would make things worse for my mum if I complained too much, so I always did my best to hold it in. Quite often during this period I would be bursting to say what I really felt but I could see my sister glaring at me: "Don't you dare say a word." She knew it would make life harder for my mum. Mum would bring stuff back from the United States and Canada – which was always really exciting for us – but I also remember being sad when she left. It was draining for me when mum was away from us, but looking back now I appreciate she was building a future for us. We just didn't always realise it at the time.

I've never been totally sure how she formulated our future plans, but I know she met my uncle in England – my uncle being my father's brother Dennis and, and his wife Sybil – and decided to make new plans for us, in a new country, away from Trinidad and Grenada. Dennis and Sybil had two children, David and Esla, with Marcelle to follow. I still see Marcelle now, she lives in Coventry. My mum clearly realised things weren't right at the Valentines and she realised we would have better opportunities in the UK. This was part of the Windrush generation and at the time England was looking for support to rebuild the economy after the war. During this period we were living in Diego Martin west of Port of Spain the capital of Trinidad and I think that's when my mum came up with the plan to move the family to England with my brother Godfrey and me going first. She told us what the plan was - basically, she said it was an adventure and promised that she and our sister would be joining us in two years time. I was nine-years-old at the time; it was 1962. We were under the impression England was paved with streets of gold. That's what we were told. There was a Calypso song about how we were moving to paradise, how the British were all welcoming. And my God were we in for rude awakening. Despite the thought of being away from my mum I knew that she always kept her promises and true to her word she joined us after two years.

My official identity was actually quite confusing for a while. In 1978 I needed to renew my passport. It came back, snipped, so it was no longer valid. I had to become naturalised Briton because before then we were members of the British Commonwealth and by right we were British citizens. They changed the immigration laws in 1971 and that's what caused so many problems. The move for independence in Grenada started in 1962. First there was Jamaica in 1962, followed by Trinidad in 1966, and then Grenada in 1974. Jennifer Hosten, from Grenada, had won the Miss World title in 1970. It's funny what you remember.

I was nine when we arrived in England in 1962. My mum had promised us faithfully that she and my sister would join us in two years. My brother and I arrived at Heathrow and that in itself was an experience. I remember being excited because I'd never been on a plane and here we were travelling to England on a BOAC flight, an airline which later became British Airways.

Oh, and another thing – nobody had warned me about the weather. It was bloody cold when we arrived and, bearing in mind we arrived in April, it was hardly mid-winter. Little did we know what was to hit us a few months later when we experienced the winter of 1962/63, which was the coldest for 30 years and remains the most perishing winter of my life. I'd never seen snow before, so there was so much that was new, but we were looking forward to the experience.

This was all new to me. For instance, we'd never seen a television. We were in a council house and everyone crowded around this tiny little box, showing black and white programmes. I remember two shows. One was Yogi Bear, the other was Coronation Street. You have to remember I was from Grenada and had lived in Trinidad, so watching Coronation Street was like watching a TV programme from a different planet and speaking in a foreign language – we couldn't understand a word they were saying in that northern accent. Come to think of it, we really struggled with the English cockney accent in Tilbury, which is where we would come to settle. I used to guess whether to say "yes" or "no" and just nodded if I thought it was the right thing to do. Truth is, I didn't have a clue what to do. People must have thought I was an imbecile, looking back, because I clearly had no idea what they were saying.

Anyway, this journey to Heathrow. Mum had told us that we must not go to anyone other my uncle Dennis - he would meet us at Heathrow Airport and we must not go anywhere else. During the course of the flight, just as we were approaching landing, I had a fizzy drink and then we hit turbulence as we began our descent. I rushed off thinking I was going to be sick and by then the seatbelt signs came on and, although I wasn't sick, I still felt a little unwell so the stewardess told me and my brother to sit in these first class seats. We landed and the stewardess came over and told us to disembark. As I went to get up my brother flung his arm across me and said "don't move" and reminded me that our mum had told us we had to wait for my uncle. He wasn't moving until my uncle arrived. Obviously, that wasn't possible so we ended up being the last people to leave the plane, along with the pilot, who escorted us off the plane. Thankfully, we finally met my uncle and got on the train to Tilbury, which is in Essex, near Grays, Gravesend and Thurrock. As we were on the train my uncle got a dishcloth out of his bag, along with a knife, and then we spotted he had this apple. But this apple was green – a Granny Smith as it happens – but we were only used to red apples that you get in Canada and the States. My brother leant over to me and said: "Don't eat it…you'll get tummy ache." It was a shock – it was so acidic. I fell in love with it straight away. And that was my first moment in England, eating a green apple. And then, down came the snow…

I remember how cold it was. My brother and I were wearing thick Worcester jackets and trousers because it was absolutely freezing. The first thing I noticed was how alike my uncle was to my father. By this point I'd only met my father twice and they weren't fond memories. The first time was one I'll never forget. Back in those days you'd buy your trousers from a tailor, so I would be measured up and he was going to buy them for me. I was so excited and yet all I remember is that we went to the tailor, I got measured and he stank of drink. I never did get those trousers. The second time was when he came to our home with another bloke and two women. My mum persuaded me and my brother to go to the cinema. Well, my brother was a bruiser during this period, and he was literally confronting my father and my father was confronting him back. I was frightened for my brother as he was only 13, yet here he was standing up to our father. In the end, we went to the pictures to get out of the house and that was the last time I saw him. My mum stood her ground and she saw him off while we were gone. I will never know what that row was about and, in a way, I never wanted to know much about him. I felt I was better off without him because he was a stranger to me.

I saw my mum struggle throughout my life and although at the time I never noticed this, I realise all of this on reflection. It was a tough period for my mum and she did all she could to give us a better life, even sacrificing her own happiness to ensure we had a good future. I will never forget that. She sent us away; she went away herself. I look back all those years on and cannot imagine not seeing my children or grandkids for that long? Kids need their mothers. Even as a grandfather, if someone said to me I cannot see those grandkids for two years I think it would put me in an early grave – that's how close I am to my family. And that's because I remember how it was then, and those years shaped me. My mother was effectively both of my parents rolled into one.

We had two years with my uncle and aunt and those were a great two years, but he was very strict in a West Indian style. If you had to be disciplined, it would be a beating. Not a tap, but a full-blown trousers-down and a shoe. That was the way. Mum never laid a finger on us. But the way we lived meant Uncle Dennis and Auntie Sybil effectively became mum and dad. I was yearning to call someone mum and dad and it was an extremely difficult two years for me.

That discipline taught me some parental skills – not least how not to be a parent - but that's how it was in those days. These were days when you could smack kids, but these weren't smacks, but something more brutal and painful. Looking back now it was a real discipline for two boys – myself and Godfrey. Thankfully, my mum came back at the right time for us because it was becoming tough for us. That said, I didn't suffer that so-called punishment too often. I was very disciplined around time-keeping and I made sure I behaved myself when around elders. It's something that I was to learn even more at Arsenal. When the whole family – including my uncle and aunt – came to England it was about getting a better education and improve our job prospects. My uncle Dennis became a chief laboratory technician and my aunt became a midwife, seemingly delivering half of Tilbury. Those were good jobs back then.

Tilbury was a working-class area in the 1960s. Now it's a different place and very gentrified but back then it was a dock area, with working units and a migrant community who came to work. England was looking for support in transportation, the NHS and all the menial jobs that many English people were unwilling to go for. My uncle and aunt were young parents and they had ambitions. It was quite funny because if you were black and living in Tilbury then you were basically a Batson. There was nobody else of that description. Life was very limited for us as a youngster before I came to England. I had an uncle who was into music. His two sons were very talented in music, and he played a keyboard, but I was just interested in running along the beach. I don't remember being interested in sport. People ask me: "What was your pathway into football?" and literally I just ran. And I ran because I was quick. When I first arrived in England it was right at the start of the athletics season so, before we closed for the summer holidays, we had our annual sports events for our different classes. On the field you were expected to run against your peers. On this occasion, not long after I arrived in England, we had white lines marked out. I had no idea what they were. Back in Trinidad I play on a beach where you were surrounded by these trees that produced this spiky fruit. They would give you a good sting when they hit you so when you were running you would do so in a zig zag to avoid being in the shadow of those trees – to make sure those retched fruit didn't rain down onto you. Anyway, fast forward to England and I'm running on this grass track and won easily but the lad who came second said I was going to be disqualified. I had no idea what he was talking about, and it was basically because I hadn't run within the lines – I'd been zig-zagging all over the place and still managed to run quicker than anyone else. It was my first experience of running within lanes and I had no idea about lane discipline. That was St Mary's school in Tilbury, which was run by nuns. Those were good, largely happy days.

Football was new to me, and I got into it thanks to a lad called Dennis Sheridan, who was one of my best friends at St Mary's. He was my first mate at school in Tilbury, when I was the only black lad at school. As I said earlier, back then, if you were black and living in Tilbury, then you were a Batson – we were literally the only black people there. What I also remember is being on the bus with my aunt Sybil. There was a woman in front with a child and this boy kept looking around at me and my aunt, and he eventually turned to his mother and said: "Why are they so dirty?" My aunt started to explain why we were that colour, and I could see the mother of the child pulling him out of embarrassment. Yet he kept on asking questions. Sometime later, you would see a lot of black children being adopted by white families. There was a lot of that at the time. There was a notion that some of those children had confused identity because they weren't aware of their heritage, having been adopted at such an early age. They were being brought up in white households so even stuff as daft as how you look after your hair became an issue, because black people have such different hair. Another problem was the food we were eating. My aunt and uncle maintained as many Caribbean standards as they could. There was no community as such, but the problem was that English food was so bland. Fridays were fish-and-chips night. Many of us brought up on the old-style Catholic faith would only eat fish on a Friday so on one occasion my brother Godfrey, my cousin David and myself approached this fish shop. The smell was horrific. I could feel my stomach turning before I had even stepped into the shop. Back in Trinidad I had no concept of fish and chips, yet here I am seeing people putting this giant battered fish and something called chips, and literally eating it out of a newspaper. I had no idea what was going on. Now, I love fish these days but at the time I didn't know what it was and within two minutes of eating that fish I was throwing up. To this day I don't eat fish in batter. My brother, meanwhile, loves fish and chips. Me? No, it's not for me. That English food, I just couldn't cope with. It meant my family were relying a lot on cooking West Indian food, which in those days wasn't very easy to produce because you just couldn't get the ingredients, especially spices. We had to improvise. I would go for dinner at my friends' houses and couldn't believe how bland their food was. We ended up having to cook for ourselves. My cousin Esla was especially good. She would cook for us when she could.

My uncle Dennis ended up buying a house in Grays, which remains in the family. Our life was disciplined. My uncle would be working during the week and on Saturday we had to clean the house. He would inspect it when he came back from work and if he found a spec of dust then we would have to start all over again. He was so strict. It stays with me.

Salvation was on its way, not least when my mum finally arrived, two years to the day after we arrived in England. I recall the letters in the Par Avion envelopes that would come once a month and cause such excitement because you knew it was an international delivery – which meant it was likely to be from mum. Yet I also remember during the build up to her arrival I was very nervous and agitated, panicking that she might not come or that something might go wrong. I can remember being sat at home hearing the taxi arrive. We didn't know if she had arrived, was safe or anything… and then I saw my sister and mum emerge from the taxi. It remains one of the most joyous moments of my life. I can still picture it now and I knew then that for the first time in my 11 years I felt like we were finally a proper family. The four of us were now together and it was the most amazing feeling. We were going to be as one. I was so happy back then.

We moved to a tiny place in Chadwell Heath. It was between a small supermarket and a laundrette. We had a lounge/dining room and a kitchen with two small bedrooms upstairs. The door was so small that I would have to walk sideways these days. It was dark and we needed a fold down table because it was so small, but we scrubbed it and scrubbed it to within an inch of its life, which was a proper West Indian thing. At this point my mum started working at the London Hilton having secured a transfer from the Trinidad Hilton where she was head housekeeper. That's where she met her future husband and my stepdad, who was sous chef at the London Hilton. I was well pissed off at the time, because just as my mum returned this bloke appeared on the scene. He was an English guy called Desmond Moore. They got together and when they did my brother and sister were onto me saying: "Don't you dare look disappointed" because they knew I was a little bit upset over it. But he was a very supportive man. He was lucky my mum was a driving force because she strived to make everything better.

By this point I was 12-years-old and I don't recall my mum marrying a white man being an issue at the time. Back then I wasn't really aware of that being a potential issue although this was a time when programmes on TV started to change. You had the Black & White Minstrels, which I absolutely hated – these white people depicted as black people - and the other thing that irritated the hell out of me was Robinson's Jam, with the Golliwog character. All the white kids it seemed to me had them as toys, which was utterly bizarre. Within a few days of being at school I was in the queue for school and this lad called me Chocolate Drop. I had no idea what he was talking about. Anyway, when I realised what he meant, the penny dropped that I was being attacked because of who I was. I was hurt and wanted to fight people. That was the first time I realised I was being picked on because of my skin colour and I had it out with this lad. A few days later this same lad turned up with his brother and gave me a bit of a beating. I ended up going home with ripped trousers. When I got home I scuttled off and hid. I never said a word to my brother who was in the senior school, but somehow he found out and he went round there and gave this lad a right thrashing. Nobody bothered me again after that. My view was that I was always going to defend myself. I then moved to senior school and went to Thurrock Boys. The first day there I was in a fight. Somebody called me something and at break I went for him. Before you know it, I was up in front of the headmaster...on my first day at school. I would never repeat what was said to me whenever I was dragged in front of the head teachers. As far as I was concerned, I was guilty of fighting, so it was on me. I was the one fighting and I owned it, despite me being picked on or called racist names. I knew I was fair game for comments. Another one was Wog, named after the Golliwog. That was a popular name to call me because of Robinson's Jam. And then there was Nigger, which was and still is a horrible word. I was called a Racoon, because of the black face. But it was Chocolate Drop when the penny dropped. Yet I never sought interventions from teachers. I fought my own battles. I didn't want to be that snitch, and I also knew my silence would bring me some respect. And on the occasions when my brother got involved, nobody touched me after that.

We moved to Walthamstow when mum got married and my sister, brother and I all went to a school called McEntee Technical School. Before moving to Walthamstow I'd gone from playing football for the school, to playing for Thurrock Boys and was also playing for a team in Barking called Rippleway Rangers who played on a Sunday. Very soon I was playing against lads two years older than me. It was also the time my brother had left school. That gave me two problems – my brother is no longer there, and I've got the resentment against me because I'm quite good at football and taking up the place of some other boy of that age group who thinks he or his mate should be in that side. That pretty much made me a No1 target for some. I got involved in this huge scrap with an older boy. Back then there was this road where you'd meet to fight after school. It was called Monoux Grove, which these days is around the corner from the Arsenal academy. Back then the residents there used to complain about all the boys turning up after school to have fights, but you knew it was better scrapping there than at school. People would be hanging out of windows threatening to report us for fighting. Anyway, on this one occasion I had a Bounty chocolate bar. I loved them and I still love them now. I'd bought this Bounty and was walking by when a lad came along and hit my arm. I saw my Bounty spin off into a puddle. I just lost my rag and said: "I'll see you down Monoux Grove." He was two years older than me but I gave him a right thrashing. Nobody touched me again. I went home with a split lip, a ripped shirt and had to explain to my mum about the fight. A few days later some lads who were friends of the lad I had the fight with drove past me as I left school making gun gestures with their hands at me. I was fourteen and thought this was getting out of hand so had to tell my mum. From there she went to the school and reported it. But a lot of these lads ended up becoming my friends. The respect between us grew and as we got older, we grew up. By then we had the Enoch Powell Rivers of Blood speech in 1968 and tensions were getting worse. We were still living in the shadows of people displaying signs saying: "No Blacks, No Irish, No Dogs", and as you get older you realise how awful those inequalities were. I knew I was an outsider. Football was very kind to me and the players of my generation – which might seem like a strange thing to say as we continue through my journey – but I heard some horrific stories of black lads on building sites, productions lines or in factories. I heard one story of a black lad who worked at a major car company as a mechanic and was racially abused on a regular basis. Back then if you broke the production line in one of those factories, the whole manufacturing process ground to a sudden halt and would be costly to the company. When that happened, with no good reason, there were no second chances. The cost of breaking that production line was an instant sacking. Anyway, this one guy was being racially abused. He obviously had enough and picked up a monkey wrench to defend himself. He was sacked. No defence. Nobody was interested in sob stories. There was no HR, no equal opportunities. The person abused got the boot, not the aggressor. That's how it was. And it made me realise what black people were up against.

You might be reading this by now wondering where the football is. It is coming. But actually, my journey didn't really involve football. You ask an eight-year-old boy or girl now and some might want to be a football player. That wasn't the case with me. In fact, it was almost an accident – you could even call it divine intervention. As I said earlier, I went to one Catholic school run by nuns and it was very religious. And Religious Instruction had a very heavy presence on the timetable. On this one particular day there was double Religious Instruction at the end of the day, and it quickly became apparent that the lads who were in the football team were allowed to miss this particular lesson. At this point I don't think I'd ever played football. In the autumn my friend Dennis Sheridan told me about this get out clause to get out of this Religious Instruction. The teacher, or coach if you prefer, was Mr Fitzgerald who agreed to give me a trial for the school team. My friend Dennis had told me say any position bar the goalkeeper because nobody wants to play in goal. At the end of that trial, Mr Fitzgerald said: "Where do you come from Batson?" I always said: "I was born in Grenada, moved to Trinidad and then came to England." He said: "That's in the West Indies isn't it... so maybe cricket is your game?" He must have seen me welling up and starting to cry, so he told me to come back the following week. During that period Dennis and I went to the local daisy fields and would play football. He had a ball, so we'd take that. Then other kids would arrive with better balls and we would keep swapping the balls for whichever one was the best, with the remaining balls lined up along the side. Of course, what quickly became apparent is that as the bigger boys started peeling off to go home, they'd pinch the best of the balls that was lying along the side and we'd end up going home with a worse ball than the one we arrived with. It was 20-a-side during the peak of the kickabout so if you have two touches per game you'd be thrilled. That week I played so much that I got home late. And woe betide me if I got home after my uncle Dennis had got home. I remember the first time he hit us was because we got home late. He hit me, and I'd run off upstairs. He hit my brother and I could see my brother fuming and forming a fist with his hands. Anyway, a few days later I was in the school team. I was nine, going on 10-years-old, and this was the first time I'd kicked a football. Not long after that I was asked to go for trials at Thurrock Boys. I was put in at right-back – maybe nobody else wanted to go there – and I remember having a trial in that position. I was coming back after one of the trials on a Saturday morning and I knew my Uncle Dennis and Auntie Sybil weren't back. They both had a Volkswagen Beetle, those original ones that you could hear a mile away. I also knew I had to take my shoes off in the boiler room, get out of my school clothes and then clean my shoes. That was the requirement. On this occasion I decided to have a kick about with my mates and had chalk dust on my shoes. I got home later than I should have, I was getting changed upstairs and then I heard that noise – that distinctive noise of a Volkswagen Beetle approaching the house. My uncle walked in, marched into the boiler room and saw the chalk dust on my shoes. He gave me one hell of a beating. I was 10-years-old, but I never did it again. Anyway, I got picked for Thurrock Boys, we got to a final but didn't win whatever cup it was, but I do remember we played in a stadium in Thurrock – the first proper stadium I played in – and I recall it was totally foggy. You couldn't see a thing. My aunt came and all I could hear was her clapping her leather gloves together and yelling in a West Indian accent: "COME ON BRENDON", but I couldn't actually see her. I went up to get my runners-up medal and the bloke who handed it over said: "I think you're going to be a success." That always stuck in my mind. It was somebody from the county FA – I have no idea who it was. But that stayed with me. And that's where it started.

By now we were living in this little place I mentioned earlier between the supermarket and laundrette, when we had a knock on the door. It was a bloke from Rippleway Rangers. He said: "Is your mum in?" He comes in, introduces himself to my mum and said: "I've heard about your son, I'd like him to play for my team." We were living in Chadwell, so I had to go from there, get to the station, get on a train, he would meet me at Barking, he would take me to the game, drop me back at the station, I would then get the train home. It must have taken hours. And now I think back and ask: "Would I let my 10-year-old boy do that?" Not a chance.

In terms of my football education that was the best I could wish for. I was playing with lads I'd never met before. The excitement of getting up, getting the train, wondering if I was on the right train and, trying to navigate my way across that part of London, was an adventure for me – it was a little bit different to the Caribbean as you can imagine.

What I quickly realised is that if it rained the night before there was a good chance the game would be off. The first time that happened I was devastated because I'd spent all week building up to this game – it was the focal point of the weekend. The whole weekend was ruined, as far as I was concerned. So, if it rained, we would leave even earlier, meet up and have a kick about anyway so even if the game was called off, we would have some football to enjoy. Soon after, we moved to Walthamstow, and I was travelling even further to Barking. This time we had a knock on the door again and a man came in and said: "I'd like Brendon to play for our team" so I joined for a team called Walthamstow Rangers. I was 13-years-old, and for the first time ever I was shocked to see a mixed race player on the other side. It was a shock for me to see another boy who looked vaguely like me.

And then along came a guy called Johnny Ellingham. He was a very successful grocer, who ran a very exclusive fruit and veg shop. I say his shop was exclusive because it was situated in a very affluent area of Finchley, on Ballards Lane. He also ran a pretty decent football team called Mildmay, and a collection of young footballers who were all on professional books. He always looked for the best players and a number of us went on to sign apprenticeships with pro clubs. There was Terry Burton, who played for Arsenal, coached with Don Howe and eventually went to West Brom as a Technical Director, managed Wimbledon and, most recently has been working for Crystal Palace. He and I became good friends at Arsenal. Then there was Ray Clarke, who played for Tottenham, Ajax, Newcastle and Brighton among other clubs. There was also Micky Dillon, who played 20-odd times for Spurs, before moving to the States where he became one of the first to play for New York Cosmos, alongside Pele and Franz Beckenbauer. Those were good days. We used to travel on the back of his fruit and veg lorry. I would work in his shop during the summer. Finchley is a very affluent area so we would get so many tips. Simon Dee, who was a former Radio Caroline DJ, would often come in. He would always drive up and down Ballards Land in his convertible Triumph Stag. He was very famous back then. Ray Dorset, the lead singer of Mungo Jerry, would also pop in for his groceries, not long before his In the Summertime hit. He'd be coming in for his fruit and veg – how's that for a claim to fame? Every Friday, Johnny would give me a big box of fruit and say: "Here you are son...take that home for your mum." He would take so much pride in his fruit and veg. He used to have us polishing the grapefruits and melons.

33

As for the football, that was an enjoyable time for me. We were playing in the Regents Park League, which could be a rough-and-ready league at times. The one time we played a team called Flomar. They were real racist bastards; they were horrible. They hated us because we were good players. We were getting abuse, and this was schoolboy level. It was horrendous. We got into so many fights. Back then you couldn't show any weakness. I don't remember thinking about it in my head. I simply had the red mist come down and I just lashed out. What helped was that I could show people I was a good player.

Unbeknown to me at the time, but a guy called George Male saw me when I was 13 playing for Waltham Forest. George had been a great player for Arsenal under Herbert Chapman and was now one of the main scouts at Arsenal. They were and always have been one of the greats of English football; a north London giant of huge tradition. Bertie Mee was the manager at the time, having replaced Billy Wright. Don Howe was the coach and Steve Burtenshaw was reserve coach, with Ernie Wally as youth team coach. That was quite a thing when I got invited to Arsenal. It was 1966 and we met the England World Cup Winners at Highbury. I remember Alan Ball and Nobby Stiles were among those I spoke to. Nobby came out, looked at me and said: "Blimey you're tall." Little did I realise then that I would one day become good friends with Alan Ball.

Football was about to become more than just a hobby.

TRIBUTE

What can I say about my little brother?

Growing up between Grenada and Trinidad up to the age of nine years, Brendon showed no interest in any sport, even when we play cricket on the beach or kicked a football. He had to be bribed or threatened with bodily harm before he would join in! I don't think anyone expected sport to be so important in his life.

That all changed after we arrived in England in 1962 and he discovered football. From then his whole focus was on playing and being the best.

He has been a true to himself in his profession and in family life. I felt so much pride when he was awarded with the MBE and then the OBE, never dreaming that he would go on to achieve so much more. The OBE was especially out-of-the-blue. We had a surprise party for him down in London, which he didn't know about. He was absolutely gobsmacked.

I'll never forget his face when he walked in. I remember he said: "I just wish mum had been here to see it." Brendon, she would have been so proud of you.

When I look back to those early day and the struggles he faced to be accepted as a professional footballer, I smile.

I never thought that a nine-year-old from Grenada – my very own little brother - would be thought of so highly by his fellow professionals, friends and family. He has achieved so much.

He is my little brother. And I'm immensely proud of him.

Godfrey Batson

TRIBUTE

My baby brother is very charming and a family person. Godfrey and myself always used to tease him that he fell into a cesspit he would come out smelling of roses.

That reminds me of an incident where his late wife Cecily and myself went out to the cinema with Brendon in London. We were walking along the embankment, with Brendon in the middle linking arms with myself and Cecily – I said he was like the rose between the two thorns. This approaching male went past me and as he did so he deliberately brushed my thigh, so as he did so I swung around and slapped him. And because I had the other arm linked with Brendon's, he was turned around by my movement and was like: 'What's happened? What's going on?' Cecily and myself pretty much got hold of Brendon's arms and frogmarched him away to make sure he didn't get into any trouble.

Brendon has always been a family man. He is a proud father and grandfather. When the three of us were little, we'd play a game of cards – he and my mother would always cheat, much to the frustration of myself and Godfrey. We'd be playing along and see Brendon or mum scratching her nose and we knew they were up to something!

Brendon has achieved so much in his life. I am very proud of him, but the problem is Brendon doesn't like to talk about these things. He should do because he has had a wonderful career and life. We're all so proud of him.

Diann Jacobs (née Batson)

CHAPTER TWO
Arsenal

"...Remember where you are, who you are, who you represent..."

I was playing a lot of football as a schoolboy. Having been selected for Waltham Forest Boys, George Male approached me and invited me to train at Highbury, in a big indoor facility behind the Clock End, after school on Mondays and Thursdays. And that was my introduction to Arsenal. I was 13-years-old and travelling across London on my own even then.

I signed schoolboy forms when I was 14-years-old. There was a gentleman called Ken Friar, who later became a very senior director at Arsenal, who was the assistant secretary at the time. We became good friends in later years. There is a statue of a boy going to the match on the concourse at the Emirates Stadium which actually depicts Ken. He oversaw the construction of the current Arsenal stadium and it has been claimed that had he been in charge of the Wembley project, it would have come in on time and on budget. But that's another story.

George Male was my mentor going through my early years. I got to know a whole new bunch of lads and most of us were the best players in our respective boys or school teams but once we got into this group we were on a par. You couldn't get away with some of the things you can maybe do in your schoolboy teams – so you had to learn to adapt to that quickly.

I remember the one day being invited to return to training the following term. I arrived to find some of those boys I'd become friends with were no longer there. That's when you realised how brutal football could be. It made me think about how I needed to perform every Monday and Thursday. That led to trial matches and gradually I found myself playing more and more.

When I turned 15 I was playing a trial game at London Colney, which was their training home even then, and at some stage George told me Arsenal were thinking of offering me an apprenticeship. By then I was playing as a defender. George had actually seen me playing as striker initially but Arsenal had been moving me around and I was playing more as a defender. The coaches would assess you as to where you most suited. You look at Ray Kennedy, who started off as a main striker at Arsenal when they won the double, and then at Liverpool he ended up becoming one of the best left-sided midfielders I've ever seen. There was one game where I was asked to play left-back, which felt like the wrong position to me because I was so right-sided, so I threw a bit of a sulk. George pulled me aside afterwards and said: "The manager (Bertie Mee) wasn't very impressed with your attitude."

I don't recall many players making it back then. There was Terry Burton, who I thought was a terrific player, and Jimmy de Garis, who was the youth cup captain. Both were released by Arsenal without being offered a pro contract. Each one of us had an appointment to see Bertie Mee. Terry and Jimmy came out crying. I was due in but went home instead. I thought I was bound to be released if the captain and one of the best other players in the side cannot get a new deal, what chance have I got? I then got a call asking me why I didn't come for my appointment. I remember my heart pounding, but when I got offered my first pro contract I couldn't believe it.

I had heard of Bertie Mee but I didn't actually meet him until I became an apprentice, and I certainly didn't realise he was watching some of those games. The big thing with Bertie was him knowing what your attitude was like as a person, not just as a footballer. I was quite lucky to be at Arsenal because they knew how to look after youngsters. It was a privilege, looking back. They had a reputation back then for being one of the best in football. But, even then, I cannot remember it dawning on me that I might become a professional footballer. I was just playing football and being part of games was a joy for me. I knew I was getting better but I didn't know to what extent so it became a bit of a surprise when I was offered an apprenticeship and later offering a professional contract.

I knew I was competitive. And I knew that was a strength during those initial stages. I remember two lads coming down from Scotland, who could clearly play but never made it. Partly that's because they were home sick but one of the things that had helped me is that moving around was part of my life. My mum sending my brother and myself to

England, having to adapt to a new environment actually helped me a lot during my career whereas others maybe struggled and couldn't settle.

The other thing I had was that I would be really embarrassed if I didn't play well because I could be easily identified – I was the only black footballer at Arsenal at this point. I would hear coaches talking about "the black kid". I knew I had to be better than my peers. It went back to my first experience at a trial at school when the teacher had told me that cricket was my game – there was no way I wasn't going to give football my best efforts. Another time I'd been pulled in by a headmaster and told: "There's no way you're going to be a footballer." These things made me more determined and more competitive. I absolutely hated losing. I was quick and if somebody was quicker, I would hate being second. I needed to win.

I remember the meeting with Ken Friar and Bertie Mee when I signed my apprenticeship at 16. Bertie spoke to my mum and stepfather Dessie. He said: "We think your son has got a chance to make a career within the game; we think he's got a chance of progressing at Arsenal but if he doesn't we will find him a better club." That always stuck in my mind.

As you'll discover later, an injury was to ruin my playing career. And the first serious one I had was in October 1969 when we played Chelsea in the South-East Counties League match. I had only signed in June and was playing for the youth team, who were then coached by Brian Whitehouse. Back then there was a culture with apprentices to discourage immediately calling for attention if you went down with a knock, so it was quite harsh if you were actually injured. Anyway, during the game I went into a tackle and as I did so I turned. My knee just gave way. Back then we had an old physio called Bert Owen, who was a fantastic guy. I suffered this knee injury on the Saturday. On the Monday I was on the table with this knee injury when Brian Whitehouse came in and made a joke about me being a softie. At that point Bert turned around and said: "Don't joke around…this lad has torn his cartilage." It was my right knee lateral cruciate – the same knee I was to damage again so many years later.

Bertie was a former physio so at least I felt I was at the right club in terms of medical care. Arsenal were one of the first clubs to have a tip-top medical set-up. Fred Street, who later became England physio, had a private practice in Harley Street and he helped me. I was really struggling to recover from the injury – it took me so long. They had the Pavilion at London Colney and I used to have to carry Bert Owen on my back as part of my rehab. And then I got told to pick wild mushrooms in the field. They'd made me run to collect these fungi that were growing next to the training ground. I'd hear a: "Go on boy, go and get that mushroom" and I'd be sent away to run across a field to find this mushroom and bring it back to them. Thankfully they didn't make me eat any.

I actually signed professional forms on my 17th birthday. I got called into a room and all of the coaching staff were there: Steve Burtenshaw, Don Howe, Brian Whitehouse and, of course, the manager Bertie Mee. Back then it cost a club £500 to sign a player on professional forms - £250 to register the player with the Football League, and the player got £250. Leading up to that, I had this urge to go back to the Caribbean. I was only on apprentice wages before I signed pro, so I was only on £16 a week and my mum also received £16 from the club for my board and keep. So, when I was to get £250, I went straight to the bank – I couldn't get there quickly enough. This was a huge amount of money for me. Barclays Bank was the bank of choice for Arsenal and where they had opened an account for me, so I went in to see the bank manager, told him I'd been offered a professional contract with Arsenal and was to receive £250. My fare to Trinidad was £252. About a week later, Bertie Mee called me in so I could sign officially. He wished me a good career, success at Arsenal and, then, as I was leaving he said: "Oh, and by the way Brendon, enjoy your holiday in Trinidad and Grenada." The bank manager had actually called the club to tell them I'd been in trying to get a loan.

That was a great trip. It was the first time I'd travelled back to the Caribbean having been in England for eight years and I spent a good six weeks there. Six months later early bird prices came in…my sister managed to get a ticket for a fifth of the price.

1971 was a great year for Arsenal. The first team won the League and FA Cup double, while the youth team – which I was very much part of – won the FA Youth Cup competition. I was still struggling with the injury a little bit and there was a threat from the medical staff to take out my other cartilage as they felt there would be an imbalance. One of the perverse things when you had a knee injury back then is that they would put the torn cartilage in a small container with some form of gel and leave it next to your bed so you can see what's come out of your knee. Mine looked like desiccated coconut where ordinarily it would have come out in one or two pieces, at the most. That's how bad it was. My whole cartilage had literally disintegrated. Back then they would slice your knee open and whip it out. Thank God for medical progress.

By now my brother Godfrey was into body-building and there was a gym just nearby where I lived in Walthamstow. I learned a lot about weight training and conditioning there. I learned that too many muscles would mean too much weight. I was told to strengthen the muscles around my knee by doing a lot of repetitive movements with smaller and lighter weights. By the time I returned from the injury, Arsenal were already doing well in the FA Youth Cup. I came back in time for the quarter-finals, which we won, ensuring our place in the semis. After that game we got taken out by Bertie Mee and the whole coaching staff to the Hunting Lodge in Haymarket. That was one of the best restaurants around at the time. None of us had been to anywhere like that before. I seem to recall I had lobster – I went for the most expensive thing I could find. It was a fantastic night and Bertie's philosophy was: "Some of you will have a career in the game – hopefully at the top end – and you need to know how to conduct yourselves in places like this."

We had a young Welsh lad who came from a mining village, who wasn't particularly streetwise. When it came to dessert, you could see him shaking behind his menu. It went to show all that Bertie Mee said was true. I knew a little bit about etiquette as my stepdad worked in a top London hotel, but others weren't aware which cutlery to use. It was all part of our education. A good lesson for those of us who ended up making careers out of the game, but also a great memory for those who dropped out of football. And that's what it was all about – it was about teaching some of us how to behave in the best restaurants, while giving some of us an experience of something we may not experience again. We beat Cardiff 2-0 on aggregate in the final.

Bertie is someone I had the utmost respect for. He ran that club. He brought in a motto: "Remember where you are, who you are, who you represent." These are values I hold myself as a result of that upbringing. I say to my kids that when they're out, they're not only representing the Batsons but also the black community. Bertie also made sure the

Arsenal first-team when flying to games travelled in two separate groups because of the Munich Air Disaster. He introduced that, knowing that while it was possible something might happen to one party, it was unlikely to happen to both. That's the presence of mind he had. He also made us hand our passports in because he knew that footballers would be careless and forget them. I rallied against that, but in the end I had to do it. Bertie Mee adopted the philosophy of "kill one, frighten ten thousand", meaning he would make examples of people to make a point. First team or not, if you breached discipline you would be punished in some way. He left players at away grounds, for instance. He would say: "The coach is leaving at 6pm"...and at 6pm sharp the coach would leave, whether you were on it or not. He didn't wait for anyone. As young players – those who didn't live near the training ground at London Colney – you would get picked up along the way. It was usually at Highbury, Southgate and Cockfosters. Those were the pick-up points. If you weren't there, you'd have to make your own way there. He wasn't just developing players, he was developing men because he knew many wouldn't make it. It wasn't just a footballing development scheme, but a process of building your personality and character.

Every year, with each new cohort of apprentices, he would ask Barclays Bank to come in and do a presentation to show us how to use our chequebook and offer us financial guidance. He had psychologists come in to work with us, to talk about our aspirations, what we were good at, what we could improve on, ask us what we were thinking about. He would ask how we felt – it was all very positive. Fred Street introduced aerobics into the training on the say so of Bertie. He was innovative in a lot of the things they wanted to do. He was big into what is now called player-liaison work, long before it became a thing.

As a person he was short in stature, but huge in presence and when he walked into a room you just knew you were in the company of somebody very special. When he arrived for training, everyone turned up their performance. He was the boss. Some managers don't like surrounding themselves with people who might threaten them, but Bertie wasn't like that. He wanted to have the best next to him – whether it was the best coach, best physio, etc, because he had that confidence in his own abilities as a manager.

There was a lad at the time called Russell Allen. He was a good player, a bit of a scallywag and he ended up being sacked by Bertie Mee. His dad Ronnie Allen was one of the great players in English football during the 1950s; he had great timing, a good passer and brilliant distribution. His son was very similar in style, but he got the sack after the quarter-finals of the FA Youth Cup. That was Bertie's philosophy: kill one, frighten plenty. He made an example of him for a misdemeanour. He ended up going to Tranmere after that, while I ended up working for his father at West Brom. It was very brutal how it ended for Russell. We'd been abroad on a tour and were called into a suite when we returned. Bertie stood up and said: "You all did so well representing our club. You were one of the youngest teams, you did us proud. But one of you let down the good name of Arsenal with his behaviour. Russell Allen, get your boots, get out of this club and never show your face at this club again."

The poor lad burst into tears as he walked out, yet he was one of our best players. That was Bertie – he was a stickler for discipline. I often wonder if Russell would have had a more successful career if it were not for his wayward ways.

Don Howe was the most fantastic coach in terms of precision. He made things very clear in what he wanted from you. Arsenal won the double thanks to him and Bertie, along with some very good players and staff members. Don had the team playing in a very straightforward way – up, back and through. The training drill was that from the back you would knock the ball up to the forwards, it would drop back into the midfield and then you started from there. George Armstrong was always the outlet. It wasn't about getting bogged down in midfield, but about going from the back to the front with quality, get it back into midfield where you would start to play – up, back and through – simple but effective. Don Howe made it very clear to the players what was needed. He made it simple, easy to understand, and it worked. He knew what the players needed. He was also very good at demonstrating what you had to do – I had no idea what he was like as a player, but it was clearly very evident that he was some footballer.

We'd have pre-match meetings where Bertie would come in and tell us what to do, before handing over to Don and leaving the room. Don would turn to us and say: "Forget everything he's said...here's what we'll do." Don looked after all of the tactical elements of that Arsenal side.

Back then Arsenal, were already thinking about pre-match fuel and nutrition. I remember going to reserve games on the train and we'd eat fillet steak, egg on top, beans on the side and then, after that, rice pudding. Sometime later we went on a pre-season trip to Scandinavia and noticed they were on a high glucose diet, so we brought that back and we'd be having tinned peaches on top of cornflakes. From that we started having pasta – again, long before other clubs.

By that 1970-71 season, I was already training with the first team quite a lot – often to make up numbers in training drills. I felt part of that first-team set-up, which was important to my development as a player and person. When you joined Arsenal, the pathway to progression was made very clear: the first-team would change in the home dressing room at Highbury, the reserve and youth team players would be in the away dressing room. And then there were the tracksuits. Youth team players had blue tracksuit tops, the reserve team players had green tracksuit tops and the first team players had red tracksuit tops. Your ambition was to get a red tracksuit and claim your place in the home dressing room.

At the end of that season Don left Arsenal to join West Bromwich Albion as manager. He was replaced at Arsenal by Bobby Campbell, who would manage Chelsea some years later. There was a suggestion that when Don left, Bertie Mee seemed to lose that sparkle and he never quite had that same chemistry with Bobby, who was quite a brash bloke. Bobby used to call me Shaft after the film at the time and we got on well, but it looked like he and Bertie was never the same as Don and Bertie.

My first-team debut came against Newcastle a year later. I was described as a dark-limbed footballer by some of the newspapers. That's how it was back then. I came on for Charlie George at half-time – he was unwell in the dressing room - and was told to go on into midfield. We lost that game 2-0. It was cold, and miserable, and wet. And I remember the chants. I heard lots of monkey chants; I heard references to my skin colour. My own feelings were of nervous excitement. It went by me in a blur as far as the game was concerned. What I do remember was Malcolm MacDonald was playing and there was an altercation between him and Alan Ball – so there was big Malcolm, with his teeth out, angry and snarling, against little Bally with his high-pitched voice. It wasn't a fair contest.

That was my first time as a substitute, back in a time when substitutes weren't always used. I'd been among the travelling party but never made it to the bench, and the day I did get named as a sub, I went on. What I didn't realise at the time was that I was the first black footballer to play a first-team game for Arsenal. That never came into my mind until many years later – but what did stick out were those vile chants. Looking back, I felt proud being the black bloke on the team. You have to remember that when I came to England I had never even kicked a football, and here I was playing for Arsenal's first team. Arsenal guided me through it.

As part of our education at Arsenal we had to sit behind the dug-out during games and analyse the games as they went on. So, one of us would have to count how many tackles we'd made, another would count how many throw-ins we'd had and so on. It was like an Opta Stats service for the 1970s.

By that season I began to think that I wasn't going to be in Arsenal's long term thinking and it seemed Bobby Campbell wasn't that keen on me as a player. They signed Jeff Blockley from Coventry in 1972, which didn't bode well for me. Arsenal had moved Peter Storrie into midfield, and Pat Rice became the right full-back. I was trying to get into that back four but was finding myself overlooked. My performances weren't strong enough and I knew I wasn't convincing Arsenal enough. And I never quite got that red tracksuit. Even though I played 10 games for them, and often trained with the first team, I never graduated from the green top. And when they signed Jeff I knew I was going to struggle.

I'd had one really bad game against Queens Park Rangers when one particular newspaper report by Julie Welch was so scathing about me that I vowed never to read any more reports about myself. Her Observer piece about me was really quite cutting – I felt so hurt about it, even though I knew I'd not played well. I'd actually been booked, was at fault for a goal and had a dreadful game. But I didn't need people to tell me how well or badly I played. From that moment on I avoided reading anything about myself in the media – I simply didn't need that added burden to my professional aspirations. That said, I looked at Jeff Blockley and realised that if Arsenal were willing to sign him then I wasn't going to be good enough to have a long-term future there.

The lads who really helped me a lot at Arsenal were Bob McNab, Sammy Nelson and Pat Rice. Frank McLintock was a fantastic skipper too. He was a great influence. But I got on with all of the lads. Pat and Sammy were like a double act – they used to call me Smokey, after Smokey Robinson. Sammy would later bare his backside and get sanctioned by the FA. His daughter was married to former cricketer Matt Prior and Sammy used to warn her to beware of photographers – which was ironic given what happened to him. Charlie George was a character. They absolutely loved him at Arsenal – he was very cavalier, had a really powerful shot on him and was straight off the North Bank. He thinks he owns the Emirates these days, but then you cannot blame him – he is a proper Arsenal legend. He was Mr Arsenal at the time and to many people he always will be. Then there was George Graham, who was nicknamed the Stroller – he was an elegant player, great in the air, but who couldn't tackle for toffee. But when he became manager with Millwall, and later Arsenal, his sides were extremely physical and nothing like him as a footballer.

We also had Peter Marinello, who came with a massive reputation and was being dubbed as the next big thing, but it never really worked out for him.

As regards my own career, Arsenal had really looked after me, but I knew I needed to find a way out. The penny was dropping that life with the Gunners wasn't for me, if only for the sake of my own career. By then I'd met Cecily and she became my wife in 1974. That's when I began to realise I had responsibilities coming up. I realised I wasn't good enough for Arsenal. I wasn't going to start deluding myself.

Arsenal had been good to me. Their development was integral to the rest of my life. It shaped me as a footballer but, more so, what I learned under the good people at Arsenal was to influence and shape my personality. And, yet, I knew it was time to leave.

TRIBUTE

Brendon is a good man and was a good lad in our dressing room. He was on the bus with me when the Youth Team won the cup in the same year we won the double – there he is, stood right behind me. I did say to him many years ago when he took the West Brom managing director's job that he should maybe hold fire and wait for the main PFA job, because he would end up as the top bloke there eventually. But it was a job he so wanted so I cannot blame him for going back to a club he so dearly loves.

He was the first black Arsenal player so his status at the club will forever be secured. He was a good player too. He left Arsenal and then Ron Atkinson took him under his wing, where he developed into a great defender.

He's one of these people who is supposedly 70 but doesn't look it. How do you do it Brendon?

Brendon and I roomed at an away game at Cardiff and I seem to recall he replaced me at Newcastle at half-time for his debut. He was always helpful to his peers, and I can only apologise if I led him astray on those games where we were room-mates. Brendon has achieved so much in football. The one thing I'll always remember is that he was and, still is, such a kind man. A perfect role-model.

Charlie George, Arsenal (1968-75)

TRIBUTE

Brendon's dedication to the game, and dedication to anything he set his mind to beyond football, has always been outstanding.

When he was at Arsenal he would join in my goalkeeping sessions – wanting to know why we were doing what we were doing from a goalkeeping point of view. He was interested in that, which isn't usual for a footballer from a completely different position.

In 1971, Arsenal won the League and Cup double. Brendon was part of the side that won the Youth Cup and I remember Brendon being part of those celebrations. He was also the first black footballer to play for Arsenal, so in many respects he was a trailblazer for the generation of future black players who came through at Arsenal. You cannot underestimate that kind of influence.

Many years later, my wife Megs and I lost our daughter Anna. We set up the Willow Foundation as a lasting memorial to Anna, with Brendon being a supporter of ours. The biggest thing I did was when I was 71 – that was to ride to all of the Premier League clubs. When I got to West Bromwich Albion I was joined by Brendon Batson, not long after his wife Cecily died. He joined me on a leg from West Brom to Wolves so he cycled alongside me. That is Brendon – always thinking about others.

He has always done everything with a smile on his face, yet he lost his wife and I know from my own experiences with Anna that you never get over something like that.

Brendon is such a personable guy. When you think of his achievements at the PFA – he got not only an MBE and then an OBE. That speaks volumes about him. He's a dedicated guy who goes beyond the normal professional footballer mentality – always wanted to put something back into the game. I'm proud to call him a friend.

Bob Wilson OBE, Arsenal (1963-74)

CHAPTER THREE
Cambridge United

"Is this the kind of player we want in the Football League?"

I was approaching 21, about to get married and I was on poor wages – even by Arsenal's standards. I knew I now needed to look after my career. It was a very uncertain time for me. I spoke to family members about leaving Arsenal, while Bertie Mee had told me not to be hasty, as had Bob Wilson, who himself was a wonderful man.

But Arsenal agreed to put me on the transfer list. My brother spoke to my mum about how unhappy I was and how I'd seen other players overtake me.

I was then told very quickly that a club called Cambridge United was supposedly coming in for me. I cost £8000 but knew absolutely nothing about how transfers worked. A guy called Ray Freeman was the coach – he'd made a reputation for himself in Norway. And the manager was a gentleman called Bill Leivers, who had played for Manchester City. Ray had watched me in pre-season and he sold me the club very quickly.

My overwhelming feeling was how flattered I was that somebody wanted me. I said yes immediately. I didn't even think about it. I was given a club house just off Newmarket Road, which while modest, was to my wife and I a lovely place…and our first home. Cambridge United were a relatively new Football League club. They got promoted out of non-league, got promoted from the old Fourth and were struggling a little bit in the Third Division. They were always in a relegation scrap and wanted to give themselves a chance to stay up, so they signed me – this young lad from Arsenal being billed as their saviour. At the end of the season we were relegated!

I didn't know much about Cambridge at the time of signing. I didn't know where it was, which division they played in, where they were in the table. I was just so relieved that somebody wanted me to play for them that I didn't care. I wanted to be good enough for somebody's first team.

Football throws people together in strange ways. There were four of us travelling in from London. We had Vic Akers – who later became the most successful Arsenal manager, when he was in charge of the women's team – Alan Harris, the brother of Ron, and Bobby Ross, a Scottish guy who was to become manager of Hayes and sell a young striker called Cyrille Regis to West Brom. But at the time we were all playing for Cambridge. We would all meet and travel in together. They were all senior pros, while I was the young lad – so that helped me integrate into the dressing room. What also helped is that I was doing a lot of my training still with Arsenal and just playing the Cambridge games. That's how it was back then.

In the 1974-75 season we started poorly. Poor Bill Leivers got the vote of confidence from the directors and, of course, in time-honoured fashion he got the sack a short time later. Meanwhile, across the way at Kettering, there was a young player-manager making a name for himself and he saw Cambridge as a step-up. And so that man, Ron Atkinson, took his first professional managerial role. I recall at the time the lads were running a book on who would replace Leivers and Ron's name wasn't even on the list. We hadn't heard of him. Suddenly, this young brash manager turned up and changed everything.

He came in as manager and thought he was the best player on the books. He was a totally different manager to anything I'd experienced. Bill Leivers had been a tracksuit manager, much like Bertie Mee. Ray Freeman was the coach, much like Don Howe. Ron came in as a manager and a coach. And he was also part of the dressing room. It was a real eye-opener for all of us. Ron would play cards with us on the coach and became part of the lads, even though he was manager. But by doing so he started to find out where we were going on the nights that we weren't supposed to be out. He would know every party we were going to – he knew everything that was going on in Cambridge. He was only 35, still very much capable of playing in five-a-sides. He would tell us: "Watch this, I'm going to stick it in that top corner lads..." while we would be thinking: "miss you bastard, please miss." But he would score, every time. He thought he was the best player, the best crosser, the best scorer, the best everything...or so he thought.

We were training in a field behind the Abbey Stadium on one particular morning. It was a real shit hole of a pitch and it was cold, so we'd have our tracksuit bottoms on. Ron came out and ordered us to remove them. He barked over: "Do you play in your tracksuits? No, now get them off." I didn't appreciate the cold so it didn't go down well with me, but Ron brought in a certain professionalism that I wasn't used to. Even at Arsenal we were allowed tracksuit bottoms, but not by Ron.

He had done his badges at Lilleshall, which was a big community for managers and coaches back then. They all became good friends and went into management. Graham Taylor, another one of the Lilleshall graduates, used to tell a story from when he was England manager. He would stop training and ask the players how many stripes were on the England socks? If anyone couldn't see three stripes because they were rolled down then he would demand the players pull up their socks and tie them up. That's how you play, that's how you prepare and present yourself. And Ron was very much from that school of thought. It might seem trivial, but it was all about standards.

I knew I was one of the main players. But it didn't start off well with me and Ron. Cecily was pregnant and we were playing Northampton away when I got the call that she had been rushed into hospital. She had a bleed. We consulted the doctor who told us to go for a scan and then told her to fully rest. The scan said the baby had a heartbeat but effectively the placenta was killing the baby and sadly she miscarried. It was a couple of months before Christmas.

All of this happened on the Friday and, thinking that Cecily and my unborn child were both okay, I thought I would carry on as normal and play the next day. I didn't travel with the team but was driven down to the game by one of the club directors. My mind was all over the place. I had a total nightmare. I actually asked Ron to come off at half-time, but he wouldn't have it. The following week Ron and I had a big bust-up in training and I just lost my rag. He told me: "You can piss off back to the dressing room if that's how you feel." So, I did just that - I walked off. On the Friday we trained as normal and then waited for Ron to name the team for the Saturday. He went through the team, the goalkeeper, the defence, and then he got to the midfield and my name wasn't called out. I could feel the atmosphere change on the training pitch and knew then he was making a point. I didn't say a word, I just accepted it. The following week – by now I'm not speaking to him at all – I was named in the reserves at centre-half against Peterborough and then Ron ends up naming himself. So, we're both at centre-half and I'm not speaking to him at all. By now he had nicknamed me Batman and he was yelling: "Come on Batman, one-two, pass here" and we'd be interchanging passes, even though I was determined to not speak to him. We got on the coach and I didn't say a word. I then played another reserve game at Gillingham and he called me in some time after for a cup of tea and said: "I like your attitude." I wasn't even speaking to him. I wanted to swing for him, even though I knew I'd probably only get one good shot otherwise he'd probably kill me as he had a significant weight advantage. More so, I knew if he didn't kill me with a punch, he could easily kill my career by completely bombing me out.

What I failed to appreciate in all of this, however, was that I was in danger of killing my career all by myself.

The best bit of advice I had came from Cecily. She knew nothing about football but said: "Brendon, you're playing in the Fourth Division...why don't you show him you're a good player." And that's when I buckled down and started playing. The following week he made me sub for the first-team, which felt even more embarrassing for me. Now, at the time, Ron would sit in the stand and if things weren't going well you'd see him launch himself from his seat and march down, his leather coat tails flailing – which would whip the fans up too. On this occasion we were winning comfortably yet he came down and asked me to warm up. I looked at the time and there were four minutes left so I ran over to the corner flag and just took my time. All the time I can see from the corner of my eye that he's looking over trying to call me back, but I just ignored him. By the time I came back it was full time – so that was me making my point.

The following week he put me back in the side. And not long afterwards he made me skipper. Now, Ron will always tell people that he thought I had a chip on my shoulder because I'd come from Arsenal, having not made it there and was now a big time Charlie. He could hear me telling stories about some of the Arsenal players and saying "Raddy (John Radford) this, Raddy that, Charlie (George) this and that..." and he didn't like it. Maybe Ron had a point, but I never agreed with that. He thought I wasn't letting go of my Arsenal days and was demeaning Cambridge, but that was not the case. I had no chip on my shoulder and

I actually wanted to say: "Bollocks to you – I'll show him what I can do." Ron was always competitive and wouldn't let anything interfere with his management of the team but I resented his treatment of me at times during those early days.

There was another reason I wasn't happy. And it goes back to one of Ron's first games in charge. Back then I had been subjected to a certain amount of abuse from the terraces but I got on with it. But on this one occasion I snapped. We played Stockport at Edgeley Park and this was the first time an opponent had given me sustained racist abuse. Among pros you occasionally had abuse, but not much. Anyway, on this occasion at Stockport, I had been subjected to abuse from County's Tony Coleman for the entirety of the first-half. I don't recall ever receiving anything on these levels before. It was relentless. On that day I was playing in midfield, as was he, so we kept clashing as you do in games. Each time he would make some comment or other. At the start of the second half we clashed and were scrapping on the ground – he was saying: "You black this and you black that." Anyway, we got back onto our feet with the referee parting us when he started making monkey gestures to me so I leaned across the referee and just hit him. I was already turning to walk off before the referee could even act. I just turned to the referee and said: "Well you've seen and heard what he's been doing" and I just left it at that.

In those days you could have personal hearings with the Football Association and, on this occasion, the referee actually came and spoke on my behalf. Ron and I drove up in his white Jaguar to this particular hearing, which was held at the Grand Hotel in Birmingham. Lo-and-behold the chairman of the hearing that day was Bert Millichip, who would later become my employer at West Brom. He was the chairman of the disciplinary committee at the FA. Anyway, I wasn't sanctioned but I remember Bert in his dulcet tones saying: "We've taken account of what you and the referee have said, and there will be no sanction...but Mr Batson, I don't wish to see you here again." So, what happens? A few months later I come up against Coleman again, and, yes I get sent off again. We're winning and it's the last few seconds of the game. I'm right by the corner flag in their half, get away from him and he kicks me, so I turn around and lashed out. As soon as I did it I knew I was off. I was sat in the dressing room, Ron walked in, turned to me and said: "Well Batman, I don't think we'll be appealing this one..."

Cecily had a very philosophical view to all of the racist abuse. What changed in my mind was the volume. I had been subjected to abuse many times. I was getting it on the street, on the Tube even in schoolboy football, which I found a lot easier to deal with. However, what changed when I moved into the professional ranks was the frequency and volume of it. Thankfully, it was very rare that you'd get abuse by a fellow professional. It did happen obviously, but not as often.

At Cambridge there were smaller crowds, smaller grounds and you could pick out people. When I went to West Brom it became like a bank of supporters abusing you because you'd be playing in front of so many more people.

Cecily didn't come to games generally, but she did do every now and again. My daughter Zoe was born in 1977 but Cecily didn't like the atmosphere, she didn't like hearing me abused and so she hardly saw me play.

There was another incident involving a lad called Robin Friday, who became a cult hero with Reading in particular, before moving to Cardiff. He'd come from non-league and built a rapport with supporters because he was a bit of a maverick. He's even had quite a few books written about him. On this occasion Cambridge were playing Reading. He was lean, sharp and he used his arms a lot – even his elbows felt sharp because he was so wiry. We had a set-to and he started calling me names. I was fine at first, I was coping with it, but then he started getting more aggressive so I started giving it back. He turned around to me, called me a racist name and I lashed out. I was sent off. Afterwards we're in the players' lounge and I was still fuming – not just with him, but more so with myself for once again reacting to an idiot. Robin came over to me and said in this strong cockney accent: "Are you okay Bren? I was a bit surprised you reacted like that because I was just told to wind you up by the manager because they said you were hot-headed." And with that he just shrugged off the whole incident and then topped it off by saying he would come and speak on my behalf if I decided to appeal it with the FA. I swear, I nearly hit him again when I heard that!

I was learning how to channel my temper but it wasn't easy. I remember going to another disciplinary hearing and they read out my charge sheet. There was a gentleman called Richard Vernon Stokes, who was the chairman at Portsmouth and on the FA's disciplinary committee.

When each charge was read out his head would shoot up and he'd glare at me. I remember him saying: "Mr Chairman (Bert Millichip), is this the kind of player we want in the Football League?" and yet I was the one being insulted and harassed. Naturally, they were all white, middle-class men sitting in judgement. Nobody cared why I was booked or sent off, yet I was the only one being sanctioned as a result of my retaliation at the abuse I was getting due to my skin colour.

I remember thinking these people knew nothing about my life and how I had arrived at this hearing, or what I'd had to go through to get myself into such a state that I'd lose my temper in the way I did. I went through that from the time I played football as a 10-year-old and here I was being judged, despite growing up with it as a black kid. I'd get it not only on the football pitch, but walking down the road – you'd get people slowing in their cars, and yelling abuse to us, telling us to "Fuck off back to your own country." It was in my DNA to put up with stuff until I snapped or lashed out – which I certainly did a lot in the early part of my career. Ron Atkinson was the one who helped me curb my temper.

There was another flare-up, this time in training, with a Cambridge player called Tommy Horsfall – nothing racist – but we were winding each other up. We had an altercation before we even went out onto the training pitch, but I remember that a lot of my own anger was about how I was reacting to things. I knew I was too angry. Matters between Tommy and I spilled over during training and I had Tommy by the throat. Ron grabbed hold of me and told me to get back to the dressing room. Afterwards he called me in to see him, over a cup of tea, and he said to me: "Well Batman...you'll always be black. So, are you going to keep on fighting or get on with it?"

The meaning was that I had to deal with this abuse. Not long after that he made me captain.

I was an angry man. It was the first time I had been exposed to this kind of abuse from opponents. You expect it from kids, but now this was my profession. I almost got to the stage where I thought: "Is this what I'll have to put up with if I stay in England for the rest of my life?" I remember a car going by one day and some kids shouting racist abuse at me – two of them were Asian boys. I have no idea if that was something to do with the notion similar to the apartheid regime where they saw themselves as being part of the white community, while the blacks were the bottom of the pack. I always wondered if those Asian boys were simply seeing us as the poor relations of a bigger racial divide.

I became friends with a Jamaican lad called Orville Coley in Walthamstow. He was the one who introduced me to reggae. But we loved music and we used to go and see Stevie Wonder, Ike and Tina Turner and as many of the top Tamla Mowtown/R & B artists of that time. There was a place called the Tottenham Royal in Seven Sisters Road. Friday was a disco night so I couldn't make that as I was playing for Arsenal at the time. I went out on one occasion as I wasn't playing but we couldn't get in. We were told by these white bouncers: "You can't come in tonight...we know you usually do, but not tonight." And it turns out there had been some fighting a previous night between white and black kids...so what did they do? They banned the black kids. Orville threw something at them and we ended up running all the way back to Seven Sisters Tube. This was just one of those things that was bubbling under. An accumulation of these things was starting to get to me. All these incidents were chipping away at me, especially where race was involved.

I was trying to make my way and to be subjected to any racist abuse was just too much for me. Those three dismissals, which were all down to racist abuse, happened in a short space of time. It was Ron's talk with me that focused my mind. And, of course, the fact that being sent-off meant I missed games. And missing games back then meant missing out on appearance fees and win bonuses. I wasn't on great money as it was, so I needed those bonuses.

I was never sure why Ron Atkinson made me captain. Yes, I would speak out and was quite vocal with my views, but he must have seen something in me. I was a bit of a leader, but it was a big shock to me to be told I was captain. How did I feel? I was proud. I felt responsibility and perhaps Ron thought that giving me more to think about would be good for me in all other respects. The other problem was that I was very superstitious - I liked to be the last one out of the dressing room – so when he made me skipper, I actually wondered what would happen but to his credit Ron let me still lead the team out...from the back. I never once led the team out, despite being captain.

In the 1976/77 season we won the Division Four championship. That was such a proud moment for me. By then I was playing right-back. One of Ron's best signings had been a great pro called Dave Stringer, who came from Norwich and later returned to manage them. He came late in his career to us and when he signed Ron moved me over to full-back because he thought I could cause damage down the wing with my pace. We were playing good stuff and totally deserved promotion. We won that division at a canter.

From a personal point of view, I felt I was so much better than the Fourth Division. I'd made the move from Arsenal and now it was looking justified. Being picked by Ron on a regular basis made me grow. He was a great man-manager and the dynamic we had in the dressing room was so vibrant. We had a lot to prove – we were a mish-mash of free transfers, youngsters and old pros. But a lot of my success I owed to Cecily. I always felt I was quick, but never always the fittest. I knew I could hold my own with anyone over 100 metres but I needed to get fitter. And in that pre-season of 1976 I felt fitter than I ever had been. Much of our training was on the Royston Golf Course in Cambridgeshire, which was a tough one because it was so undulating. I remember thinking: "This is the year I get out of this division." That fitness work gave me more confidence.

Ron would always challenge you. He wanted you to improve all the time, he wouldn't rest even if you were doing well. People played for him because he was one of the best man-managers around. The dynamic in the dressing room was so healthy – we were competitive, we were successful but there was also a lot of laughter. He would also wheel and deal. He bought in one player from Vauxhall Motors for a case of Champagne, allegedly – hence why he got called Champagne Charlie. Ron's message was constant: "You keep telling me you're a good player... don't tell me, show me." His motivation was a big part of our success. We had a squad full of so many different characters and yet each one of us at Cambridge wanted to do well for him. Back then young players from lower-league clubs would move up the divisions. Phil Neal, for instance, went from Northampton to Liverpool, while Ian Rush went from Chester City to Liverpool a few years later. I remember playing against Alan Taylor when he was at Rochdale – he didn't get a kick against me – but he went onto West Ham and he scored two goals in the FA Cup Final. So, I started to think, well, will I ever get a chance? You had scouts at every game, wanting to pick up that next gem. I honestly felt I could play in a higher division.

In 1977/78 the rumours about Ron Atkinson leaving started to gather pace. There was a lot made about the style of football, but he also knew John Bond, Malcolm Allison and some of the bigger personalities at the top of the game, so he knew how to showcase his abilities and, more so, his larger-than-life personality. He also had that big white Jaguar which had ferried me to some of my meetings with the FA disciplinary meetings and, as luxurious as that car was, it was pretty unheard of at our level of football. He was flash, and he knew it!

His final game was at Oxford away. Mick Brown was manager of Oxford – he would end up becoming Ron's number two a few years later. I remember we won that game and were already making moves to get promoted to Division Two. But we knew Ron was a wanted man and the following week it got done – Ron Atkinson left us to go to West Bromwich Albion.

Ron later told me that during the discussions the West Brom director Brian Boundy said: "We'll be taking your right-back too…"

At Cambridge I'd become close to quite a few of the players. There was a lad called Bobby Shinton, who came from Walsall, and one of my other pals was Malcolm Webster, a goalkeeper. He was someone I knew from my time with Arsenal, where we had played together in the reserves. By the time I'd caught up with him as a Cambridge player he was actually shifting furniture down near Southend and clearly trying to get his career back on track. I ended up suggesting to Ron that he comes up for a trial with Cambridge and play a pre-season friendly against Bristol City. Sod's Law, Malcolm had an absolutely nightmare, letting a tame header slip through his hands and legs. That was his first game for Cambridge and I half expected it to be his last. After the game, Ron came over to me and said: "Who the hell have you got me here Batman?" He ended up playing about 250 games for Cambridge, becoming a club legend – so my recommendation wasn't too bad, was it?

Another I'd mention was Dave Stringer. He was probably Ron's best signing for the U's. He was already in his 30s by the time he came to Cambridge, but he was so good for us at the back in defence. I was skipper and he was the one bollocking me during games. Another reason we liked Dave was because he had a small holding with chickens back in Norwich and would sort us all out with eggs. We'd all be ordering from him and hoping he wouldn't smash any during his journey from across East Anglia. He was some player though and ended up playing more than 150 games for the club.

Anyway, back to football: Ron Atkinson had gone to the West Midlands, while the rest of us were adjusting to life without him at Cambridge. We played Tranmere and, funnily enough Mark Palios, who would one day become the Football Association's chief executive, was playing that day. It was the first game after Ron had gone and I could feel the lads were subdued. While I was stretching in the showers, I heard a burst of activity in the dressing room and, sure enough, Ron had walked in to give his old team a pep talk. We won that evening. As he walked out of the door after the game, he said to me: "Say your goodbyes Batman, you've played your last game for this club." I thought he was taking the piss.

We then had a game called off due to bad weather, and I was then ill for a week, so I missed a game or two.

It turned out to be my final game for Cambridge after all.

TRIBUTE

Brendon was already at Cambridge when I joined from Luton. In my first year I broke my leg in the third game, so I missed working with Brendon at first, but it was clear from how he conducted himself just how respected and liked he was.

He was an absolutely gent – a class act. As soon as I'd established myself you realised you were playing next to a Rolls-Royce. He was a little bit older than me – five years is half a generation in footballing terms – but I looked up to him from day one.

He was also immaculate. Don't get me wrong, he had some outrageous shirts, especially in the summer but his dress sense was always spot on. He was one of the lads, but was always articulate, well-spoken and knew how to behave when he needed to. He read situations well, he had great balance on the pitch and was a very accomplished and confident defender.

We had a fair bit in common too. Both Brendon and I came to Cambridge from what were then First Division clubs. And Cambridge gave both of us a chance and platform to reboot our careers.

Brendon is one of those players you knew was going to go far. Cambridge was a smashing club, but he was always going to move on, especially when Ron Atkinson went to West Brom.

Everything about him was spot on. A great ambassador, a good influence and, as someone younger, he was a mentor for me. Brendon was a captain and leader by example, especially as he had to put up with so much abuse from racists.

Alan Biley, Cambridge United _(1975-79)_

CHAPTER FOUR
West Bromwich Albion

"....'It's now or never Batman.' I knew what that meant - I simply had to perform..."

Once again Ray Freeman was to be a major influence in my career move – albeit this time the metric used was somewhat different.

By 1978 Ray had moved from football and was making a name for himself as a merchant for Pieroth Wines, who were quite a high-end company. I quite liked my wine, so I'd occasionally buy a case or two from him. It was during March of that year that I had a wine-tasting evening to hopefully put some orders Ray's way and had invited a few friends around to our house. It was all very relaxed and, of course, the wine helped.

Anyway, Ray was there, and the phone started ringing. I had a habit of never answering the phone, least of all when we had company. Cecily answered and said John Docherty, the new Cambridge boss, was on the phone and was asking to speak to me urgently. Whatever it was, it couldn't wait. I reluctantly wandered over to the phone, to be told: "Brendon, we have done a deal with West Brom. Ron is going to call you in about 10 minutes. You're off to West Bromwich." I wasn't consulted, asked, or even given a choice. I honestly thought I'd had too much wine! I had taken the call upstairs and before I'd even made my way downstairs, I had a call from Ron while everyone else was knocking back the wine. I called Cecily upstairs and told her the news.

That was a Wednesday evening. On the Thursday I signed for Albion. On the Saturday, West Brom played Coventry and drew 3-3. On the following Tuesday we played Birmingham at St Andrew's and won 2-1. That was my first game for the club. Birmingham was a horrible night for me, but we won – with the two Browns, Tony and Ally, scoring. I then played against Ipswich the following Saturday and Tony scored twice for us again. You'd think from my memories that they were enjoyable games to be involved in – far from it. They were an absolute nightmare for me. I was terrible.

My debut had come at Birmingham. It was just awful. Thanks to my earlier experience at the hands of The Observer, I was no longer reading what newspapers thought of my performances, which was probably just as well. The media back then were different. Ron had a rapport with the Midlands press but also the national media, including people like Ray Matts, Joe Melling and many others. But, personally, I wasn't a fan of the press. I had stopped bothering with press reports, be they good, bad or indifferent.

On that night against Birmingham, I was simply overawed. It all happened too quickly for me. I thought I'd have to speed up my game because I was playing at a higher level, but actually I was to find that the top level was much calmer. I was trying too hard. I walked down the steps at St Andrew's and slipped on a banana. I didn't even see it. It was wet as it was, so that didn't help. Both the Birmingham and Ipswich games were horrendous for me.

What didn't help was that I was coming in for an established Republic of Ireland international called Paddy Mulligan. Paddy had an acerbic tongue and thought of himself as being quite witty. I didn't like him, mainly because I thought he was very insulting to people and would claim jokes at the expense of others. But, more so and importantly for me, he and Ron Atkinson didn't get on. Ron told me I would have to win my place because, at the time, Paddy was injured. In fact, against Coventry in that 3-3 draw, the right-back was actually Bryan Robson, just a few weeks after he'd played as a left-back for us by all accounts. Before that debut at Birmingham, I was in the dressing room and Paddy happened to be in there. He went round all of the lads wishing them all the best and then he came to me. The dressing room went quiet, he held out his hand and said: "All the best…I hope you have a fucking nightmare." Now the lads thought that was funny, but I think he meant it. Sure enough, I had a nightmare.

I played in those two games and then had to sit out some games because I was cup-tied. That actually helped me because it took me out of the firing line, knowing I'd had two stinkers. In training we would have five-a-side games and that's where my confidence grew. The players could see I wasn't as bad as they thought I was in those first two games. Ally Robertson, who is a great mate of mine now, said at the time: "Fucking hell, you can play after all." It was only later that

I found out some of the players regarded me as a bit of a spy in the camp, because I'd come to Albion as the Cambridge skipper and may be feeding back to Ron. But it really wasn't like that and I certainly was not like that.

I was starting to settle down, I was training well. I even had some confrontations in the five-a-sides. John Wile, who was our captain, had been interim manager before Ron Atkinson came in and he was almost testing me out. I wasn't backing down. He could tell I could look after myself.

April was when it all changed for me at West Brom. We played eight games during that month, including a crushing FA Cup semi-final defeat to Ipswich. But it was towards the end of April that we got absolutely battered by Aston Villa. That was on the Saturday, and we had a game against Everton on the Tuesday. At the time I was still staying in the Europa Lodge hotel by The Hawthorns. On this occasion Ron was staying there with Colin Addison, his assistant manager. I came down for breakfast on the day of the game. As I'm eating Ron came and joined me. Without even looking at me he said: "It's now or never Batman." I knew what that meant - I was in the side, but I simply had to perform. He didn't need to spell it out to me – I'd played twice, I'd played badly, and this was going to be my third strike. We won that game 3-1 – Cyrille was to score a brilliant goal that day – and I ended up playing the final matches of that particular season. Not once was I on the losing side.

It was the turning point I needed.

The Ipswich semi-final was tough for the team to take. I was cup-tied, still living in Cambridge and I had just got in my seat at Arsenal's Highbury stadium when Brian Talbot and John Wile clashed heads for the opening Ipswich goal. We ended up losing 3-1. It's a really strange feeling when you're at a club but not allowed to play. I wanted the team to win, and I wanted the excitement of going to Wembley, but there was a part of me that thought: "Shit, how will I feel missing out on that?" What I do remember that day is that we were always second. Ipswich were much more vibrant and more committed to everything. No matter what we did that day, Ipswich did it better. We had players of equal billing, if not of more ability in some respects, but on that day they did us because they handled the pressure far better than we did. I subsequently found out that Ron had been filmed on Football Focus doing a piece at Wembley for BBC. It was suggested that all four FA Cup semi-final managers – including those at Arsenal and Orient in the other game – had been invited to do a promotional film at Wembley. Three of them refused, but Ron accepted it. And it was as good as a team-talk for Bobby Robson by all accounts. He simply showed them the clip and it wound them up.

As it happens that game opened the door for me as we took a while to get over that. Had we got to the final my career might have gone a different direction as Paddy Mulligan might have kept his spot.

That Everton game established me in the team. West Brom was a dressing room of big players. Ron had already primed me. He thought I'd be a good influence to help the personal and professional development of a young lad they'd brought in a year or so earlier. I didn't know much about Laurie Cunningham, but he was quite shy. The one thing Ron did say is that I would be joining an extremely professional set of players. That might seem like a normal thing these days but back then football culture was different. Footballers would train, go home and then forget about football, often spending their time in a pub, bookies or both. The West Brom team showed me a different level of professionalism. The players were staying after training, working on their fitness and generally doing a bit extra to improve as individuals. The first game I saw the team play after joining was against Coventry. I watched from the stand and was particularly drawn to the left-back; a kid called Derek Statham. He was only 18 at the time and I remember going back to Cambridge to collect my things on the Monday. I said to the lads: "I've just seen some young lad playing full-back, and I've never seen anyone play full-back like him." He was exceptional. He was just phenomenal. He was doing drag-backs in his own box. If I'd tried that at Cambridge, my old team-mate Dave Stringer would have booted me out of the ground, and here was a teenager Derek Statham, in the First Division at West Brom, playing with such ability and grace, when he was barely old enough to legally buy a pint.

Ron also told me I'd enjoy playing with Willie Johnston. And he was right. What a character he was. I used to train with Willie on the cinder track that ran alongside the pitch at The Hawthorns. We'd both wear spikes to help us with our sprinting. He was bloody quick, even at that stage of his career when he was in his 30s.

And then there was Bryan Robson. He would walk past you and you wouldn't realise he'd even walked past. He was so quiet. How on earth he didn't play in the semi-final against Ipswich, I don't know. He should have done. You could already tell there was something there on the pitch, but his personality and character was to catch up – to a point where he became the focal point of every team he played for, including ours. Ally Robertson was jovial, but uncompromising on the pitch. I'm glad I never had to face him as a striker.

Laurie, Cyrille, Derek and goalkeeper Tony Godden were the young guns, coming through. They were all technically exceptional players. One of the best was Lenny Cantello. He was playing on the right-hand side of midfield when I first broke into the team, and he helped me settle into the side. I used to love to attack and when I did that, Lenny would fill in for me which gave me the confidence to push forward at every opportunity.

Laurie and Cyrille are probably the two players that everyone will associate me with – for obvious reasons. We were black. And we were all playing in the same football team. I had heard about Laurie when he was at Orient. He was like a Formula One car when he was accelerating. Seeing him in training was incredible. His actual driving and directional sense was less impressive. On my first day of training at West Brom, he and Cyrille offered to pick me up from the hotel by The Hawthorns. We only had a five-mile journey or so. The instructions were clear: We had to join the M5 at Junction 1, next to the hotel, drive a couple of miles to the junction with the M6, take the southbound carriageway, continue along the M6 for about half a mile, come off, and the training ground was pretty much there. It all sounds simple doesn't it? Not for Laurie. Instead of taking the left-hand lane as the M5 joined the M6, he took the right-hand carriageway, sending us up the M6 towards Stoke-on-Trent and Manchester. It seems like we were travelling for ages – much longer than I'd been told it would take – before Laurie casually said: "We're lost..." Note, he said we're lost, not I'm lost. And, so, we were. What a way to make an impression on my first day in a new job!

Going back to that Everton game, on April 25, 1978. I was told many years later that it was the first time Laurie, Cyrille and I all started a game for West Brom. At the start of my time at the club myself and Laurie weren't starting games so it took a good two months for us all to be named in the starting line-up.

In any case, the 1977-78 season was over and we were off for a post-season trip. But not to the usual location of Spain or Portugal. I could have lived with that. This was slightly different. And I first got wind of it when I signed for West Brom. Ron dropped in a comment at the end of our discussion pretty much along the lines of: "Hey Batman, by the way, we're going to China in the summer." I actually hated end-of-season trips because they were generally an excuse for people to drink lots, get into arguments or fights, maybe play some golf and lay around a pool. I had a baby daughter Zoe, so I didn't want to go anywhere for three weeks, let alone a post-season trip. When I came back a few weeks later she wouldn't go near me for days as she thought I was a stranger. Cecily had her so close to her that all she knew was her mum. That was very hard for me.

On the pitch, things were looking better. The culmination of getting knocked out in the semi-finals, me getting into the team and being in China for the best part of a month, where we played five games, was very important to me establishing myself in the team.

China was an end-of-season trip like no other. Initially the FA had wanted England to go there but for whatever reason that didn't happen. Bert Millichip, who was our chairman, was steadily manoeuvring himself into a senior role with the FA and so he decided to volunteer us for the trip. From our point of view, China was an ambassadorial trip, with a big political agenda. We also had BBC cameras with us as part of the World About Us documentary series with Julian Pettifer. China was a great experience - I thoroughly enjoyed it, even though many of the lads hated it. I went back 40 years later and to see the way it had developed was amazing. It was very different when we went there in 1978. Going from cosmopolitan areas like Birmingham or London, it was one hell of a shock to all of us.

But before that we went to Hong Kong for two days, before moving onto China. During our stay in the hotel in Hong Kong there was high jinks when Ally Robertson threw a bucket of water over Derek Statham – or at least Ally thought it was Derek. It was, in fact, Sir Bert Millichip, who was showing some Chinese delegates around the hotel just as Ally launched the bucket. Sir Bert wasn't impressed: "Alistair, I think you'd better return to your room." On the same day I too became the innocent victim of a drenching. I was lying on my bed, with my suitcase open next to the bed. My clothes got absolutely soaked. Like Sir Bert, I wasn't very impressed either. To this day I don't know who it was.

We then moved onto China where we were greeted and treated like royalty, escorted everywhere, and given local currency but told it was a closed economy – so we couldn't take it out of the country. We were leaving coins in our rooms as tips and those coins were collected and being taken out to us when we moved onto the next hotel, because if someone had been accused of mishandling that money or taking it, they'd have been in huge trouble. Honesty was everything out there. Whenever you'd go abroad you could draw comparisons between countries. So, you could say certain things about England were similar in some respects to somewhere like France, which might be a little like Spain, which might have some things that are relevant to Portugal, and so on. You couldn't do that in China. It was like nowhere else back then. There would be huge boulevards, with big state buildings running alongside them. And then at, say, 4pm, these big empty roads would suddenly fill with thousands of bicycles emerging, with everyone dressed in grey or blue. I remember seeing one guy squatting in the road with a red flag – it turns out there was a pothole next to him and he was trying to warn the other road-users. The food? I thoroughly enjoyed it – well, most of it! It wasn't like the Chinese food we have in the UK. There would be loads of courses – sometime as many as 20 it seemed.

We had excursions, but some of the lads opted out. They'd rather have a card school than go to the Ming tombs. I remember Bertie Mee being on the trip actually and that was a big thing for me because I had learned from my time at Arsenal that you had to be a good tourist – make sure you explore and make the most of the downtime. And, to be honest, nobody wanted to stay in the hotel rooms anyway because they were so basic. I remember Bryan Robson smashing up a room and throwing the Chinese money around saying they could take any damage to the room out of that. He was so bored. So many were.

We then played cricket against the English press. One of the directors, a lovely man called Tom Silk was a decent cricketer. As he was running up to bowl, the elastic snapped on his shorts and so while he was in the throes of bowling, his shorts were sliding down his legs but he kept on going. It was that day Ally decided to get a white towel from one of the rooms and hoisted it up the flagpole. What we didn't realise was that was extremely disrespectful in China. All those incidents with buckets of water being thrown around, rooms being smashed up... and they took the most offence against a towel fluttering from a flagpole.

The saviour for us were the games. We won all of them and that allowed us to release much pent up energy. The matches were bizarre experiences. The stadia were huge, with a lot of people attending but fans weren't allowed to make a noise. There were 90,000 in Bejing and you could hear a pin drop – apparently it was considered impolite to clap and make noise. Mick Martin wore an old man mask to our first training session and as we came off the coach, he turned to face the waiting public and some of the people ran off. They thought he was some kind of evil spirit. It was during the trip that our interpreter learned some new words. Our physio at the time was George Wright, who could be quite short-fused. When we were ready to leave the stadium, George would always be impatient and be yelling: "Come on, lads, let's fucking go." The interpreter asked: "What is this word 'flucking'?" so George told him it was an Anglo-Saxon word for "hurry up". This interpreter was part of the diplomatic corps and I often wondered if he used that "flucking" word to hurry up others...

The one guy who wasn't with us in China was Willie Johnston. He was with Scotland in Argentina at the World Cup but it didn't end well for him. He was sent home after failing a drugs' test. Before I continue, I should add that footballers make jokes about everything. At times nothing is off limit, even these days. Willie said that Ron had met him at the airport and told him he had got him a new deal with Boots, The Chemist. I felt very sorry for Willie. He took a hay-fever remedy to help him sleep but it was apparently a performance-enhancing drug and on the banned list. Willie claimed that there was no way it could have been performance-enhancing given how badly he played.

So that was China. At least we were back home, right? You'd be wrong. We flew to Syria a few weeks later as part of our pre-season. Ron Atkinson didn't bother coming on that trip, not surprisingly, and we had Colin Addison looking after us for those two games against local teams in Aleppo. What I remember about that trip was flying back after our final game where it took us three attempts to land. We were on a military cargo plane and I recall hearing this bang, looked at the back of the plane where a door had opened there were the skips with our kit and equipment but also there were several military guys sitting on the skips. It was a white-knuckle ride for us. I had done a bit of gliding and flying so I knew a little bit about aircraft discipline. I know that when it's windy you have to come in quick to avoid the effects of the gust with the aircraft at an angle to the runway and then straighten out for the landing. Each time we came in, as we were about to land the power would go back on, and we'd go around again. On the first attempt Derek Statham was taking the piss out of Tony Brown, who hated flying. But after we failed to land for the second time even Derek went quiet. When we did finally land on the third attempt, I could see the grass to the side of the runway coming towards us very quickly – we didn't so much land as bang down onto the ground, before straightening out on the runway. If we had clipped the grass verge, we'd have skidded off the runaway. It was quite scary. It wasn't a good experience for any of us, even those of us who were relaxed about flying.

We were getting noticed as a team. There was a period where we almost lost big Cyrille to French club Saint-Etienne. They came in with an offer of around £750,000, which was more than Hamburg had spent on Kevin Keegan a year or so before, so they weren't messing around. Cyrille was still only 20, so it was probably too early for him to move. It wasn't unusual to see our players being linked with moves back then.

When I first joined West Brom, one of the first things Ron said to me was that I might not get a chance to play with Tony Brown much because he's coming towards the end of his career. Bomber, which was Tony's nickname, had been a brilliant player for the club since the 1960s and was well into his 30s when I joined. He ended up becoming one of our key players, especially in that 1978/79 season when the team just seemed to click. He was very infectious, like a perpetual schoolboy. As players we always felt that Bomber would grab you a goal. Ally Brown isn't related to his namesake, but they often shared a telepathic understanding that meant Ally would do so much of the hard work, which Bomber and Cyrille would finish off. Ally was one of my room-mates for a number of years, and actually quite insecure that he didn't score enough. I would always be telling him how he occupied defenders, creating space for Bomber or Cyrille, or how he would stretch defenders to create more room for Pop to run into. I've seen people compare Bomber to Frank Lampard both being goal-scoring midfielders...but Bomber scored more. And that's saying something given how many times Lampard netted for Chelsea and England.

As for Bryan - or Pop or Robbo as he was known- initially he reminded me of the former Ipswich and Liverpool player John Wark in the way he would ghost into space without anyone apparently seeing him. It was quite a quality to have. He obviously went onto develop over the years, not only into a box-to-box player, but a very good player technically. The only player I saw give Pop a hard time was Craig Johnston, the former Middlesbrough and Liverpool player. Craig could read him, stay with him and was immensely fit. Not many could do that, but Craig did.

Pop was so competitive. He didn't always say much back then but if you weren't on your game, you'd get the stare from him. He was never a shouter much like Bobby Moore who wasn't demonstrative either – more so someone who would lead by example and expected others to reach his standards, and that is exactly how Pop was. You knew if you weren't on your game, Pop would be all over you with that stare. There was an incident in the season before he went to Manchester United, we were 2-1 down towards the end of the game and attacking on my side. I managed to win the ball, deep in my half, I knocked into Pop, who returned it to me. I played it to Gary Owen and then from nowhere Pop wins us a penalty. I've barely crossed the halfway line, yet he'd already made that ground up to get into their box and win us that spot-kick. Bryan wasn't so quick in acceleration but he had the longer-distance energy and pace to burn people off. You may see his runs coming, but you could do little about them because he just had the legs to get into goalscoring positions. If you want to see what else Bryan could do, check out his goals in the opening England game of the 1982 World Cup. The first was all about anticipation, reading the movement of defenders around him and executing the shot with his left foot; his second was a fantastic header. He also read the game exceptionally well and was strong in the tackle. When there was talk of him going, I did a piece in the Sports Argus newspaper saying that you want to keep your best players but knowing we couldn't deny him that move. West Brom, even then, were a selling club. People forget I only played with Laurie for 15 months because he went off to Madrid, likewise Lenny Cantello, who moved to Bolton. The club simply didn't invest enough. Laurie went too soon, Lenny went for the wrong reasons. We got David Mills, who just didn't work out for us – for the individual, or the club. Remi Moses, a terrific little player, also left us. You don't get many Laurie Cunninghams, Bryan Robsons or Remis...and yet when we did, we sold them.

The 1978/79 season was one hell of a campaign for us. In many ways it was a let-down because we finished the season without winning anything. But equally we won a lot of friends playing some fantastic football.

We started off with three straight wins. And what was very clear at the start of that campaign was how much Laurie had developed during that summer. We saw glimpses of it in China but he was on a totally different level to what we'd seen of him before. Elsewhere, Pop began to emerge – he seemed to be getting better and better. And the player who had a major influence that season was Len Cantello. He was particularly dominant that season in a lot of games. One of the reasons Lenny left at the end of that season – which was to be a big mistake in my view – was because Ron Atkinson felt in many ways that he was too dominant over Bryan, which I just couldn't understand. Pop was always going to be the Bryan Robson we came to see as captain of Manchester United and England, regardless of anyone else in that team. Yes, Lenny was an influence on Pop, but I felt Ron thought that it was holding Pop back. And at the end of that season Lenny was to leave over a few quid. He never reached those heights again in his career and it was very damaging to us too. We knew we couldn't keep Laurie, and we knew we'd struggle to keep Bryan, but to lose Lenny the way we did – to Bolton, who were no great shakes – was really disappointing.

That first game in 1978/79 was against Ipswich Town, played in the bright sunshine. It was our first meeting with Ipswich since that FA Cup semi-final defeat but, this time, we had Robson and Cunningham playing. I just wonder what would have happened had those two played just a few months earlier in that Highbury game. Those first six or seven games I don't think we played as well again that season – we were absolutely fantastic. We beat Bolton at The Hawthorns when Frank Worthington was playing for Wanderers. We got a corner and I was the last man back. Frank turned to me and said: "Fucking hell, you're a good side aren't you?" They were four down at the time!

Then there was another game, just a week later, where Brian Clough couldn't praise enough for a no score game where we absolutely battered Nottingham Forest. We were just brilliant at the City Ground, with Peter Shilton being the best player on the field. Ally Brown was one-on-one with Peter three times and each time he was denied. That performance was noticed by Clough, who spoke so highly about us – it also summed us up at that time. People were taking a shine to us. And this was a Forest side which won the League and was heading fast towards the first of two European Cups.

Funnily enough a few years later I went to a forum with radio presenter Tony Butler, who was well-known for being the voice of West Midlands' football during the 1970s and 1980s. There was myself, Trevor Francis and Brian Clough. That was one hell of a good night. During the evening I was relating a story about how we'd gone to see one of the Forest games during their promotion year. Cambridge were due to play Swansea only for the game to get called off, so Ron Atkinson took us to see Forest play Millwall. One of my former team-mates at Arsenal David Donaldson was playing right-back for Millwall and being given the absolute run-around by Forest's ace left-winger John Robertson. At one point John crossed the ball into the box for the far post, David went to head it away for a corner and somehow managed to steer it past his own goalkeeper...something I'd do in the years to come! Anyway, a few years later I'm at this forum recounting this story when Brian stands up, points at me and says: "Yeah, but it was a fucking good cross wasn't it?" And that was Brian Clough one of the real characters in the game.

Anyway, back to Albion. We absolutely hammered Chelsea 3-1 at Stamford Bridge – it should have been a lot more too – and then went to Leeds and won by the same scoreline. It just seemed that we could beat anyone. Training was great. We would play five-a-side and Ron still thought he was the best player but by now, surrounded by those West Brom lads, I think it's fair to say he wasn't. The one thing Ron did well was surround himself with a good No2. His first assistant with us was Colin Addison and then Mick Brown came in. With both men you thought you could go to them with any issues. Colin especially was a very bubbly character. Ron was bubbly too but he was the manager, who occasionally had to say the harsh things. Colin was the perfect supplement to that relationship. He was terrific and, to this day, I'm very fond of him.

We played Coventry in October 1978 and that was a special day for us. They were wearing this awful brown kit that will probably forever be associated with that game, but they had some useful players in their side. People like Jim Holton, Ian Wallace, Steve Hunt - they had footballers who were established top-flight players, yet everything that could go right, did go right for us. It clicked that day. We had five goal-scorers, including little Derek Statham. We beat them 7-1 and felt there was something very special brewing.

It's quite interesting that when Ron Atkinson came into West Brom there was a perception that he was a lower league manager. He had been preceded by John Giles, who was a world-class footballer in his own right, and Ronnie Allen, who was a West Brom legend. So, Ron had a lot to do to change that perception of him. The one asset he had was this ability to be absolutely unfazed. His confidence was off the scale. He made sure the players enjoyed training sessions, but he also wanted us playing a certain way – with two full-backs, myself and Derek, being able to attack and support the forward players, like Cyrille, Laurie and Ally Brown then players like Pop Robson and Bomber supporting them. It's no wonder we had this confidence about us whenever we attacked. Bomber, Cyrille, Laurie and Ally Brown all scored double figures for us that season.

Oddly, it was that particular year that a young goalkeeper called Bruce Grobbelaar joined us for training. He had previously fought in the Rhodesian Bush War and it was very clear to us that he was some character. We went to a training camp in Oxford, and he was taking the lead in the cross-country running – I'd never seen a keeper at the front of the pack, yet there he was. He just shrugged and said in that strong Afrikaan's accent: "You learn to run fast when they're shooting at you."

At the time we had Tony Godden and Mark Grew, so it was always going to be tough for Bruce. And then he realised he couldn't get a work permit, so we thought that was that – only for him to rock up at Crewe a few months later. It turns out that after he'd left us, he'd realised he had some family members in Scotland and qualified for a work permit after all. Our loss was definitely Liverpool's gain, as Bruce went onto become a mainstay of the brilliant Reds' team of the 1980s. I'll say this for Bruce, he had one of the most horrendous golf swings I've ever seen. He'd absolutely shank it and then yell: "I'll see you on the green" and we'd not see him again for ages. He certainly wasn't shy.

Anyway, back to the football. December 1978 was a special month for us. Off the pitch it wasn't a great time. It was the winter of discontent across the country, and we were about to enter one of the coldest periods of the decade, just as we were hitting our peak.

We beat Middlesbrough 2-0, we beat Wolves 3-0 at Molineux, Arsenal away 2-1 on Boxing Day and then came the Manchester United game. The build up to Old Trafford was a succession of wins. Cyrille scored a brilliant goal at Molineux. I chipped the ball to Ally Brown, who did a chest pass that split Bob Hazell and George Berry, allowing Cyrille to knock it in. It was one of those games where everything worked well. Arsenal was even better. Liam Brady was playing that day and I recall Pop was running the show in midfield – again, it was a brilliant attacking display by us. And then came Manchester United. We were on a roll. We felt – probably knew – we could have beaten any team in the country at that point. Collectively I'd say we were playing at 75 per cent plus. And what I mean by that is at any given period a team will inevitably carry one or two who maybe aren't playing at their best. In December 1978, we didn't have anyone who wasn't playing at near the best of their form. It was close to being the perfect team, with exceptional performances from people like Bryan, Cyrille, Ally Brown, Lenny Cantello and Laurie. We weren't just winning games, we were leaving stardust on the pitch.

Anyway, back to Old Trafford. That was such an open game. The scoring went 1-0 to them, 2-1 to us – with Lenny scoring one of the goals of the season - 3-2 to them and then we scored an equaliser with the last kick of the first half. It was quite funny because Ron had already left the dug-out and gone back to the dressing room thinking we were losing 3-2. He got out this piece of paper with his half-time notes and said: "I cannot believe you're losing...this is a travesty." We were all looking at each other and then I heard Bomber pipe up: "Hey, I've just scored." And with that Ron screwed up the piece of paper and said: "Well, go and win it then." He made us feel about 10 feet tall. In the second half it was just one-way traffic. We were never going to lose that game. What struck me most is that Cyrille was being thwarted repeatedly by Gary Bailey, who was producing these spectacular saves and regarded by some to have been the best United player on the day. But in the end Cyrille scored that goal that everyone remembers, with Laurie racing down the right, playing it into Ally Brown and then Cyrille smashing it in, raising his arms in celebration and just that big smile and those dimples looking straight back at us. That became his trademark. Even the United players from that game appreciate they were part of something special. And yet I still think the Arsenal game was better. It was probably more of a personal thing for me because I came away thinking that my decision to leave Arsenal was vindicated. I knew I was good enough to have played for them. As a team performance that was fantastic.

What is now of greater significance perhaps is that the United game was the first time that racism had been called out. ITV were filming the game for The Big Match highlights show and the commentator was the well-known Granada TV commentator Gerald Sinstadt. The abuse we received that day was very audible but often ignored so to hear it mentioned by Gerald was to his credit. I remember once speaking to John Motson and I asked him why he didn't mention the racist abuse that black players were getting. He would happily refer to someone throwing a bottle or brick onto the pitch, but not mention racist abuse... so I asked why? His reply was along the lines that at the time there was another chant by supporters as the goalkeeper took a goal-kick that he claimed could be mistaken for racist abuse. I said that was utter rubbish – if we could hear it, so could he. I'm not making this an attack on John Motson, because he was a great commentator, who was hugely respected by all within the game, but he was one of many who took a similar stance in not calling out racist abuse. It makes me think they were being silenced by their bosses, which is why it was so surprising and refreshing that Gerald Sinstadt called out the Manchester United fans on that particular day. Everyone has their own memories of that fantastic match, but for me one of the biggest moments was hearing, at last, a commentator speaking out about the horrific chanting. I admired him so much for having the conviction and presence of mind to do that. I was watching it at home the following day and was just shocked that a commentator on national TV would make reference to it.

It was during that period we played Valencia in the UEFA Cup. European competition was new for us as a team. I'd been playing for Cambridge the year before and here I was playing in Europe. We beat Sporting Braga, which was a fantastic experience. But Valencia was the night. During the course of the game I remember thinking: "Thank goodness I'm not the one marking Laurie." Who was having the game of his life. I had Lenny in front of me, along with Laurie. We did the usual thing – kept them quiet for as long as we could and even when they scored after 20 minutes we gradually got a hold of the game. You knew if you gave the ball to Laurie you had time to get yourself organised – Gordon Strachan and Ryan Giggs were another two who were good at that. You knew they could just hold that ball, allow you to regroup, return into your team shape. We drew in Spain and I knew we'd win at home. Valencia had the great Mario Kempes playing, who had won the World Cup with Argentina just a few months earlier. Ally Robertson had threatened Mario with all sorts of violence – he even gave him the old finger across the throat. Poor Mario didn't turn up at all that night at The Hawthorns.

As for the game, if you look outside The Hawthorns now you actually see the statue that replicates one of Bomber Brown's goals that night. Laurie had actually under-hit a cross and Bomber had to instinctively volley it because he didn't have the time to do much else. Of course, what nobody ever mentions is that I'd beaten a couple of players and passed to Laurie before he crossed it. They never mention that bit of skill! Every time I see that statue I'm taken back to that goal. In the next round we played Red Star Belgrade. Now, that was an experience. I believe there were 98,000 there that day but unofficially there were reports many more actually attended. We were naïve in those two legs. We lost the away leg 1-0 after giving away a lot of stupid free-kicks, but we thought we would claw it back in England. The irony is we were 1-0 up at The Hawthorns and looking for a second when they broke away and scored so we went out 2-1. It was down to our inexperience in Europe – Liverpool or a Brian Clough team wouldn't have allowed that to happen, but we were new to that as players and Ron was new to European football as a manager. We simply weren't streetwise enough. Sadly, we never learned our lessons from that because we didn't ever adapt our UEFA Cup games under Ron Atkinson. We played our normal way and came up against sides who knew how to adjust to continental football. We should have been better than Carl Zeiss Jena and Grasshoppers of Zurich in subsequent seasons, but we let ourselves down by not learning our lessons.

Thankfully, things were looking better in the League. Or so we thought. That was the winter it didn't stop snowing. It was 1963 all over again.

We were due to play Bristol City on New Year's Day and we knew the game would be in jeopardy due to the snow, so a lot of fans came to clean the terraces and the pitch. Joe Royle was with Bristol and, as one of their more experienced players, he was desperately trying to get it called off. What they didn't realise is that Ron had been in the States and found out about these boots that had pimpled soles rather than traditional studs. In front of Joe, Ron asked Bomber to put the boots on and asked him to sprint down the pitch – probably thinking that if the oldest player is fine with them then all will be okay. Ron turns around to Bomber and asked: "Hey Bomber, how was that? Is it okay for us to play?" And, with that, Bomber gave him the thumbs up. So, Ron turns back to Joe and says: "Joe, he's 35 and he said it's fine so what's the problem?" We absolutely murdered Bristol City, beating them 3-1. We played with elegance, while their players slipped around the pitch. Ally Brown got into a bit of trouble that day. He always had a mischievous streak in him and, whenever we faced a penalty, he'd roll up a bit of mud and throw it over the kicker's shoulder. I told him to stop doing it, but he didn't listen. We were 1-0 up approaching half-time when Bristol were awarded a penalty and as Tom Ritchie ran up to take it I could see from the corner of my eye that Ally was up to something. And, sure enough, Ally had rolled up a snowball and launched it straight at Ritchie, who stuck his penalty a mile wide. The referee spotted Ally's mischief and ordered a retake – which Ritchie duly scored. Thanks for that Ally!

We were absolutely loving football at this point. Every day in training was a great day. There were times Ron would actually have to stop training because we were enjoying it so much and didn't want to stop. He was worried we'd pick up a knock or simply be too tired for the match. We went top of the league for the first time in 50 years a few days later. We were 1-0 up at Norwich in what wasn't a great game for me. The freeze-up was starting and I was playing on the side where the stand had put a shadow over the pitch, so the ice hadn't thawed. We had a corner on our left, so I sneaked off to change my boots and called over to John Trewick to cover for me. I was desperately trying to get my boots on as quickly as possible. We swing the corner in straight to their keeper's hands and I can already see what's about to happen so I'm desperately trying to get back on the pitch but the ball isn't going out of play and Colin Addison, our assistant manager, is stopping me from going back on because he's convinced I'll be booked – he's practically got me in an arm-lock. I was just hoping somebody would commit a foul or kick it out, but nobody did. And, sure enough, Norwich scored and, yes, it came down my side. I wish I'd taken the yellow card after all. We were playing some fantastic football and games couldn't come quickly enough for us.

And then came the snow and the frost.

That break killed our momentum. Our next game was about three weeks later against Liverpool, who beat us 2-1. Anfield was the only ground that I never got a point. I always lost up there. Our form was just never the same again after that. We had to scramble in so many games and our performances started to drop off. We didn't have that same fluency any more. We lost 1-0 to Bristol City and never recovered. We played Chelsea on a Thursday – they murdered us, but we won – and ended up playing eight games in April. We were basically living in hotels, barely training and merely ticking over until the next game. Mentally we didn't even think second place was important. We had already qualified for Europe and it felt like an anti-climax at the end. I look back now and I'm disappointed we didn't do more to claim second because it was in our grasp. A point against Forest in our final game which was at home would have been enough, but we conceded a late Trevor Francis goal and they moved up into second above us. Very disappointing, looking back. While writing this book, I heard the sad news of Trevor's death. He a fabulous player, and a really nice guy, who I first played against in a reserve game at St Andrew's when I was at Arsenal. You could tell he was going to be a very special player.

It was that summer we had the Len Cantello testimonial when an all-white team played an all-black team. I've no idea who came up with the concept. Everyone was claiming it – there were some saying it was Ron's idea, others saying it was Cyrille's idea, other people were saying it was down to the testimonial committee. Back then we had a lot of testimonials – John Wile, Bomber Brown, Ally Robertson, John Osborne and others, so people were looking to do something different. I thought it was a great idea and it was a huge success for Lenny. And there was a real response from the black community. In terms of our approach, I know Cyrille has since spoken about how much he wanted to win that day because there was a feeling that as black people we needed to be seen to be working harder to be accepted. Without saying it, I think it would be fair to say we all felt that before the game, mainly because we all had a similar background, a shared journey and we had all experienced some form of prejudice. So, yeah, I'd say we knew and appreciated that for us this was way much more than just a testimonial. I think it was Garth Crooks who rallied us and said: "Let's beat these bastards." There were some obvious names in the team – myself Cyrille, Laurie, George Berry, Bob Hazell for instance – but we started to get people coming out of the woodwork, wanting to be part of the team. Vernon Hodgson, who I didn't know but was emerging at Birmingham, was one of those. Ron Atkinson immediately said he wanted to manage the black side – although Cyrille was quoted as saying his choice of manager would be Enoch Powell (who had made the famous Rivers of Blood speech a few years earlier), which was typical of Cyrille's humour. Anyway, as Ron was rallying everyone around this black kid suddenly appeared in the doorway. Nobody knew who he was. After a few minutes Ron eventually turned to him and said: "What's your name then?" It was Noel Blake, who was just a young lad at Aston Villa. He just turned up and asked to play.

This wasn't a normal testimonial game for us. At the time we were hearing people saying it was divisive and it wasn't good for race relations. We didn't see it like that. We just saw it as a way of getting people through the turnstiles, to showcase the progress that black players were making. It certainly wasn't intended as anything more than that. This was something else to give Lenny a bit of recognition for his 10 years at the club. But, yes, we also thought it was a positive message for black players, not least as we ended up winning 3-2. And yet looking back it's one of the games people have heard so little about. There was a documentary some years ago but until then it had been barely mentioned. But it was never intended to be a social milestone; it was merely a different idea to a testimonial. It was a way of raising money for someone who deserved it.

Losing Lenny was a blow. He would dominate games – he was so important to us. We lost a good player, Bolton never really saw the best of him and Lenny wasn't the same player after leaving us. People talk about Laurie leaving for Madrid, but he was the sprinkle of gold dust and, we were never going to compete with the club who came in for him. Lenny was so important to us in other ways and we paid for it. Coming to us were Peter Barnes and Gary Owen. They were steeped in

Manchester City for so many years, so it was a surprise they joined us. Peter was a record signing for £748,000 – which was a lot of money back then. They were two different characters but very funny in their own right. Barnsey was away with the fairies at times. He scored quite a few goals for us and had one of the best first touches that I've ever seen. He and Derek Statham were excellent in that respect. Gary Owen came into the void left by Len Cantello but he was such a different player. It would be unfair to compare Gary to Len, or Peter to Laurie, because they didn't have the same attributes as the players they replaced. What I do remember is us going on tour to Yugoslavia and recreating the old Superstars TV programme, including one discipline in open water, swimming between rocks. Gary Owen told us he could swim, jumped in and we could see him waving – we thought he was drowning, with all that flapping away. He was hilarious. He was a better footballer than he was a swimmer.

We struggled massively the next season. We were tipped to be one of the title contenders and yet we had an awful start to the season. It's quite funny looking back because at the time we were given club cars and the registration plates on the cars were all similar. The cars had clearly been registered at the same time, with all of them featuring the letters D-Y-M on the number plates. The papers picked up on that and had a field day, as you can imagine, not least given our poor form. We ended up mid-table and were scrambling around the bottom for way too long throughout that season. We lost Cyrille to injury for a long time, which didn't help, and the whole dynamic of the side changed when Laurie and Lenny left. It felt like a hangover from the previous season. And it was very forgettable for us, with few highlights. There was one game we played against Palace where Remi Moses made his debut. Ron was miked up for that, doing commentary during periods of the game. Imagine that now. When I first join West Brom and played a few games in the reserves Ron had asked me what I thought about the younger players. I told him that I thought Remi and Martyn Bennett would be good players. In that Palace game – which was Remi's debut – we were two nil down, but he absolutely took over in the second half. He was outstanding and we went onto draw 2-2. That was the turning point for us that season. Remi was one hell of a player and someone I've always had a lot of time for. Once he got into the side, he was never out of it. For a young player he was strong-minded, refused to back down and wasn't overawed by any of his opponents, no matter who they were, despite still being a 19-year-old. I recall sharing a room with him during one of our European games and our conversation was basically me saying: "Good morning Remi" and then "Goodnight Remi." That's how quiet he was. He was desperately unlucky to suffer with injuries, as was Martyn Bennett – a big, strong and hard-as-nails defender, who got picked for the England squad but never played due to a back problem that was to blight him for the remainder of his career.

It was during this season that Pop also started to dominate games on a regular basis. In the season before he joined United – in 1980/81 – he was the best player in the League. He was a brilliant reader of the game, which is why he got into the positions to score so often. He had massive determination. I remember just before his move writing a column for the Sports Argus as he was getting some negative publicity about the interest from Man United. I stated that West Brom should do everything in their power to keep him because we stand a better chance with him in the team rather than letting him go for a record fee to Manchester United. I did my best to take the sting out of that whole situation. Without doubt had he stayed for another season we would have had a better campaign in 1981/82.

There was another reason for our decline. In September 1980 we lost Tom Silk, who was an increasingly influential director at West Brom and, at the time of his death, effectively our de facto chairman. We were playing Everton away and beat them 2-1. John Gidman missed a penalty and we had given him dog's abuse as he prepared to take it. It had been a great game that night for the team and after the match we filtered back to the dressing room on a high following our performance. The mood soon turned when we were told the horrific news that Tom's light aircraft had crashed in southern France. He and his wife were on their way back to watch our game on Merseyside...but they never made it. It was a brutal thing to hear. He was popular among the players – especially during the trip to China, when we really got to know him. He was approachable, had a brilliant sense of humour, with he and Ron Atkinson being like a music hall double act. He was called Torremolinos Tom - he would get the Champagne in, and Ron would say: "Hey Tom...what do you think of this Champagne?" And after a few bottles he'd be informed it was the most expensive one on the wine list. Tom was effectively being lined up to be the next chairman when Sir Bert Millichip completed his transition to the Football Association. Sir Bert had been a very respected, successful figurehead but Tom was dynamic and would have given the club a completely different, fresh vision. He knew football, but he also knew the value of growing the club – he was a very ambitious man. Sadly, it was never to be. And I don't think West Brom ever recovered from that.

We were on the downward curve by 1980/81, even though we were to finish fourth. I really do think Tom might have arrested that trend. You just felt that in that moment the club was winded beyond belief. We had people like Sid Lucas, a director who called me a barrack-room lawyer – he didn't like me advising other players. Absolute nonsense. He was calling me that because I'd been giving my views about Bryan Robson's potential move to Manchester United in my Sports Argus column. The Sports Argus was a Saturday pink newspaper in the West Midlands. Each club in the area would have a guest player columnist, and in 1981 it happened to be me. The club didn't like me saying what I thought. But I was honest. We were in decline – which was to be proven after Ron Atkinson left and Tom Silk died.

John Silk, who was Tom's brother, was very different. He became chairman some years later, during the late 1980s, when the club was in an even worse place. Our total trajectory changed in that one moment in September 1980 when Tom lost his life. The ambition went completely. We started to sell big, without replacing what we had. Players need that lift. We were all ambitious and we didn't shy away from competition. These days it's a squad game and you rotate. Back in my day if you were rotated, you were dropped. But I didn't mind that. That was football.

1981 was to end with us finishing fourth. We hadn't really challenged for the title and it felt like the end of an era, with hindsight. In fact we were to have a major say in the League title's destination – when I say we, I mean me. I scored my first League goal in our 3-1 win against Ipswich in April. Just a few days later I made the error which gifted Ipswich's title rivals Aston Villa a victory in our game at Villa Park. That defeat, and our win against Ipswich, essentially gave our neighbours the momentum to finish off the job. The 1980/81 season ended as an anti-climax, but things were about to get worse.

1981/82 was bad from a football point of view. We played three semi-finals and didn't score a goal – we played twice against Spurs in the

Milk Cup and QPR in the semi-final. That was also the season Albion replaced Manchester United-bound Ron Atkinson with the wrong manager. West Brom interviewed Ronnie Allen and Alan Mullery. After going through the interview process they decided that Mullery was going to be the next manager but somewhere along the line somebody made a mistake and informed Allen that he'd got the job instead, rather than Alan. What a mistake to make! By all accounts Ronnie was asked to stay behind to sign the contract, while Alan was back on a train to Brighton, totally oblivious of the mistake. It was too late to call him back. Alan Mullery has since told the story himself but at the time you're thinking: "No, surely not...?" but, yes, it did actually happen.

When I joined Albion in early 1978, I'd heard stories about John Giles, who was regarded as a Messiah, and Ronnie Allen who was referred to as a joke. So, when Ronnie was reappointed as manager in 1981, you can imagine how that went down. At the time Ally Brown was my room-mate but he'd done off to play for Portland Timbers over in the States during the summer. I never answered the phone in our house, but Cecily called me over, demanding that I take it. I picked up the phone and all I heard was: "Brendon, tell me it's not true...they've not reappointed Ronnie Allen have they?" I had no idea who it was calling me at first. It was Ally. He couldn't believe it and he clearly wasn't impressed.

Another reason the players didn't like him is that in his first spell, back in 1977, he had lost the players within his first training session! Apparently, Allen brought his wife down to training and she was sat on a deck chair from the side of the pitch, blowing a whistle and calling players out. I couldn't believe what I was hearing.

For a long-time Ronnie was the club's all-time leading scorer. He became Albion manager around the period that Tony Brown started to close-in on his record. I'm told he used to wind-up Tony, promising him there was no way he would claim his record. And as manager I guess he could decide whether Bomber played. I'm told Ronnie had been a phenomenal player – the records suggest he was - but as a manager, I just didn't rate him.

More to the point, for the first time since joining West Brom, I was beginning to wonder if my future might lie elsewhere.

TRIBUTE

I am so fond of Brendon. He always stood out because not only was he one of the lads, but he was quite an intellectual too. Well-mannered, a lovely and polite guy – not something you'd always see in football. He was a very thoughtful man who was a gentleman off the pitch, but more than comfortable with the pressures that football brought.

When you're at a club you sometimes look at new signings and think: "I'm not so sure about him," and whether he will catch on. But I never had that with Brendon, because we knew he'd been at Arsenal as a kid and with that kind of background you know you're going to be getting a player who must have been showing something. You don't play for Arsenal if you're not talented.

He was calming on the pitch. You'd rarely see him flustered and very few could knock it and run the ball past him. Brendon didn't look quick on the pitch but that was deceptive. He was extremely quick, he could defend, his positional sense was very good, and he fitted in well into what was a very strong team at that time. It was only a matter of time before he made the shirt his own. And once he did, he never looked back.

As a person we became good friends and although we don't see that much of each other these days, I look back on our time as team-mates with great fondness. Brendon was also a top role-model – I can imagine a lot of kids looking up to him. He was a good footballer and an even better man.

Len Cantello, West Bromwich Albion (1968-1979)

CHAPTER FIVE
Ron, Ronnie, Ron...

"...You'll have a bit of pain, but you'll have to get on with it..."

Ronnie Allen's time in charge was an unhappy period in my career. The stories I'd heard from his first tenure didn't bode well. I really couldn't get my head around why they had even considered him knowing so many of the players didn't like him – of course, it made more sense when we realised the club had made that awful mistake.

He left the club in the lurch in his first spell by going to Saudi Arabia. Some of the stories I heard about him as a manager and coach were just unbelievable. I honestly thought some of the lads were joking when they were telling me, but I was to find out just how real those stories were.

Ronnie came in and it quickly became apparent that it wasn't going to work between us. Remi Moses had already gone to Manchester United to join Ron Atkinson and Pop wasn't far behind him. I then started hearing whispers that he considered me to be "Ron's Man" and that I was a "cancer" in the club – those were the exact words that were being fed back to me by people in the game.

During that season he signed Martin Jol and Romeo Zondervan. Jol was a midfielder but there were very strong rumours that he was being signed to replace me – even though I was a defender. I've no idea how that was going to work, not least as Martin wasn't a full-back, but these rumours were gathering momentum, so I went to confront Ronnie about this. When people you're mates with in the press are starting to say: "Watch your back Bren," and things like that, you know that someone is laying down poison. And I was told it was coming from my own manager. At the time the Halfords Lane stand at The Hawthorns was being rebuilt so the club's offices were technically in a series of portable cabins opposite the stadium. I went into his office and I had it out with him – he was denying everything, being extremely defensive. But, equally, he didn't give me any kind of reassurance either, which pissed me off even more. I stormed back out after saying my piece and slammed the door shut. And then all I heard was the door creak and fall

85

off its hinge. So, there I was having just told the manager what I thought of him and now I'm trying to wrestle his office door back onto its hinges. That pretty much set the tone for our relationship.

There was a farcical situation at the hotel before the Leeds game that season. I was hearing all of these rumours about Jol signing and while we were there, preparing for the game, I went to the toilet and as I came out Martin Jol was coming in. It was such an awkward moment because he knew who I was and his reaction to seeing me made me think he'd been told that I would be gone by the time he turned up.

Martin and Romeo were great players by the way. This was a period where more and more players were coming in from overseas. Martin was perceived as a bit of a hard case but I never saw him that way. He was actually a lovely man, he had a presence but he was a good player. Romeo was a lovely footballer. He reminded me of Remi in that he had lovely feet and could move the ball comfortably and with such short steps. He was one of these footballers who wasn't quick, but he was quick when he had the ball at his feet – he was a very technically good player. Both of them integrated well.

The 1981/82 season was a huge disappointment for us. We got to two semi-finals and lost both, without scoring a goal across three games. And we could easily have got relegated, which with that set of players would have been an absolute disgrace. During that season I asked to leave because of what was going on with Ronnie Allen's whispering campaign. I had a call telling me that John Bond wanted me at Manchester City but then the directors made it clear I wouldn't be leaving. I'd been on the transfer list for most of the season but, eventually, as we went on those cup runs, they asked me to come off the list so I did. It was a very unhappy time for me and the club, because of those accusations.

With hindsight that was probably my biggest mistake. I wonder what would have happened had I gone elsewhere but I was blinded by the cup runs.

The semi-finals were a big regret. To not score a goal was just shocking really and we played so badly, especially in the FA Cup semi-final. But first we had the League Cup semi-final double-header against Spurs. We drew the first game 0-0 and I was forced to miss the second game because I suffered a hamstring injury, which was the first time I'd ever suffered such an injury – and it happened during a warm-up in training the day before the second leg, which made it even more frustrating. They put an injection into the injury, which turned out to be a massive mistake and caused me problems for a long time afterwards. I was watching from the stands. Micky Hazard scored the one and only winning goal, with Jol and Tottenham's Tony Galvin being sent off during that match. Very frustrating.

I managed to get back well in time for the FA Cup semi-final against Queens Park Rangers, who were a second division side at the time albeit a very good footballing team. Leicester and Tottenham were the two other sides in the semi-final so we were rubbing our hands, thinking we'd got the best draw. We were playing well at the time, albeit we were picking up more draws than wins. That game at Highbury was one of the biggest games of our careers but it was an absolute non-event. It was one of the worst games I've been involved in and don't recall a single worthwhile contribution I made to that game. Rangers were managed at the time by Terry Venables, who would go onto manage Barcelona and England, and he turned up to that semi-final with a game plan. We all said Tony Currie was the one we had to be aware of, because he could control the game with his passing. Their plan was that Gary Micklewhite would block Derek Statham and Micky Flanagan would block me, and Bob Hazell would man-mark Cyrille. And it worked, because both myself, and Derek – who provided so much attacking width – were totally snuffed out. Worse, Tony Currie had the run of the pitch and we couldn't do anything about it.

But the tone for this match was set before we even kicked-off. Gary Owen was dropped. I was actually going out for a walk outside our Kensington hotel before the game when John Wile pulled me over and said: "He's left out Gary." I could not believe it, yet Gary didn't know. There is no way you can drop a bombshell like that in the team meeting, which is exactly what Ronnie Allen was planning to do. John told me to leave it, so I was walking around knowing Gary wasn't in the side and, worse, didn't even know yet. We went into the meeting, Ronnie went through the side and then it got to No10 and it was Nicky Cross, with Martyn Bennett going in as a third centre-half. And at that moment Ronnie managed to kill the entire atmosphere. Players knew instinctively who would be playing so to see us suddenly change a system when we've been going well was madness. And if you're going to make a major selection decision like that at least make everyone aware in advance. We had spent the whole week training with different personnel so there wasn't even any inkling that Gary wouldn't be playing. It was an abysmal way to treat him and I believe Gary never properly forgave Ronnie for that. I'm not blaming that decision by the manager for the way we played, but it certainly didn't help. It was an appalling way to handle such an important decision.

It went downhill after that. we went onto lose nine of the next 10 games after that. Allen's assistant Gerry Summers took the full brunt of my anger. We had a meeting, where myself, John Wile and Ally Robertson effectively took charge. We were regarded as the Three Contemptibles because we were deemed the old guard taking on a manager who wasn't showing any signs of arresting our decline. We were on the slide, we were going down, but we all knew that we were good enough to play in the top division.

Gerry Summers always said I got him and Ronnie Allen the sack. That's absolute rubbish. They got the sack because they took a side that had finished fourth the previous year, and just about stayed up on their watch. Gerry was formulaic with his training. It was the same every single day. We were doing the same warm-ups, the same drills, the same training sessions...all in the hope it would change the result. We were doing the same thing over and again, hoping for a different result. The definition of madness, Einstein called it. In one session Gerry was making us play five-a-side, in a small area, but with full-size goals. There was no passing, no tackling because the pitch was so small, we effectively could have a shot within one pass. It was ridiculous. Under Ron Atkinson we had sessions that were so competitive that he had to stop them at times, but here we were playing some kind of five-a-side on a tiny pitch but proper goals. It made no sense, but Gerry's reasoning was that we used the big goals because that's what we played with on the Saturday. A team meeting was called and during the course of it I just lost it. I told him training was a joke and he just got up and walked out. I thought that was me done. I suggested we go playing golf, go for a swim, doing something different – anything to get us smiling again and restore some spirit. We needed a change of scenery.

That period really underlined that Allen was weak as piss as a manager because he had no authority. He was a strange character. He had no appetite for confrontation. We were losing one of the games during that slump and he walked in at half-time and said: "So, what we going to do lads?" and I'm thinking "You're the fucking manager...you give us direction and guidance." I'd never seen anything like it. He wouldn't change anything. Summers didn't help. Previous assistant managers like Colin Addison and Mick Brown would report back to Ron Atkinson but would not drop the lads in it. There was a trust there. We didn't have that with Gerry.

We were losing games. Mind you, we beat Wolves on May 1. We always seemed to do well against Wolves. That was the game Cyrille and Derek Monaghan scored with Andy Gray knocking out Romeo Zondervan. Andy was a good old warrior but I took a swipe at him for doing what he did to poor Romeo. I actually missed him! He got the foul anyway and as he prepared to take it, referee Neil Midgley called me over and said: "Brendon come here...you've got something in your eye." He actually had his hanky out, offering it to me. He then leaned over to me and said: "You do anything like that again and I'll have you sent off..." I didn't do it again. It's also what you call clever refereeing!

Leeds was the big one. It was the penultimate game for us. We knew that if we beat Leeds we'd be staying up. A win for us would also mean that either Leeds or Stoke would be going down – depending on results in the final game of the season. Anyway, we were 2-0 up against Leeds and the fans started wrecking the ground and spilling onto the pitch. It was the first time I had seen police horses on the pitch at The Hawthorns. The next day we could see blood, trainers and all sorts of debris on the terraces. With about a minute to go I saw a horse on the pitch and said to the referee: "Ref, you've got to call time, there's a horse on the pitch." I cannot remember who the referee was, but he turned around, blew the whistle and we all sprinted off the pitch. That meant it was between Stoke or Leeds to see who would go down. And Stoke's final game happened to be against us – they couldn't have called it any better. For the first 20 minutes Stoke didn't have a kick and then they scored from nothing. There had been strong rumours that Leeds fans would be coming up to that game to effectively try to get our game called off if Stoke took the lead. I think collectively we just thought: "Fuck this, we're safe anyway." We ended up losing 3-0 but Stoke didn't actually play well. The funny thing was about 10 minutes after the game, we were still in the dressing room at the Victoria Ground when the door swung open – in came Stoke manager Richie Barker with a couple of bottles of Champagne, wishing us a happy summer. Can you imagine that now?

More to the point, that was the end of Ronnie Allen. I don't like to speak ill of the dead but I cannot see what on earth possessed Albion to re-appoint a manager who was so poorly thought of in the first place.

Mind you, it didn't get much better for me. Coming in next was Ron Wylie, who had previously been manager of Coventry. I didn't maybe clash with Ron as I did with Ronnie, but it was still a very tough period for me. It was also going to get much worse for me on a completely different level, though I didn't know it yet.

Things started quite well under Ron – although only after we'd got our customary defeat at Anfield out of the way on the opening day of the season.

We then beat Brighton 5-0, Manchester United 3-1 and Stoke away by three goals to nil. That suggested all was well, but it actually quickly fell apart.

We played Watford at Vicarage Road at a time when they too were looking good, having been promoted from Division Two. For some reason Ron Wylie put Martin Jol at sweeper against a side that we knew would play 4-2-4 against us. They were playing long ball, so they could then pounce on the second ball. If you take a midfielder out, like we did, then it's not going to end well. We needed midfielders in there to fight Watford toe-to-toe.

We were second at the time when we played them. Martin (Jol) actually said: "What the hell are you doing putting me back there when my strength and their strength is in midfield?" We lost 3-0 and got battered. We had Ally Robertson and John Wile, who were rarely beaten in the air – yet Ron Wylie thought we needed a sweeper behind them, against a team that played high up the field. It was madness. And that was down to Ron Wylie and his assistant Mick Kelly, who was just as bad as Gerry Summers in many respects.

Mick wasn't the most popular. I always remember when I was injured watching a functional game in training, first team vs reserves. I was watching from the side-lines just as the ball fell for Romeo Zondervan on the edge of his own box, he had a quick look around before he pulled the ball down, turned and knocked a great ball to one of his teammates – an excellent piece of skill. Mick Kelly called a stop to training and went absolutely ballistic at Romeo, telling him never to do that again. Typical old school coaching.

That defeat at Watford set us back. We went down to Ipswich and that's when it all went wrong for me. We seemed to have this thing about losing heavily whenever we played Ipswich. It was one of those games where Eric Gates was playing in what we would call the hole these days. And we couldn't mark the sod because he was such a clever player. The game was drifting away from us and in the final 10 minutes or so the ball broke giving a 50:50 challenge - I got to it first. One of their players came in slightly after me – it wasn't malicious, just one of those things. As I toe-poked the ball away, his momentum came down onto my foot and my knee twisted. That injury I had as a 16-year-old finally caught up with me. The next day my kids were at horse riding and as I walked up the steps to a viewing gallery my knee locked. It's where the cartilage drops in between the joint. That's when I knew I'd done my cartilage.

A guy called Harry Willis had tried to help me. He was a great guy and a top physio who actually mentored physiotherapists and used to work pro bono when I was at Cambridge. It was he who had me working on my hamstrings because he could tell from my running style that I would suffer issues if I didn't look after them correctly. He was actually at the Ipswich game and knew straight away what had happened. Harry called me down to Cambridge and told me about a surgeon called David Dandy, who had pioneered the arthroscopy some time before then. A rugby player had got back playing within 10 days through this new technique. He was the first surgeon to champion this in the UK. It was a less intrusive, less traumatic form of treatment. The only trouble was that he was away in Texas for several months. I thought: "Bollocks to that, I'll be fit by then," so I went under the care of another surgeon, recommended by the club, who I later found out was not an orthopaedic specialist. I had the operation but could tell after about three months that my leg was withering. There was no definition. After five weeks I kicked the ball and the pain was absolutely immense – I had never experienced pain like it before or since. At that time all I was concentrating on was getting back to full fitness but here I was struggling to even kick a ball. I wanted to be back some time in the New Year of 1983, ideally. It clearly wasn't going to happen.

I fell out with Ron Wylie because his assistant Mick Kelly told me: "You'll have a bit of pain but you'll have to get on with it," which I couldn't believe. Anyway, I went back to Harry Willis and told him I had a problem – I couldn't even bend my knee properly. I went down to see him and was asked to apply this giant sock, from my foot right up to my groin, which they then pumped air through to try to straighten the leg and remove any obstruction. Ipswich Town's George Burley was in the bed next to me also being treated for a knee injury – his knee sounded like a rusty bicycle chain every time he moved it, but he was able to carry on. Anyway, after this procedure Harry called me into his office. I walked in, he shut the door behind me, sat me down, looked at me and said in his broad Yorkshire accent: "This could finish you." And that's when I first realised my career was on the line. I just burst out crying.

Basically, we had to start again. By now David Dandy was back in the UK and the plan was that we'd do a new procedure. I went back to Albion, told them what I wanted to do, but Ron Wylie said: "No, no, no... you cannot do that, you're under the club's jurisdiction."

My reply was to the point: "I couldn't give a fuck what you think Ron." This was my career. I had my operation on the club's recommendation, it didn't work, and now I had the chance of another operation – I could either do it with Ron's blessing, or without. Either way, I was going. The club had made an absolute pig's ear of my first operation and there was no way they were going to stop me from trying to save my career.

By now it was starting to get to me. Results weren't going well for us and I remember being in M&S in Sutton Coldfield trying to walk down the steps and having to hold onto the bannister because my knee was still causing problems – it was basically like moving down the hill without a brake, there was no control in my knee. At this point two Albion fans spotted me, walked over and said: "When are you going to get that cowing leg of yours fixed Bren – we need you back?" I'd had enough. There was only so much sympathy I could take, and I decided at that point I needed to get away.

I went back down to Cambridge and met David Dandy, who asked for new scans. He took one look at my x-rays and said: "You need to finish."

And that was that.

I started to cry, again. I had two young kids, I couldn't even play with them properly because of the pain. I pleaded with him to operate again on my knee and let me worry about the recovery. I was desperate. He agreed to that and operated on me. I was travelling down to Cambridge on the Monday and staying until the Friday – I did that from March to the end of the season. That became my life. I ended up staying in a caravan in Cromer for a week, just for a change of scenery and it was bloody freezing. Back at Cambridge, I was joined at physio sessions by another Ipswich player, Paul Mariner, who at the time was also recovering from a major injury. I worked really hard in a sand track that week and the one thing that was apparent was that I was carrying my right leg, my stride pattern was shorter and, even though I thought I'd done well, it was clear looking back that things weren't right.

I came back for pre-season in 1983. I managed to get through that but struggled a bit. Even so I thought I'd be fit enough to start the season and I remember going to see Ron Wylie and he made it very clear that in his view I wasn't ready.

I missed one hell of an opening day game. We played Villa away and we lost 4-3 – it was an outstanding game, even though we were unlucky to lose. Instead of making a comeback in the first team as I had hoped I was playing in the reserves up at Chesterfield and the pitch was like glass. It wasn't their first team pitch, but one of the others and it simply wasn't up to standard. It was hard and awkward to play on. As I was running forward during the game, a lad came towards me, mistimed his tackle and caught me on my right leg and, yes you've guessed it, my knee went again. I went straight down to David Dandy to tidy it up again and starting the process all over again. I remember Ally Robertson saying that he could tell I was fine running forward but the twisting and turning was the problem. He could see it; I could feel it. He was right. If I could run forwards in a straight line, without twisting and turning, I could salvage my career. If only football was that simple. Every time in training we did doggy sprints – where you run to one cone, run back, then run back to the next furthest cone, back again and so on - I would be fine running forward, even if I'd lost a yard of pace. I felt I was still relatively quick, but I knew I was struggling as soon as I had to twist and turn.

I had a tough decision to make but it was a fairly easy one because my body was telling me that I couldn't carry on anymore. No matter how hard I'd tried, it just wasn't going to happen. I called it a day just before Christmas 1983. By then I was having arguments with Mick Kelly, Wylie and others. I'd just had enough.

This wasn't an overnight process. I got injured in October 1982 and 14 months later it was all over. My wife Cecily was brilliant throughout. There was one occasion where I just snapped at her and yelled: "Leave me alone", because it was getting too much for me. That was so unfair on Cecily, who was so supportive in every way. I was so focused on getting back that I left our domestic life to her. She was great – she looked after the home and kids, allowing me to go down to Cambridge to try to recover. She left me alone to concentrate on that and I cannot imagine I was an easy person to live with during those months.

Harry Willis's words that this injury could finish my career had changed my outlook, even though it never made it easier. There were periods where deep down I knew it was game over and it wasn't a case of getting fit to play elite football, but merely a challenge to try to get fit and running again like any normal 30-year-old would. My knee wasn't allowing me to do that so even though I had it in the back of my mind, I was having to consider what would happen as I got older. I remember years later Paul McGrath at Aston Villa being managed through the tail end of his career by people like Graham Taylor and Ron Atkinson because he had so many issues with his knees. He ended up playing until he was nearly 40, with minimal training, because he could get through the games, but I couldn't even manage that.

I've always been quite self-critical. I explained earlier why I wanted to leave Arsenal, because I couldn't see myself having a career with them. My view was that I hadn't been convincing enough to be in their team. I then got to Cambridge, realised I was quick, but not fit enough. I was seeing other players at my level going onto First Division clubs. So, I decided to get fitter over distances, because I knew I needed to react to better myself. When it became clear that my knee wasn't going to recover, I knew I had to think about my future.

One of the things that prompted it was Stevie Coppell announcing that he was retiring, also through a serious injury. At the time he was the chairman of the Professional Footballers' Association, when I was on the management committee. Gordon Taylor, who was the head of the PFA, had a word with me and asked if I would consider replacing Steve as he saw me as the next chairman of the PFA. Gordon is a fantastic man, way ahead of his time, who wanted the management committee to be reflective of the membership, so I was the first black player to be elected onto the management committee. To be the chairman of the PFA you needed to be an active player so when Steve retired Gordon approached me, but I had to tell him that it wouldn't be fair as I was struggling myself. I didn't want to take the chair only to find that I had to stand down straight away. It would have been a waste of time, so Brian Talbot took over as chairman.

It was almost a relief for me to actually announce my retirement. I'd found it very debilitating being asked by people when I was going to be fit. That used to really get me down. To tell people I wasn't going to make it made it feel like a weight was lifted from my shoulders.

A few months later, Wylie was gone and John Giles returned as manager, bringing in Nobby Stiles and Norman Hunter as his assistants. West Brom were playing third division Plymouth at The Hawthorns in the FA Cup fifth round. There was a massive buzz around the stadium that day with Giles returning and a big expectation that we would reach the quarter-finals and maybe even make the final. But it was a strange day for me because a part of me was so desperate to see my club, my mates on the pitch, and the fans, get to a cup final...but a part of me just couldn't believe that the club were making progress towards a cup run and I wasn't part of it. I was convinced I'd be missing out on a cup final. As it happens Albion lost 1-0 to a Tommy Tynan goal and that was sadly to set the tone for John, who never repeated the form of his first spell in charge.

By then I'd stopped feeling part of it. I took the best part of 15 months to retire. I was now a statistic. One of 40 or 50 players who retire each year.

My good pal Garth Wooldridge, whose company Swan Housewares had been one of the first Albion shirt sponsors, got in touch with me after I had announced my retirement and wanted me to have a testimonial, as so many players did back then. I didn't want one but John Osborne, the former Albion keeper who had left just before I joined, also spoke to me and convinced me that it was the standard way for supporters to say goodbye. I reluctantly agreed, provided it would be done quickly.

As far as my team-mates were concerned well, yes, they were sympathetic but a part of them would be thinking: "Thank God it's not me," and I cannot blame them. That's the nature of the game. It's a sport built around the team ethic, but one that is so fiercely individualistic. Everyone is out to get what they can out of their own career. John Rudge, who was a long-time manager of Port Vale, was at a reserve game and he said that he could tell I was carrying my leg. My right leg was lagging behind. When you've got fellow professionals and coaches telling you what they can see, then you appreciate it was never going to happen.

By the end I just wanted to recover enough movement in my knee just so I could play with my kids. And yet I had a manager in Ron Wylie, trying to tell me to get used to the pain in my knee every time I kicked the ball – which was utterly ridiculous. I didn't hold any resentment to the club at all but I did wonder what would have been had David Dandy been in the UK, and not in Texas, when I first suffered the injury. My knee wasn't a good knee – I knew that – so the outcome might not have been different, but that first knee operation didn't work. And that first knee injury I had at 16 could easily have finished me off – so in some respects I was grateful to get another 13 years of playing.

I'd had some happy times as a player and my period at West Brom had started with such promise. I do look back now and wonder how on earth we didn't win a trophy or two.

I remember one day a letter arriving at the club. It was telling me that myself, Derek Statham, Cyrille and Peter Barnes were all being called up to the England B squad. At the time there were a lot of players who never quite made it in the top division straight away. That was my route and I knew I had to work extra hard to make it at Cambridge and West Brom. There were quite a few players in my position. Viv Anderson had been called up and Kenny Swain got in ahead of me too. It didn't help that I carried an injury before the 1982 World Cup. And, obviously, after that I got injured and never recovered. I wasn't really that focused on the World Cup – my main thing was to make sure I played in the first-team, wherever I was. From the moment I became established at Cambridge I was never dropped for anything other than disciplinary issues. There was another thing going on at the time. If you look at the team we had, Bryan Robson barely won any caps until he joined

Manchester United, Derek Statham only won three caps, Laurie and Cyrille won a handful of caps. There was a train of thought in the local press that the England manager would always go for a player from a London club or fashionable club, rather than someone from West Brom. But I never subscribed to that. Managers have in their mind how they visualise their teams, how they want them to play, and who they think will fit in. There's a great story about Jack Charlton coming into the England team and after one of the games he said goodbye to Alf Ramsey and said: "I'll see you at the next call up boss," to which Sir Alf replied, "If you're selected Jack..."

And with that, there ended my England career. I played three times for the B team, against the US, Spain and Australia.

The only other time I had a chance to play a sort of international football was when I was offered an opportunity to play in South Africa during the off-season of the regular football season. One of the big petroleum companies was involved with it. I recall Cyrille went, as did Gary Owen, but it wasn't for me. I got approached and just said: "No." I had a chat with Cyrille and warned that he might have difficulties over there due to the apartheid system. We were promised that wouldn't impact on us, but all the same, I was very uneasy about it.

Cyrille later told me that he was in a bar somewhere in South Africa when a white bloke walked in and pushed him aside. Cyrille ignored it and then the bloke did it a couple more times, as if to say: "I'm getting a drink first." Cyrille apparently turned to this guy and said: "Mate, if you were in London now, acting like this, you'd be dead." It wasn't a pleasant place to be and I couldn't go there against the political backdrop.

I recall some years later Ted Croker, who was the secretary of the FA, wanted to know if I'd be interested to do a presentation in Zimbabwe at some awards ceremony. I said I'd happily do it and while I was there I was sitting by the pool a day before the ceremony when I saw this guy running down to me with a piece of paper. This guy was clearly panicked that I might have been one of those players who had gone to South Africa. He basically said that had I ever been there then I wouldn't be allowed to attend the ceremony the following day – which was ridiculous given I'd been flown over there at somebody else's expense and on the night before the ceremony it suddenly became a problem. That's how political the whole situation was regarding South Africa. I had to actually sign a declaration that I had never been to South Africa.

I know some England cricketers went over to play there as part of a rebel tour. I simply didn't want to be part of something that had such a racial divide. The cricketers, for instance, said they wanted to go into the townships to educate people. That was nonsense because people were being brutalised there. They simply went for the money. And that's fair enough. It's their choice, their conscience. But just be honest about the motive.

As for playing for one's country, some of my other team-mates could certainly consider themselves unlucky not to earn greater recognition.

Tony Godden, our goalkeeper, was an outstanding shot stopper and if you remove Pat Jennings of Northern Ireland, Ray Clemence and Peter Shilton from the equation then he was as good as anyone. He organised things well, was a wonderful character and a key member of the team. Derek Statham was a confident lad and when I first clapped eyes on him, he was doing things that I'd never seen from a full-back. I thought I could play, but Derek was something else. He was doing drag-backs in his own box, ran with the ball, beat players in his own box and was more like a winger. He was extremely talented and unlucky to come up against Kenny Sansom in the fight for England's No3 shirt. Both were worthy contenders to be England's left-back. Another thing with Derek: he was a joker and immensely skilled at forging signatures. The number of times he'd sign several names on one ball – I'm sure there are people out there thinking they own an item with Cyrille's signature or Bryan Robson's autograph, but there's every chance it was done by Derek.

John Wile and Ally Robertson were typical of a brilliant pairing. You think of Colin Todd and Roy McFarland at Derby, Dave Stringer and Duncan Forbes at Norwich or even Alvin Martin and Billy Bonds at West Ham. We had John and Ally. They were good footballers in their own right, but together they were even better. Ally used to sniff out danger before it happened and wouldn't let many go past him. John was just a natural leader: imposing, demonstrative and a winner.

I've already talked about the importance of Lenny, who was so influential to me settling in at West Brom and was to become a good mate. And then there was Pop – who was never the most vocal of people, apart when he'd had a drink. He was probably the best footballer

I ever played with. He played hard on and off the pitch and was a phenomenal talent. He was an instinctive leader and it was no surprise to see him win nearly 100 caps and win trophy after trophy with Manchester United. At times it was like he was superhuman.

Tony Brown played just behind our front players. When I signed Ron Atkinson warned me that he was a great character, but that he probably wouldn't play much because of his age – he ended up playing pretty much every week for the next two seasons. He still has that enthusiasm now and a brilliant sense of humour. He has a statue outside The Hawthorns and rightly so – nobody else has scored more, or played more, for West Bromwich Albion.

As for the other Brown, Alistair, he was my room-mate. I nicknamed him Action because he reminded me of the Action Man figure. He was so under-rated and would do a lot of the hard-work for Cyrille and the others. I always felt that if he'd had more confidence in his own ability, he'd have been even more of a player. As a room-mate I was his skivvy. "Can you make me this?" or "Brendon, will you get this for me?" I was his butler, basically.

I'll come back to Cyrille and Laurie later on, but a word about one or two others. David Mills was a lovely gentleman, who just had such a rough time of it. He just never settled sadly. And John Deehan was another who was unlucky. We were 2-0 up against Brighton and he had one of those games where he had several opportunities to make it 3-0 but just couldn't convert his chances. Brighton eventually came back and scored two goals in the last six minutes and I think Ron just lost faith in him. He was a great wit, always had a smile on his face and a lovely bloke.

I married quite young so I wasn't really a party animal although I enjoyed a night as much as anyone. Cambridge was a university city so there were lots of students, lots of parties and, yes, lots of temptations. I used to enjoy going out, but I wasn't a drinker. I found the pub scene in London was terrifying – lots of gangs. When I lived in Walthamstow, we would often be challenged if we went into a pub with mates. If there was, say, 12 of us, a group of lads would say there were 20 of them and away we go. A friend of mine had a pint glass smashed in his face for no reason other than a minor disagreement with some bloke. I just hated that culture, if you can call it that.

Thursday and Friday were traditionally pulling nights, while Saturdays were when you went out as couples, and I was mainly going out with Cecily anyway. Some of the other lads well, yes, every night could be pulling night. I don't mind lager, but I had a taste for dry white wine at the time. We had student nights out in Cambridge but when Ron turned up he seemed to know of every party where we would be.

What I remember about West Brom was Ron telling me that I was joining a very professional bunch of lads. I was captain at Cambridge but knew I needed to keep my head down until I got myself established in the team. But I do recall going out with the lads for my first time to the Four In Hand pub in West Bromwich after a game. Lenny Cantello was in the chair and was looking around I can already picture the others. There was Bryan Robson, Ally Brown, Ally Robertson, Cyrille, Derek Statham, Tony Godden – pretty much all of the drinkers, and me. John Wile and Bomber Brown didn't really go out much, so they weren't there. Lenny was going around each one of us and it was: "Guinness, mild, lager, lager, lager, Guinness, lager..." and when it came to me I said: "I'll have a dry white wine." Lenny looked at me with utter disgust and said: "Brendon, you'll have a pint." I am not joking when I say that I had two sips of a lager shandy and then I heard a thud on the table, with a voice piping up: "Right, whose round is it next?" Everyone else had finished their drinks before I had hardly started mine. I quickly realised I was out of my depth in this drinking squad. These were professional footballers and professional drinkers. People always used to say Pop had a reputation but in training he would be at the front in the distance running. I thought we trained hard at Cambridge, but it was a different level at West Brom and make no mistake Bryan Robson was always at the front, no matter how many drinks he'd had the previous night.

Another time I remember going out with Laurie and Cyrille to a club called Maxwell's in Birmingham. Anywhere with Laurie and Cyrille would be fraught with danger, not because of anything they'd do, but because they were black and, secondly, because the women would gravitate towards them. We were having a drink this one time and I could see Laurie getting a bit agitated. The next thing I could see him talking to a group of white lads. You could tell he was really animated about something. He came back and I said: "Laurie, what's wrong?" and he said: "They're looking at us." Well, yes, three black lads who play for West Bromwich Albion are out for a drink, so of course they recognised us. Laurie didn't seem to take that into account but was convinced they were after trouble. Anyway, he goes back and the next thing he's dragged them over and we're buying them all drinks.

I was one of those players that could never sleep peacefully after a game. After home games I would go home and relive the game over and over again. Away matches, we'd come back to the ground and then go out for a few drinks. Liberty's nightclub in Birmingham was very popular, as was Maxwell's, and then there was Holy City Zoo, owned by former Wolves and Villa striker Andy Gray – and it was a flipping zoo as well, let me tell you.

I've always been of the view that some of the football stories don't travel well – much like some wines I guess. They might be funny within the confines of the dressing room or out with your team-mates, but they can be off-putting to readers.

I did occasionally go to Liberty's on a Thursday. But we weren't meant to be out 48 hours before a game. We were due to play Liverpool at The Hawthorns on one occasion. Derek Statham was out on the Thursday night at Liberty's and was spotted by the assistant manager Mick Brown and Brian Whitehouse, the youth team coach, who also happened to be in the same club. On the Friday he got a letter saying he'd been fined two weeks' wages for a breach of club rules but Ron Atkinson didn't say a word to Derek. On the Saturday morning of the game we had finished our pre-match meal and team meeting and were about to leave the hotel for the match when Ron said: "One of your mates is in trouble... and you can get him out of trouble with a result today," without saying who it was. Ron didn't have to do a talk in the dressing room, because Derek was running around each one of us trying to get us going. It was hilarious. Anyway, we were 1-0 up during the first half when at one point Tony Godden, after catching the ball from a corner, then proceeded to drop it as we were all pushing up to the halfway line. We heard a roar from the Liverpool supporters. Poor Tony hadn't noticed Kenny Daglish, who was behind him, ran round nicked the ball and scored. Derek wasn't happy afterwards.

When things went well Ron was relaxed. You knew that Wednesday before a Saturday was your last night out before the game. But he also liked to have 'club functions' as a way of building team spirit. I remember we went to a Greek restaurant on one night out, with the

101

tradition of plate smashing being enthusiastically enjoyed. I could see out of the corner of my eye Peter Barnes walking around collecting plates from other tables and stacking them up. He was basically building up a collection of plates to start throwing onto the floor. The thing is that these weren't the clay plates that are smashed and then put back into the kiln, but quite expensive dining plates and we were frantically trying to stop him from smashing these plates. Anyway, I remember this as being the night that an argument broke out because we had the girlfriends and wives there and they started to bicker about who should and shouldn't be in the team – which is never a good thing – and the next day Ron made an announcement telling us that never again would he be allowing other halves to come out because it seemed to be a recipe for aggravation. And I don't think poor Peter ever did get to throw those plates.

But my biggest issue around Christmas 1983 wasn't about my next drink or night out, but where my next salary would be coming from. I had to decide which path to take next. Ron Atkinson felt I could have gone onto manage as long ago as when I was at Cambridge but at the time I wasn't sure if I was good enough to play at the highest level, let alone manage.

I was approaching my 31st birthday, and now having to decide what to do for the rest of my working life.

TRIBUTE

Brendon was a really great player and a good professional on and off the field. He was a brilliant signing by Ron Atkinson.

Quite a few of the lads called me 'Pop', after the Bryan Robson who played for Sunderland. Brendon continued with that throughout my time at West Brom and at times I think he probably could have called me a lot worse!

You always encourage people around you but if they started to do the wrong thing and if anyone got slack or lazy, I'd get annoyed and give them the stare. Thankfully Brendon never had too many of those but I'm pretty sure he gave me a few rollockings over the years because the one thing he did was make big demands of players around him. He was a great team-mate and an extremely underrated member of our team.

When we came to the fore in 1978 it was people like Cyrille, Laurie, Bomber Brown and myself who were getting the accolades and attention from the media and pundits, but it was the likes of Brendon doing their job properly and doing it well that enabled us to prosper as a team. For me, he was one of the most under-rated members of that side – a great footballer and team-mate, and a brilliant ambassador for the sport.

Bryan Robson OBE, West Bromwich Albion (1972-1981)

CHAPTER SIX
Cecily

"I'm going to marry that girl."

I was introduced to Cecily by her aunt Maysie Samuel who was affectionately known as Grandma Maysie. She was Cecily's mum's sister. Sadly, I never met Cecily's mother as she died very young. I missed her by about two months. That was in 1970.

Cecily came to England and was sent to a secretarial college in Hampstead. Sometime around May time she came up to look at the school and visited us as my mum and grandma Maysie were good friends back in Grenada. Cecily was brought to the house to meet my sister Diane so she would have a girl friend and wouldn't feel isolated. I set eyes on Cecily and was struck by her. I was about 18 months younger than her and my first words to her did not impress, she told me later. After she left, I said to my brother: "I'm going to marry that girl." I was only 17 and I thought she might be a challenge. And I was right – she was a flipping challenge as well! Grandma Maysie decided to play cupid as she quite liked me so gradually Cecily and I came across each other more and more. Thank you Grandma Maysie.

I was going back to Trinidad later that year and going across to Grenada so Cecily, who was back in the UK, told me to pop over to her house while I was over there and meet her family. I turned up and her elder sister Cutie opened the door – she was almost identical to Cecily. I jumped in shock when I saw her. I met her brother and was due to meet her mother, but she got delayed somewhere so I missed out on that. Sadly, the following year she passed away so I never did meet her. I later found out Cutie wasn't her sister's proper name, it was actually Yolande.

It was my 18th birthday party when Cecily and I really hit it off. My mum threw me a party and that's when we got together.

That was in 1971. At the time Cecily was at an exclusive college in Hampstead – girls from all over the world would go there. She wasn't my first girlfriend though – far from it – but there was something about her. She was a bit of a force, a big challenge for me and I enjoyed the chase. There was a mutual link there because we both knew so many people in Grenada, albeit independently – we had a shared background of people we knew in different circumstances. I think we were all probably related in some way.

Anyway, we got married in 1974 but not before a further drama a year or so earlier. She finished college and only had a student visa. We went back to Grenada and her visa was about to run out but we were assured it wouldn't be a problem. While we were in Trinidad to get our flight, we got a call from Cutie to say immigration had been in touch and revoked her passport. We couldn't get it sorted so I came back to the UK. We ended up apart for 10 months - I actually proposed over the phone – but to be honest I did wonder if this was my chance to get away and maybe move on. But I couldn't. It was then I began to realise how much I missed her and wanted to be with her.

You have to remember I was being schooled to become a footballer, so I never really got into that pub scene. I found it quite a violent environment, especially for young lads. It was smoky, claustrophobic and I just didn't like it. We couldn't go out 48 hours before a game and I never indulged that social drinking like some of my mates did. That was a British culture. I did like parties though. We had what we'd call Blues' Parties – where people from the Caribbean would put boom boxes in, charge money and play music. They were all illegal, but were the big thing in the black communities. That's one of the reasons I wasn't fond of end-of-season trips because you'd have a group of lads after a long season, going away and getting drunk. It was a recipe for a fight, and that wasn't for me.

Cecily wasn't impressed by my background. She wasn't part of that football crowd. When she told her dad that she was courting a footballer, the first thing he said was: "What happens if he breaks his leg?" I remember going back to Grenada at one point and I was in a lounge in Barbados waiting for a transfer when I came across an elderly gentleman, extremely well-dressed. He asked me what I did for a living and, when I told him I played football for a living, there was an utter look of disgust across his face as if to say: "You've been in England all that time and all you've done is played football?"

Thankfully, Cecily's family accepted me for who I was. A lady I called my aunt Auntie Lyndi, real name Lyndonna Webster, was married to Rudi Webster, who played cricket for Warwickshire and was from Barbados. He was ambassador to Barbados for Australia. Auntie Lyndi was a constant presence in my life. Woe betide if I didn't go to see her when I was back in Grenada. So, conversation with Cecily and her family was easy. We all knew so many people.

Cecily wanted to get to know you before she warmed to you. But when she got to know you, you'd be a friend for life. She was no-nonsense. If she had something to say, she would say it. You knew where you stood with her. As my career grew, she could spot people who were around me for all the wrong reasons. Footballers now are like rock stars but, even then, we had hangers on. And Cecily hated that. Our best friends were on the outside of football generally, which suited both of us.

There was a fantastic warmth to Cecily once she got to know you. And, another thing: her gut instincts were invariably correct too, often to my cost.

In terms of my professional career, Cecily was always supportive. She didn't have a clue about football early on. I was always told by my mother to be bold. Don't be afraid to make bold decisions and the trick was to make sure you got the big decisions more right than wrong. I always stuck to that which is why I decided to leave Arsenal. I knew I wasn't good enough for the first team at that time, but also knew I was better than the reserves.

I lived not far from the Abbey Stadium in Cambridge. It was exciting for me because, although we got relegated, I'd become a regular in the first team. Off the pitch, life was also exciting. Cecily and I got married on June 15, 1974, at a church in Chingford. It was one of the most joyous days of my life. Cecily looked beautiful – I couldn't believe how lucky I was.

At this point she was looking for a job but had become a brilliant seamstress. She made Zoe's wedding dress when she got married and it's a craft she passed down to Zoe. For a while she worked in Fortnum & Mason when she had finished college. She loved fashion and was always so stunningly dressed.

It was at Cambridge where I first came across racism on the pitch from a fellow professional. Cecily barely came to matches as a result of those incidents. I had a cousin called Laurie who was 6ft 6ins. He was at the game at the Abbey when I was getting stick from some of the fans and Laurie confronted those fans. Even though nothing untoward happened, it put her off for pretty much the rest of my career. Of course, Sod's Law, there was another game she went to – in April 1981, when I delivered that horrendous back-pass at Villa Park which pretty much handed the League title to Aston Villa.

On that night I had permission not to go back on the coach. Ron was going berserk at the way we had lost the game with me the main focus of his anger. I was always the last one out of the dressing room, as I was before games when I walked out onto the pitch. On that evening at Villa Park, I must have had a face like thunder. Cecily said something totally innocently and was shocked I was so angry, so she said: "What's the matter?" Well, I just lost it and went: "What's the matter...what's the matter?" She didn't get that as a footballer I was still in that zone having made a mistake that pretty much handed the League title to our West Midlands' rivals. I won't have been the first nor last footballer to react like that after a game, but it's not a reaction I look back on with any fondness. Sadly, it's all too easy to get lost in that moment when you're a professional sportsman.

In 1978, I went from being a Third Division footballer to one that was challenging for the top six in the First Division, alongside and against international footballers and high-profile names. Cecily was very supportive. She was very balanced throughout. Zoe had been born the previous August and it was a tough time in some respects as we were stopping at the Europa Lodge Hotel in West Bromwich and Zoe just wouldn't settle. One day I came back from training to find Cecily had packed her bags and just said: "Brendon, I'm sorry, I can't cope with this, we're going back to our house in Cambridge."

We ended up buying a house in the summer and moved up as a family. The China tour was particularly hard because I was away for nearly a month. I got back and couldn't wait to see my daughter, yet when I got home she was hiding from me. She didn't recognise me. She wouldn't come near me. She was nicknamed Cecily's shoulder broach because everywhere she went, Zoe was clinging onto her. Poor Zoe was so confused about who I was, but Cecily took everything in her stride. She was a fantastic mother and a wonderful wife – totally understanding.

It reminds me of a time when we got to know a gentleman called Jack Downing, who was an auctioneer and ran an estate agents called Allsops. We bought our first home in the Midlands through Jack. He was also a big West Brom fan and quite a character. He had a loud booming voice, and also had a glass eye covered by a patch. He'd often tell us the story of how somebody slapped him on the back during a game, prompting his false eye to fly out! Jack was a fantastic guy and used to come by to see how Cecily and baby were doing, mindful we were new to the area – he was a real gentleman.

The Three Degrees period brought other marital challenges. It was okay to start with. Cecily didn't mind it at all, but I got the impression some of the lads thought it was one photo too many and, of course, there were always the rumours: "So, Brendon, which one was yours?" Even to this day I'm asked which one I was paired up with, but it really wasn't like that.

We actually went to see The Three Degrees when they were appearing in Birmingham. I was married at the time and yet I would still have people coming up to me asking: "So, which one are you with Brendon?" because at the time there were suggestions about Cyrille and Sheila Ferguson. Anyway, on this particular night we – myself, Laurie and Cyrille – were guests of the Three Degrees who were performing at the Night Out venue in Birmingham. I was really not keen – and I know Cecily wasn't – but she urged me to go just to keep in with the spirit of it all but because of that I was late arriving. The show had already started and so I had to be escorted down to the front – the girls were already on stage by this point – and all I heard was "Thank you for joining us Mr Batson." It was Sheila Ferguson calling me out during the concert. From having a subdued torch showing me the way, I suddenly had a spotlight shining on me. It was all quite embarrassing.

Cecily was having to roll her eyes and just accept that we were thrust into this. She knew it was no more than a few publicity shots from my point of view. I think the bigger problem was with the lads. Some of the others thought it was too much, but we got away with it because we were a good side and played great football. I just detected that some thought it was a distraction – it was all about Cyrille, Laurie and myself. This actual publicity period only lasted for a few days, but it kept on being referred to because we were so good on the pitch. And this was leading up to our peak in the build up to Christmas 1978. Even now people associate that side as being the Three Degrees – which is grossly unfair because that was a bloody good side and we happened to be three elements of that team.

Games were a problem for Cecily, especially night games where I'd come home and spend the night kicking her during my restless sleep as I relived the game and played it all through my head. Poor Cecily ended up with bruises on her legs at times because I was still making challenges and tackles as I dozed off.

We also had an incident on the London Underground. There was a guy on the other side of the carriage who yelled something and, although I couldn't hear him, I felt the atmosphere change and Cecily grabbed hold of my arm as if to restrain me. And then he repeated it – the gist of it was that we should go back to our own country. The young white guy next to us defended us, while Cecily was holding me back because she knew I'd want to confront him. This guy kept on shouting as we got off the train and went up the escalator. At the top of the escalator this bloke kept going and so I went up to him, grabbed him, but luckily, the guy sat next to us on the train had informed some of the security staff. Cecily and I tackled these incidents together.

The best way of describing how Cecily supported me was to not ask me how I was when she knew I was in a bad place. I would tell her if I needed support. I didn't take my football home, unlike some footballers. You would get some partners asking: "Why aren't you in the team?" and Cecily wasn't like that. I was enjoying being a father. We had moved to Launceston Road in Walsall in June 1979 and my next-door neighbours had two daughters who were roughly the same age as my children, which was lovely for the kids growing up. I kept my work at work and liked to enjoy my home life, away from football. You couldn't hide results, but I avoided talking about it.

I wasn't an easy patient when I was injured for that final time. I picked up the injury in October 1982 against Ipswich. It wasn't long until I knew a return to football was a long shot. I used to leave on Monday morning continue my rehab in Cambridge and come home on Friday night. Cecily was amazing. She left me to it.

All my best decisions were when I consulted Cecily. My worst ones were made when I didn't speak to her. She would just say: "Brendon, are we ok?" and that would be it. She always had my back.

The trouble is that I didn't actually know what lay ahead for me? Management? Maybe. But I wasn't sure about that and there seemed to be few opportunities full-stop, let alone chances for black men. I've no idea what kind of manager I'd have made.

Speaking of managers, it's probably the right time to reflect on those men I worked for. I admired Bertie Mee – he was unbelievable. Small in stature, huge in presence. He had a great coach in Don Howe. I cannot stress enough what a wonderful man Bertie was. I appreciate that Herbert Chapman was a special man in Arsenal's history, mainly due to his impact at Highbury in the 1920s and 30s. And then there was Arsene Wenger at the turn of the 21st century, who revolutionised English football in so many different ways – not least around nutrition, conditioning and how they should behave away from the pitch. But Bertie Mee bridged those successes. And he was only the second manager in the 20th century – and one of only a handful of managers – to lead a men's team to a League and FA Cup double.

As an organiser Bertie was brilliant, but Ron Atkinson was a motivator – he would make you feel like you could do anything. His training was enjoyable. People said he wasn't the best tactician, but I'm not so sure. He could guide us and see what was needed when necessary. Actually, if you think back to when he was a commentator then he really was one of the best analysts out there so the notion that he wasn't strong tactically was incorrect. He could read the game, he could tell you why it was happening and what might happen next. His knowledge of football was, and remains, absolutely immense. His memory for details when it comes to football is astounding. He remembers things that I've long forgotten. Perhaps the force of his personality meant that his football insight got overlooked, I don't know. What he did do well was make demands of you to do your job. He once said that players get themselves into the side, and players play themselves out of the side. Ron gave us the licence to take the handbrake off and be expansive within our play, provided we did our jobs. I learned the hard way at Cambridge that if I wasn't playing well then I'd be out.

Ronnie Allen and Ron Wylie? I didn't take anything from them. I had no respect for them, and little time for their coaches.

Mick Brown and Colin Addison, however, were two great foils for Ron Atkinson and the players trusted them implicitly. They were totally different characters. Both had integrity and you never once felt they would breach a confidence – they were a strong buffer to when things weren't going well and we were searching for something to happen during a bad run. They would boost your confidence where maybe a manager might be on your back and angry. Compare that with Ronnie Allen, who was briefing the media about me just after he took over.

In any case I went down a different route by accepting the job with the Professional Footballers' Association. I needed to get away from the Midlands. There was only so much sympathy I could take. It's a big mental health challenge but back then we didn't concern ourselves with things like that. Until that major injury I didn't miss many games for West Brom. I envisaged playing into my mid-30s but the longer I was out, the more philosophical I became about the whole thing.

I decided to make a move away from the area and Gordon Taylor sold the PFA to me. He was the secretary of the Professional Footballers' Association and wanted to expand it. He was a great visionary. I knew I'd have to grit my teeth for 18 months to make it work, because it was sold to me as a long-term project. I moved up to Congleton – a halfway house between the Midlands and Manchester. It was a nightmare because I still had to drive to Manchester, where the PFA was based, and football was London-centric. We moved in August 1984, so the kids could start school the following term. By September I knew I'd made a mistake. I was moody, I was getting techy. I went for a run one evening and when I got back Cecily could see I wasn't right. She said: "We've made a mistake haven't we? We shouldn't have moved?" She didn't say you've made a mistake; it was we. Within two days we had a For Sale sign outside the house. And we ended up moving back to Walsall in August 1985.

Cecily was extremely decisive. She wasn't averse to bold decisions herself. Her dad was Cecil Kenrick Sylvester. Everyone referred to him as CK. Just before he passed away, at the grand age of 97, he released a book, which was a great little read. We all got brought up on making bold decisions in the hope we would get them more right than wrong. Cecily would give me the encouragement and belief. When I quit football my salary was washed away at a stroke. Cecily just said: "Bren, we'll be okay."

And she was right. As usual. The next chapter was about to begin.

TRIBUTE

I first came across Brendon when I was a player at Tranmere and he was at Cambridge. He was obviously a very well-respected player, but the real connection with Brendon came some years later when I was with the FA and looking to change the disciplinary system. I decided I needed somebody who was well-respected, not only within the game, but among players. Brendon came to mind straight away because of his previous work with the Professional Footballers' Association. He was somebody who I felt I needed, not just because of his experience and standing, but because we were having some difficult times with the PFA due to some issues going on at the time between certain players. I knew Brendon would bring great value to our working dynamic.

What he did in terms of bringing together the players side was second-to-none. That formed a long-standing friendship too.

He was also heavily involved in the Equality, Diversity and Inclusion as an ambassador. He was chosen because he was the best guy and the best person for the job. Over the years Brendon has done some fantastic things, and a lot of that is down to the way he carries himself. If you are to talk about the real heroes of football's campaign against racism, then Brendon would be viewed as being extremely important to that entire cause, not least because of his professionalism and personality, but also his will to eradicate discrimination from the sport. He has been a driving force in promoting fairness and inclusivity. Football owes him a great deal.

Mark Palios, Tranmere Rovers executive chairman

TRIBUTE

Our paths first crossed when I was at West Brom, with him being an ex-player. But when I started with the FA, Brendon was already doing some work to improve diversity and inclusivity. I liaised directly with him regarding this particular initiative and worked closely with him to try and drive it through.

Brendon has always been so passionate about making the game better and improving diversity in the industry. He was a pioneer, an ambassador, a person that would strive to push the importance of diversity and opportunities across football.

That is a really easy thing to say but you need somebody to actually be willing to take that on and Brendon has always done it stridently. He was driving it passionately, making sure it wasn't just an agenda item under any other business at the bottom of the list.

The other thing I'd say about Brendon is that he did all of this in a brilliant way. He was humble, respectful, rational and showed a great understanding of the political landscape within the game itself.

One of the things that has made a marked difference is around visibility within the game. Brendon had a big thing about this in that there should be black coaches in the game to offer those aspirational beliefs to the current black players that there is a route through for them. Before Brendon took this on there wasn't much of a pathway, with very few role models in the managerial and coaching sectors. Brendon has helped enable that by driving through initiatives that allow this.

Dan Ashworth, Newcastle United sporting director

CHAPTER SEVEN
The Professional Footballers' Association

"...All 594 First Division players were balloted and returned a 90 per cent support for whatever action the PFA deemed necessary..."

I'll come onto my PFA career shortly. But first a little about my managerial and coaching spell.

My what? Yes, there was a time I considered being stood on the touchline.

It was becoming apparent that I was really struggling with that final injury. I already had my preliminary coaching badge so then went to do what would now be the equivalent of a UEFA A Licence, under the auspices of Charles Hughes. This meant spending two weeks during the close season at Lilleshall – the so-called university of football coaching, in Shropshire - which was one hell of an experience. I knew I needed those qualifications if I wanted to develop any aspirations to become a manager. So, I went there and was alongside a good group of former and current players and wannabe coaches.

When I sent off applications for managerial and coaching roles I very rarely even got a reply. I did get one from Cambridge United – in fact I got an interview – perhaps out of respect that I'd been captain there, but I wasn't offered the job. I had an interview but at the time what was very en vogue was the concept of player-managers. In effect clubs were getting two roles filled for the price of one. The problem was that by then I couldn't play anymore, but it was also felt that, at 31 as I was at the time, I was too young to go into management. That was the first and only interview I had. I spoke to Ron Atkinson about it, and he told me that the timing wasn't right and then the offer came in from Gordon Taylor at the PFA – Ron said that would probably be the best option for me.

I remember mentioning to somebody when I still had managerial ambitions and that person said: "Brendon, you haven't got a chance... you're too outspoken. There's no way you'll put up with the bullshit from the Boardroom." He was probably right.

As for Lilleshall, those few weeks in Shropshire make me smile now. It was under Charles Hughes, the coach guru at the FA, who was all about the long ball. He felt that it was the formula for success and had written lots of coaching books and journals about his philosophies. We all had to buy his book The Winning Formula to actually get onto the course in the first place; it was a requirement. The book was effectively the basis of how English football should be played and coached. Everything – the coaching, the drills, the disciplines on the pitch - was about his principles of football.

We had to report on the Sunday and had a tutorial with Charles in the evening. One of the games he highlighted for us as part of our learning was an international match between USSR versus Brazil. He stood there, with a big pointer, showing us this game. But before he did, he said: "Who here thinks Brazil play the game in the right way?" Now, bear in mind this group was made up in part of current and former players literally everyone put up their hands. Then he ran the clip, and it showed Brazil knocking the ball around and each time they passed it backwards, or sideways, he'd stop the clip and ask: "Could they play it forward?" He then cited a statistic that if you have more than three consecutive passes then the chances of you scoring decline dramatically. Anyway, we're watching this game and Brazil have kept the ball for about two minutes – USSR, or the Russians if you prefer, cannot get near them – but they lose it just outside the Russian box. Brazil won it back immediately; bang, bang, bang and score straight away. Charles stops the clip and says: "And there you have it. Three passes, goal." I found it hard to accept that philosophy.

We also had to submit papers which were to be assessed based on the topic of our coaching assignment. David Burnside, the former West Brom player from the 1950s, happened to be one of the FA staff coaches tutoring us. He had a look at one of my papers and said: "Brendon, they think you're anti this learning?" And in a way he was right - I couldn't accept the principles they were preaching. But I stuck at it. My comparison would be that people said Mohammed Ali didn't have a knock-out punch but what they didn't see is that for six rounds Ali would be tap-tap-taping to tire his opponents out with jabs, and then that same tap-tap-tap would end up knocking somebody out in round seven. That's exactly what the Brazilians were doing. The Russians were so anxious once they gained possession that they lost the ball almost straight away. Liverpool had a similar philosophy of keeping the ball when they had their great sides of the 70s and 80s. It was a passing game, as Manchester City do under Pep Guardiola. They push people forward, while keeping possession – so when they lose the ball, they win it back straight away. So, yes, I spent a lot of my time at Lilleshall biting my tongue having to listen to things I simply didn't agree with.

I was alongside people like John McDowell, from West Ham, Micky Flanagan of QPR – not long after our semi-final defeat at Highbury, there I am playing cards with him at Lilleshall – the former Manchester City player Willie Donachie, who later developed into a brilliant coach. But a lot of pros clashed with Charles Hughes's coaches and the methods. Even then it was beginning to feel outdated. Yet, despite my misgivings, it was a learning process which in the end I enjoyed especially being among fellow professionals.

We had one session where we defended the ball. We were told that when the opposition have the ball you have to close down the ball and that you must be no more than two-to-three yards away. Then we had another session defending corners – where they put two men defending the corner. I said: "Hang on, we've been told you cannot be three yards away...now we're told you can be 10 yards away and that it will prevent their corner from being effective, whether it's an inswinger or outswinger." It was utter nonsense, and it wasn't for me. Some managers, however, were very keen on the methods. Graham Taylor, a very successful manager who went on to manage England, was a Hughes acolyte and when we played Watford you could tell that they wanted to get the ball down the pitch quickly and cause their damage from there. They were successful at doing that and it was effective.

Another session was on attacking play getting into the opposing box on the angle the object being to shoot across the goalkeeper for the far post, the principle being that if the keeper gets a hand to it he may push it out to the attacking players following up. We had repeated this exercise times when they stop the session and one of the FA coaches asked: "So what's this called when we shoot across the keeper on the angle?" We're all looking around wondering what he meant as to us it was obvious – we were shooting for the far post. He said: "It's called

POMO – position of maximum opportunity."

So, the theory was that when we see a player bearing down on goal on the angle and preparing to shoot we should consider it a POMO. Anyway, we had one coach from the West Country who was running around shouting: "POMO, POMO…" which doesn't sound great when you're yelling it at someone on a football pitch.

It's no surprise really that I came to the conclusion that management and coaching wasn't for me.

It was the Professional Footballers' Association that was to be my calling. And I was to become involved in one of the most exciting and progressive periods of football. The game was to undergo radical changes off-the-field during my time at the PFA, not least when I initially became assistant secretary.

I had been a member of the PFA since I was 16-years-old when I first signed as an apprentice for Arsenal in 1969. I had been the delegate at Cambridge, just after arriving from Arsenal. When I joined West Brom, John Wile was the delegate in name only basically – so he gladly handed over to me. That was an exciting time for the PFA – during those late 1970s – as I'd been part of the freedom of contract discussions when Derek Dougan was chairman. I remember we had these regional meetings that, at several times, were like the Nuremburg Rally – we were going to go on strike, we were perceived as these troublesome militants and the press said it was going to be the demise of the lower leagues, with our response basically being: "bollocks to you".

I spoke to Ron Atkinson, who gave me some advice. I spoke to my mate Garth Wooldridge, but it was Gordon Taylor who sold me the prospect of being part of the future of the PFA. Gordon was a brilliant innovator and I joined in May 84 as his assistant secretary.

And what did Gordon do? Well, the first thing he did was to piss off on holiday, leaving me in charge – where I had absolutely no idea what was going on.

I was trying to get to grips with my role at the PFA during this period, while being extremely unhappy about having to move my family up north when we had been so settled in the Midlands. It didn't help that Zoe was being racially abused during her time at school there. It was an absolute nightmare.

As far as the PFA was concerned, we only had one set of rules and regulations to refer to then, which was the League handbook – our bible basically. Gordon went off on holiday, so we had players calling the office but not wanting to speak to me because they were so used to being put through to Gordon and probably thought I didn't know anything. And those who did speak I would stop them in their tracks and say: "Oh hang on...I have another call coming through," and ask if I could call them back in five or 10 minutes, just to give me some time to quickly look up the appropriate regulation that I needed to refer to. It really was that chaotic. I had to pretend I knew what I was talking about. I can remember the one day I was so worn out heading back to Cheshire that I was falling asleep on the train. Thankfully I managed to wake up before I ended up in London or somewhere else. And yet somewhere along the line I had this seminal moment where suddenly people actually wanted to speak to me. It was to be the start of a brilliant 18 years.

But first you need to know about my journey with the PFA. I joined Cambridge in 1974 and knew nothing about the PFA. I became a delegate and it was quite apparent that football was starting to change from a footballing point of view.

There was a Commission of Industrial Relations recommendation that players should be given freedom of contract at the end of their contract, legal representation in disciplinary hearings, the PFA to represent players in contractual discussions – obviously before the days of agents - and the PFA to have greater representation. But everything was pretty much loaded towards the first point of allowing footballers to be able to move freely when their club deals came to an end.

This was commissioned in the mid-1970s and it didn't really come into play until 1978. By now I was becoming heavily involved with union matters. I started to go up to Manchester for the AGM when Cliff Lloyd was general secretary and the very charismatic Derek Dougan was chairman. He and the PFA management committee along with Cliff were guiding us through the freedom of contract negotiations. I remember in 1976 going to regional meetings so the PFA could explain what it would mean. In essence it meant that at the end of the contract if you couldn't agree terms with your existing club you were free to leave and join another club of your choice. But if the existing club wanted a fee for the player they had to make an offer no less favourable than the previous contract – excluding signing on fees. If the clubs couldn't agree a deal, then it would go to a tribunal where a fee would be set.

There was all sorts of scaremongering, not least that it would mean the demise of the Third and Fourth Divisions because players would be asking for too much money. But what it meant for individuals is that you couldn't be prevented from taking up employment elsewhere. The retain-and-transfer system had come into disrepute with the George Eastham case in 1963 when he put in a transfer and demanded a move. Under the retain-and-transfer system the club could keep a player's registration and prevent them from moving, while also refusing to pay them if they had requested a transfer. Eastham challenged this successfully, citing an unfair restriction of trade. Now it had moved forward, and I don't think there had been another industry where you could ask for a fee so that someone could simply move their registration from one organisation to another. Things are obviously different now with the different age groups and more freedom. Now what you see are many clubs inserting buy-out clauses in players' contracts – in some countries like Spain they're actually compulsory, or like those that Erling Haaland was signed up to, which enabled him to leave Dortmund for €60million. Clubs are very much aware that if you want to make an enquiry for a particular player then they know the parameters. That has brought some regulation to the transfer market and clubs know what they have to pay.

Players are in a stronger position now. In 1978, when freedom of contract was first introduced, there followed an influx of foreign players coming in. This caused a backlash and accusations of "cheap foreign labour" and such like. People were suspicious of these footballers, thinking they were taking the jobs off British players and blocking opportunities for our own footballers. That accusation was misplaced as what it actually did was introduce different types of footballers, people like Ossie Ardiles and Ricardo Villa at Spurs, Arnold Muhren and Frans Thyssen at Ipswich, who not only lit up the top-flight, but helped to improve the standards of play. What it also did was benefit the younger players who were learning from their new team-mates about new ways of training along with conditioning and fitness techniques. Look at the way the young Class of 92 Manchester United players looked up to Eric

Cantona, for instance.

The intention was that this was supposed to welcome players in to our top two divisions who were of the highest calibre, rather than be used by clubs in the lower leagues. The criteria and process was that you would have players from the top tiers of football who were better than what we had here. But that was misused. It got hilarious at times because whenever a club was losing a player they would say he was the next George Best and wanted top dollar for the transfer fee, yet if they were a buying club then they'd be painting a picture of someone who might not make it. The criteria stipulated that this was supposed to attract the elite foreign players to England. What happened in reality was that while you had some great players coming over, you also had a few lower league clubs bringing over players from the continent which, in effect, started to put a premium on the British players – a problem which still exists today to some degree. What you also found was some clubs bringing in foreign players and paying them much less, so there was some abuse of that system. What also came in later was that the player had to have played a certain amount of games for their national team and that country had to be in the top 75 of the FIFA world rankings - unless there was a compelling reason as to why that player should get a work permit, something which Aston Villa managed to enable when they signed the Trinidadian player Dwight Yorke during the early 90s. He was too young to have the international experience, but Graham Taylor spoke so highly of him that he managed to convince the authorities to facilitate that deal. But, even then, he had to play a certain number of first team games for that club, or you'd risk losing that player – which immediately stacked all the risk onto the club.

One of the big initiatives was funded by the state during the 1980s. The PFA championed the Youth Training Scheme, the YTS as it was known, which enabled clubs to take on a number of apprentices with support from the Government, with the proviso that the youngsters had to also continue with their education. A lot of clubs wouldn't have been able to do this without the financial help so that was quite an important development in our timeline. These were generally three-year schemes where the players weren't technically employed by the club but were on a training programme and could be signed on as a professional player when they got to 17-years-old. That said, the stat remains that 75% of footballers who come into the game at 16-years-old are gone by the time they hit 21 – so to have one in every four making it through that period means you need something for these youngsters to fall back on if they don't make a career in the game.

The PFA has continued to help many of those players. We've had ex-players come through who have gone onto get bursaries for university courses. One of the most successful one of those is the physiotherapy course at Salford University. And as students many of them were getting excellent grades because they'd experienced injuries and the treatment of injuries at their clubs. This all helped as they pursued their qualifications before many went on to get jobs in football. Media and journalism courses have also been popular among many current and former players.

One of the big wake-up calls for football came in the early 1980s when Bristol City almost went bust and the famous Gang of Eight (Peter Aitken, Chris Garland, Jimmy Mann, Julian Marshall, Geoff Merrick, Dave Rodgers, Trevor Tainton and Geoff Sweeney) saved the club from going under by effectively terminating their own contracts. The PFA were key to those negotiations. It was increasingly obvious that many clubs were struggling with more and more clubs receiving PFA loans to help them pay player wages. We effectively became like a bank, handing out loans to several clubs including Hull, Darlington, Halifax and Wolves. We were giving loans to clubs to stop them going under and to pay the players' wages only. One of the reasons for doing so was obviously to protect our members livelihood but also the clubs as community assets. You've got to remember what football clubs bring to a locality, be it providing business to local shops, pubs, restaurants and other commercial spin-offs in those areas near a stadium that make money on matchdays. And, of course, for supporters their football clubs are an important part of their lives. It's maybe a cliched thing to say, but football clubs really are the lifeblood of many communities.

By the early 80s we were already seeing football changing. Shirt sponsorship had already been introduced and were permitted for televised games from 1983. Until then you had clubs with two versions of each shirt – one without a sponsor for TV games, one with a sponsor for games where there were no cameras present. And it was also in 1983 that clubs finally stopped sharing gate receipts. Up until that point away teams got a percentage of ticket sales with the split being about a third for the away team minus any costs and levies. But the big clubs didn't like that because you'd have Manchester United and Liverpool asking why they had to hand over a split of more than 40,000 ticket sales when a Luton Town or Oxford were getting just a few thousand through the gates at Kenilworth Road and the old Manor Ground. The League used a term called the Natural Wastage Policy saying you shouldn't have to rely on a share of the gate receipts. The counter argument from those smaller clubs was that without us you've got no match. That was never going to wash. Whereas before football had been sport with a big S and business with a small B, the movers and shakers at the top end of football were casting envious eyes at how sport was being run overseas, especially in the US, and they wanted a part of that.

The voting structure within the league enabled the smaller clubs to block the big clubs from getting their own way with any kind of progressive ideas. Those big clubs were getting fed up of that, not least as there was a train of thought that it was starting to put them at a disadvantage with the major European sides. They basically wanted to keep more money for themselves.

There was a new breed of directors coming into English football who were watching what was happening in America, and how you could bring more money into a sport, the razzmatazz you could generate, the benefits of commercialism in football and the many avenues of revenue generation.

Now you had a whole generation of football owners starting to think about how your supporters could be customers, who you can sell a shiny new product to, by not only getting them into the stadiums, but then convincing them to buy merchandise to generate even more income. I heard one owner refer to the football stadium as a "profit centre" where you're not only getting people into the stadium, but you're giving them a whole matchday experience that extends beyond the 90 minutes of football. It's the same premise as supermarkets that put sweets near the checkouts, knowing that children who are shopping with their parents will pull their mum's sleeve to try and convince her to buy some chocolate. The business focus was about how you can maximise your profits within the stadium for the customers who were rocking up every week. It's all about not only getting them into the stadium, but taking more money off them when they do come through the turnstiles.

You would hear more and more about these directors who wanted to change football. There were discussions about removing promotion and relegation, you'd hear more about location being a key factor in determining if you'd be invited to a new super league and even whether you had adequate stadium capacity. It wasn't just on merit, this was going to be an invitation-only venture.

That concerned us, especially the welfare of the membership. Players traditionally had a pathway throughout their career, without the glass ceiling to restrict them, having ambitions to play in the highest division they possibly could. They also wanted their own rule book, so you would effectively have two sets of rules and regulations in respect of the terms and conditions of player contracts.

One gentleman at the forefront for greater change was David Dein, who was growing in influence at Arsenal as the co-owner and one of football's go-getters of that period. He was behind the Emirates project and to give you some context of the impact of new stadia, you only have to look at how matchday revenues compared. Bournemouth, in 2022 for instance, were making £210,000 per matchday, while Arsenal were bringing in £3.1million. Manchester United actually make £3.96million on a matchday – which is more than Bournemouth make over the course of the entire season. Both north London clubs have relatively new stadia, with huge capacities and massive corporate potential. That's where the revenue opportunities can be found – football, in the 1980s, simply wasn't maximising its revenue capabilities.

David was a big driver. He could see how things were continually changing in the United States and the money being brought in through broadcast revenues and sponsorship. Football was restricting its commercial opportunities by basically thinking about 45 minutes of two halves, whereas US sports were treating sport as a day-long event. It was David who called for half-time to be extended to 15 minutes rather than 10, because it offered more opportunities for fans to spend money on the concourses. One chairman of another club opposed that on the basis of citing what the manager would say to his players during that extended period, with no appreciation whatsoever for the financial gains that could be made. Amusingly, another chairman also resisted calls for two substitutes to be introduced during games as it might mean having to hire a bigger coach for away games. That was the mentality that football was locked into – a very parochial, small-minded one.

During that period in the mid-80s things were beginning to change forever in English football. In the space of one month, we had the Bradford and Heysel tragedies. We had a scenario where our stadiums were deemed unfit – in the case of Bradford City where tragically 56 people died in a horrific fire – and a scenario where our supporters were deemed unwelcome overseas because they couldn't behave.

The Heysel tragedy unfolded before the European Cup Final between Liverpool and Juventus. It was just appalling to watch and subsequently 39 people died following clashes between rival fans in a stadium that was unfit for such a match. As a result, English football clubs were banned from European competition from 1985 until 1990.

That had a massive impact on English football, because it meant that during the late 1980s there was a whole generation of footballers emerging who didn't get the experience of playing European club competitions. This meant that many of the best players and managers in England were moving abroad or to Scotland for European matches. You also had an England manager in Graham Taylor who, while he was in charge of the national team between 1990 and 1993, was picking from a pool of English players who had experience of European club competitions but were coming towards the end of their careers, or emerging footballers who had no experience of the European Cup, UEFA Cup and Cup Winners Cup and therefore didn't have quite the same education or experiences of the older players. It cannot be underestimated how important European competition was to the development of our best footballers, because of the different technical elements of the game overseas. Being exiled for five years really did create a huge void in our footballers' knowledge. At the same time Italian football was growing particularly with so many players being attracted to Serie A clubs, many of whom were playing in stadia that had been rebuilt for Italia 90. English football had to find a way of making itself attractive, not only to footballers but to supporters and, more so, investors.

Sir Bert Millichip, my old chairman at West Brom, was the head of the Football Association and it was his decision to withdraw clubs from

European competition. It was a brave decision, but it felt like the only decision. And then we had the issues surrounding Norwich City, Oxford United, Coventry City, Luton Town and Wimbledon. These were all unfancied clubs who had won domestic cup competitions that would have ordinarily guaranteed them European football, and the kudos that would bring, but were now being denied those opportunities. We, at the PFA, even sought legal advice on behalf of Norwich, who won the Milk (League) Cup in 1985 and would have ordinarily taken part in the UEFA Cup in 85/86. We actually looked into whether the ban could be challenged but we knew we had no chance of doing so. I had a lot of sympathy for those players, many of whom missed out on their only opportunity to experience playing in European competition. My good mates Cyrille and Laurie won the FA Cup with Coventry and Wimbledon respectively in 1987 and 88 but at least they'd tasted European football with West Brom earlier in their careers, but not everyone was as fortunate, and it was a very damaging period for those players in terms of their exposure to bigger audiences and their potential earning capacity. Everton might argue they never recovered from Heysel – they lost Gary Lineker to Barcelona, Trevor Steven and Gary Stevens to Rangers and, most notably, Howard Kendall to Athletic Bilbao. English football's reputation was being trashed, led by a Margaret Thatcher Government who had little time for the national game as it was. Hooliganism was being exported and it was to the shame of English football.

When the ban was finally lifted in 1990, Manchester United actually won the European Cup Winners Cup at the first attempt, but it took a while for English clubs generally to get back into the swing of things because they'd been out of it for so long. It wasn't until 1999 that an English club won the Champions League trophy, that being United again – some 14 years from that initial ban being imposed. It took a while for those clubs to catch up.

The other significant moment of 1985 was English football's failure to secure a rights' deal with the broadcasters – so, effectively, between August and January 1986, there were no domestic games screened on TV. No live games, no highlights, nothing. For fans of my old club West Brom this was probably no bad thing as we went into a sudden decline that ended up with our relegation that season. But for Manchester United supporters, especially those who couldn't get to games, they missed out on their side winning the first 10 matches of the season. Imagine now a scenario where there were no football games on TV.

I remember reports and leaks at the time that top-flight clubs were fed-up of the voting structure favouring the lower league clubs. There were suggestions that the big clubs were going to pressure the second division clubs into breaking away – or cutting them off altogether. That panicked the third and fourth division clubs in itself.

You had people like David Dein of Arsenal, Martin Edwards from Manchester United and Everton's Philip Carter being the big hitters, as part of the Big Five, which back then was made up of those three, plus Liverpool and Spurs.

The voting structure was the problem. The big clubs wanted greater influence and initially the Premier League was going to be structured around two divisions, taking into account location and capacity as well. They wanted to streamline the top division into 18 clubs – something that has never happened – while making sure it was loaded towards the biggest clubs.

It was also this period that the non-league doors were being opened into the Football League. Up until then any club finishing bottom of the fourth division had to reapply for re-election into the Football League. But this change meant that the bottom team would be relegated from the Football League into what was then called the Conference, with Halifax being the first club to be demoted in 1987, with Scarborough replacing them as the first club to be promoted from non-league into the Football League.

Back to the so-called Premier League, I recall one Friday night when I had a call from Gordon Taylor to say there was a crisis meeting in Plymouth of all places. Gordon was going to drive down from Blackburn to my house, with me taking over the driving duties from Walsall to Plymouth – ideal for someone who hated driving, especially on motorways! It wasn't how I intended to spend this particular Friday night, let me tell you. We were going into separate rooms, having separate discussions with various owners and chairmen. I don't think I got to bed until about 6am in the morning. And that was the start of it. Philip Carter and David Dein were certainly there, as were so many others.

In terms of being the heads of the PFA, we also needed to make sure that the viability of the 72 clubs in the Football League was maintained, especially as this was still a period where footballers were moving up and down the leagues. It was important to keep those career avenues open so the integrity of the clubs remained. There was a great deal of intrigue as to how things were going to develop – one thing was for sure, there was a growing appetite for change to bring football into a new era. And they needed the PFA onside with this, knowing that the players, our members, trusted their Association to look after their best interests. Players wanted to know that their contracts and terms and conditions were protected no matter what happened. It was important no regulations could be changed without the agreement of the PFA.

That Plymouth meeting was one to sound us out about how we would react to something that would almost certainly be happening. The word breakaway was never mentioned during that meeting, but it was clear that there was an appetite to restructure the Football League and it was a precursor to what was to follow with the formation of the Premier League.

When the Premier League was talked about in the first instance there was a lot of discussion about location and ground capacity, rather than around merit. Football was heading for seismic change. What we didn't know at that stage was when it would happen. The revenues were dwindling, English football was in a bad place and people were losing interest with the domestic game. The big clubs were looking at this in the knowledge that competition was not only with the smaller clubs in their own division, but with the big clubs in Europe.

The arrival of the Premier League in 1992 was the seismic moment in English football.

We had the one forum, the Professional Football Negotiating Committee (PFNC), which eventually became the Professional Football Negotiating and Consultative Committee (PFNCC), with a chief executive designate in Rick Parry, and Barclays Bank as the nominated sponsors. We wanted to make sure the players' hard-earned rights in respect of their contracts were honoured and enhanced where possible, for as has always been the case, it's the players who are the stars of the show. Without the players there would be no Premier League, so that was always our negotiating card.

Between 1986 and 1992, there was a hell of a lot going on behind the scenes. Gordon Taylor, who was outstanding in his leadership of the PFA at this particular time, and I could see that there would be this huge separation between the top-flight and the rest of the league. We wanted to see an equal distribution of the wealth that would flow from the formation of the Premier League. In the end the distribution formula agree was a 50 per cent basic award so each club receiving an equal share, 25 per cent for appearances on TV and then the remaining 25 per cent distributed as a ladder payment based on a club's league position at the end of the season so that the clubs finishing higher up the table would get more money.

The Premier League project, as it was, became known as The FOG – Fear, Opportunism and Greed – courtesy of a club chairman who was opposed to the idea. It was like food envy. You'd be effectively eating at the same restaurant as everyone else, but you'd be envious of what other people were eating. I recall one chairman in the Premier League talking about the Football League being a wasteland and wanting to pull up the drawbridge. His club were relegated at the end of that season.

That penultimate season of the old Football League, back in 1991/92, perhaps brought most perspective into how much football was about to change. There was no sponsorship of the Football League until about October and when they finally got one it was worth £1million and spread across 92 clubs. And yet just a few months later the first Premier League UK TV rights deal was announced to the tune of £304million, being distributed between just 22 clubs. That lasted until 1997, when the next deal was introduced at more than double that, £670million. By then we were down to 20 clubs. That's when you knew money was going to be the overriding factor.

In that final year of the old model, Gordon and I went around the clubs talking to players and what it meant and how important their support was. In the Football League handbook was a stipulation for the PFA to receive 10 per cent of any broadcasting contract, which had been negotiated by Cliff Lloyd back in 1955. That was fantastic foresight but what nobody saw then was the impact that overseas' TV deals would have. The PFA have tried to receive an entitlement to those, but never succeeded. And while the 10 per cent that we were entitled to from the Football League was there in black and white in the handbook, we never actually took the full amount. Nevertheless, that was our starting point and a strong bargaining position. In March 1992, the Premier League – then led by chairman Sir John Quinton – offered us a minimum guarantee of £1million. Sir John, who was also the former chairman of Barclays Bank, called that a fair and reasonable offer but we didn't agree to that. We wanted 10 per cent of any new deal up to £15million and five per cent above that figure. It was at that point we took it to a strike ballot. I was going around the regions telling the players that unless we got our way their Association could be undermined and all the hard-won benefits they enjoyed could be placed at risk. More importantly it was only fair that their association should receive a reasonable share of the monies coming into the game from television for the overall benefit of all members. That's how bad it was. However the Premier League were, insultingly, only offering the PFA £1million from a £304million contract. You're joking, right? There was no way we were going to agree to that.

All 594 First Division players were balloted and returned a 90 per cent support for whatever action the PFA deemed necessary. There were a lot of harsh words between ourselves and the Premier League, but we finally agreed a deal on April 27, 1992. The most significant part of it was that the PFA would receive a minimum guarantee of £1.5million, consisting of 10 per cent of the first £10million income band and five per cent thereafter.

The essence of it was that players had it in their contracts that they were obliged to play football matches. But crucially, there was nothing in those contracts about playing in front of cameras. Basically, we took a view that if the cameras were there then they would refuse to play. And this wasn't just live games, but recorded games too – so in fact this impacted on all games as every match was televised, which was part of the new appeal of the Premier League.

There were rumours of Gordon Taylor leaving us for the Football League in 1989 before all of this. Aston Villa's Doug Ellis, John Smith of Liverpool and Norwich's Robert Chase opposed it. I've no idea why. I don't think they could cope with a union man being in charge. The FA also came calling too during that period.

Thankfully, Gordon stayed with the PFA and it was to our benefit and the benefit of all members that he did.

You cannot deny the Premier League has been a massive success. There were concerns that with matches being televised people would stop going to games in the same numbers but that didn't happen. The Premier League has become a worldwide brand, with more than 230 territories showing it. Not only the players and coaches, but even referees have become worldwide stars. It has been packaged together brilliantly into the product it is today. The only concern I had was to see a better distribution within the game, rather than the lion's share being retained by the big clubs. You only have to look at the struggles to get into the Premier League for those who aren't in there. It's created a huge and even dangerous gap that many clubs are trying to bridge and struggling to justify financially. It has distorted football and it would be much more of a level playing field if they rethought the distribution of money. But why would they? The big clubs want that to themselves. Turkeys don't vote for Christmas.

Another aspect of looking after players was making sure those 40 or 50-a-year who retire through injury are taken care of. The money was also used towards youth development, social projects, community projects, pension rights – a lot of stuff that went on that wasn't visible to the public, but was benefitting our members.

The Bosman Ruling was also a big moment during my time with the PFA. This was a legal challenge brought about by Jean-Marc Bosman, whose contract had come to an end with Belgian club Liege. He wanted to change clubs and move to French club Dunkerque, but they couldn't afford the fee Liege were asking for and so withdrew from the deal. Bosman found his wages reduced by 70 per cent by Liege, who no longer considered him a first-team player. Bosman took them to the European Court of Justice citing restraint of trade and, after a long court case, the ECJ found in his favour. It meant that players could now move to a new club at the end of their contract without their old club receiving a fee.

That completely changed the landscape once more. Players were employees and we had to make sure they matched the advancements of the game. The George Eastham case started it all. When he took Newcastle to the High Court, the PFA effectively paid £15,000 towards his legal fees. Had we lost that case it would have completely bankrupted the PFA. Freedom of contract in 1978 then became a precursor to what followed with Bosman and the freedom of movement.

There were even discussions in England about total freedom of movement. There is no other industry where this is the case other than perhaps the Forces. In football you effectively own the registration of the player and the fee demanded is for the transfer of that registration. You can see how this would unbalance the status quo and in particular in terms of youth development. But in respect of EU laws and freedom of movement they had to go with it, albeit with some conditions.

It has benefitted footballers. If you have a talent you always feel you can exploit it. I was the PFA delegate at Cambridge when Freedom of Contract came in and the media were saying it would be the demise of the third and fourth divisions. We had just won promotion to the third tier but as players we wanted the freedom to pursue our own destiny, without being shackled to a club in any shape nor form.

And, of course, there are clubs driving up the value of players artificially. There's a huge element of commercialisation that has gone hand in hand with the Premier League.

When FIFA talked about taking the World Cup to America there was genuine discussion about shifting the game from two halves to four quarters because they could see the commercial value of more breaks. And then there could be some branding on the pitch, and even more branding in the penalty area, because that's where the action occurs. These were things being discussed. They say the two most expensive slots in sport are the Super Bowl and Augusta, where the US Masters is held.

Pre-season used to be a trip to Europe or to the British seaside if a club wasn't as rich. Now clubs are going to America, or Asia, or Australia. Football is a money-spinner in every respect.

Where are we with football right now? Well, we are already seeing the diminishing of the FA Cup. Arsene Wenger talked about developing his players through the FA Cup and, actually, once they got to the latter stages, he was playing slightly stronger sides. I always thought they missed a trick by not offering a Champions League spot to the FA Cup winners. This isn't a revolutionary idea, but equally the big clubs weren't keen on it.

You see the same teams in the Premier League competing for the title and for the top four positions. I think we might, in years to come, see a Premier League II where they block off the bottom 48 clubs. But then why would those Premier League clubs want to dilute in any way the riches currently enjoyed with a further 24 clubs? That would be something they'd have to overcome but I've always felt that an element of self-preservation occupies their thinking - where you remove some of the jeopardy, so instead of three up and three down, you end up with one up and one down. I am sure the very big clubs would like to close it off in some way. Relegation and promotion isn't what those mega clubs want – as was the proposal from The European Super League as a way of ensuring that these clubs exist in their own bubble.

The supporters are crucial to this in many ways. I think the supporters' reaction to the European Super League shocked many, especially outside of England. This is what people grow up with, it is what people hook onto – the football club is your football club. And you stick by it during those good times and bad times. And jeopardy is part of that experience. The uncertainty of result is the allure of any sport, despite Manchester City seemingly being the dominant club right now.

But then I can see the other side. I've got friends who support West Bromwich Albion who say they can enjoy watching them in the Championship because they prefer to see them winning games. In the Premier League that isn't the case. Gary Megson, who was boss at West Brom when I returned to work there as managing director in 2002, always told me to look at the wage bill. You will generally finish where your wage bill is for that division.

The Premier League isn't that competitive in terms of winning the title. Leicester City was a perfect storm and one that may not happen again. Football is rock and roll now. Many fans just want to see the best players. The ambitions to win anything are a distant dream for most clubs – it's all about staying in the Premier League and benefitting from the riches. Each season for most is to achieve in the region of 38 points, which usually avoids relegation and is all that matters. You can talk about the development of the club, the wellbeing of the club, the match day experience but what really matters is being in the Premier League. Supporters actually own the club; the directors are the guardians. Fans remain the heart and soul of a club. There is a realisation for many supporters that expectation far outweighs reality.

I do look at the Premier League now and the number of foreign owners and wonder if they might seek changes so that relegation and promotion is scrapped. I really do think they will try to make it a closed shop. The European Super League proposals didn't shock me one bit. That had been rumbling for years and it may return at some point, because football is about generating revenues and the self-interests of those clubs involved. The interests of the likes of Liverpool, Manchester City and United are different to those clubs who aspire to just be part of the Premier League. We are the only country with, effectively, a five-league structure, if you count the National League, but I cannot help thinking the sand will shift at some point.

The Premier League is the bully in the playground, and I do think there are some involved who would like it to be sealed off – effectively giving a chunk of money to the Football League – and would like to acquire the England team, because that's also a money spinner. What I mean by that is the England team becomes part of the Premier League brand, with the FA being left to look after grass roots football. Having the England brand under their portfolio would be huge for the Premier League, not to mention offer huge commercial opportunities. The appetite for exploiting the game at the top end remains undiminished.

I appreciate the PFA has had an image problem over the years. It was irritating because a lot of it is rubbish. Some of the agendas were being driven by the clubs and certain elements of the media. You always had to ignore what was being said because our job was to protect players. Not many clubs wish to know about players when they've left the game.

A case in point is the debate around neurodegenerative diseases (NDD) where people are pointing the finger at the PFA, saying: "The union should be dealing with that" and looking after these players. The PFA refer such players to the charity The Players Foundation (formerly The PFA Charity) so that we can offer them as much support as we possibly can. However, the charity of which I am chairman is not in a position to pay for full residential or nursing home fees. We simply don't have the money. What we are able to do is financially support research into the causes of this dreadful disease.

Sometimes players don't know what the Union does for them, and I accept there is a lack of understanding of the many aspects of the work the PFA does on behalf of it's members.

First and foremost, one of the most important things was the negotiation and establishment of the standard contract whereby all the terms and conditions have to be met. The Bosman ruling had a massive impact too. The PFA are there to protect players' rights, provide support by way of educational, financial, legal and wellbeing services as well as offering advice in such areas as personal development. All of these services are funded through the money we get from the shared TV rights. There are many former players who need medical attention as a result of injuries sustained during their playing days and the PFA can offer financial support if a corrective procedure is needed. A hip replacement for example can cost up to £15,000.

Gordon Taylor gets a lot of unfair criticism, yet he is one of the best administrators in the game. He even got approached to join the FA many years back. People criticise his salary, but I've never heard anyone say he did a bad job for the players. He did an amazing job in negotiating the terms and conditions and numerous benefits for the members over the years. He strengthened the players' contracts. When the Football In the Community Scheme was first suggested during the mid 1980s, there was a lack of enthusiasm from the Football League to get involved. The PFA therefore launched a pilot scheme involving six clubs in the North West using former players to act as community officers. It proved a huge success and has evolved into the current day charitable Foundations which clubs now administer. A great deal of credit at that time goes to Micky Burns who headed up our education department and his assistant Pat Lally who oversaw the scheme.

Things are different now – the Premier League has made sure of that – but there was a time when very few footballers could retire and lie on the beach for the rest of their days. Even now it's a different landscape in the EFL, where you may have players on short-term or even monthly contracts. The reality is 75 per cent of players are outside of the Premier League. You also have between 40 and 50 players a year having to retire through injury – I was one such statistic myself. And you have young players whose dreams have been shattered for one reason or another. The PFA has always been about looking after its members whenever and whatever the circumstances.

The one story that perhaps gained more traction than many in recent years is the Jeff Astle tragedy. I had a vested interest in that because I knew Jeff. One of the few games I played for Arsenal was against West Brom and then I later got to know him when I played for the club. Jeff was great fun. When you saw him approach you from a 100-metres away, you'd start to smile, because he was such great company. By the 1990s he started to sing on the Skinner and Baddiel Fantasy Football Show, which went down brilliantly and brought him to the attention of a whole new audience. It was some time after that when Jeff disappeared off the radar, and you would hear rumours that he wasn't well. I remember speaking to Tony Brown, one of Jeff's best friends, to ask what was going on because nobody had seen him or Jeff's wife Laraine for some time. I asked if there was anything the PFA could do to help so in the end Tony spoke to Laraine and she said I could go to see him. It was very clear that Jeff wasn't well. I suggested the PFA could help financially with some refurbishments to the house to make it easier for Laraine and the family to cope. I went back to Gordon and said what we needed to do to which he readily agreed. The work needed was completed but sadly within a few weeks Jeff passed away.

I went to the inquest sometime later and remember seeing a famous picture of Jeff making a diving header with such power that the ball appeared to be deflated at the moment of impact. I recall the coroner's summary when he concluded that the damage suffered by Jeff to the front of his brain was most likely caused from the heading of the old leather footballs. Since then, there have been studies that suggest players are three-and-a-half times more likely to develop some form of dementia than the general public, so there is no question there are concerns.

And then concussion comes into the conversation because there is heading of the ball and there are concussive injuries, where you can clash heads or receive blows to the head through dangerous use of the arms and elbows. There was also the release of a famous film, Concussion, starring Will Smith about players in American football who suffer brain damage in the course of normal play. Research remains ongoing into this. The PFA takes a lot of criticism around these issues, but whenever it's been asked it has always funded any research in this area.

The notion the PFA has been passive is nonsense. The criticism we get is around what we do for the families but any oversights we have put right. We are now in a place where we have been asked to fund care home costs. Now, the average care home costs about £40-50,000 per year. We have about 50,000 former members. The maths doesn't stack up. More than that, that's what the state is there for. We have engaged with health experts and we have supported families with care in their homes, be it respite care, or top-up care. What we cannot do is meet the costs of care homes. People like Chris Sutton and John Stiles (son of Nobby) were saying the PFA weren't helping their fathers and having to go into care homes. In England if you have assets in excess of £23,250 or more (excluding your home), then you have to fund your own care. They wanted the PFA to fund it. Because we had big reserves in the charity it was felt that we had an obligation to help these people suffering from NDD but these reserves were to meet the obligations of all our beneficiaries who are in need of help.

Once they move into a care home, that should be funded by the state. But certain people and media think the PFA are responsible for that. If every former member came to us and demanded we fund their care then the Union or the Charity would be bankrupt overnight.

I look back on my time with the PFA with great pride. I was part of an exciting era when the whole landscape changed. Securing the financial wellbeing of the PFA was part of that, making sure we looked after our members and safeguarded the future of the union. I went from uncertainty when my career ended with West Bromwich Albion, to being thrust into the PFA at the very point that football was about to completely changed. I had 18 years as deputy to Gordon Taylor and I wouldn't change it for the world.

The main thing is that the members – and yes that is a very old-fashioned term – won't always appreciate what the Union is about and what it does for them. And that's fine in a way because it means they've maybe never had to turn to us, but make no mistake, that it's helped protect them and the industry they work in. A story from the player associations in the States is that when things go quiet they create a crisis, because they want to remind their members what they're about. We never quite needed to resort to such measures and yet the organisation has been fantastic not only for the players but for the game itself.

More people involved in the game and media would do well to remember that.

TRIBUTE

I had been on the PFA management committee for a few years, having been delegate at Birmingham City and Bolton Wanderers. It was quite clear that we were going to need to grow the PFA and I knew that would be a huge challenge – I also knew I needed good people around me. I identified Brendon as someone who would bring great value to our organisation. He impressed me a lot whenever I met him.

His career as a player was ending, he had been a good delegate, and I had a high regard for him. He was a cool customer, always had a lot of dignity about him, a great personality and was very interested in the PFA. Brendon had been a player of some distinction – especially as one member of the Three Degrees – but it was apparent he had so much to offer off-the-pitch. I invited him to be my assistant and, thankfully, he chose to do that. It started off as a temporary arrangement, but it quickly became permanent because from day one he was a first-class colleague.

He was always calm, always measured and we became a good team – he was especially passionate about inclusivity and representation across all communities, which is something I was very happy to endorse.

I remember being in Rotterdam with Brendon when Sir Alex Ferguson won his first European trophy as Manchester United manager in 1991. Brendon, Mick Hucknall of Simply Red and myself watched that European Cup Winners Final against Barcelona. That was a wonderful night.

I also remember some of the challenging times we had in the 1980s and early 1990s trying to keep pace with some of the seismic changes that the game went through, not least the European ban and then the advent of the Premier League and all that brought to our members.

Even after leaving us in 2002, he retained strong links with the PFA. I knew he wanted to try his hand working for a club – which he did with West Bromwich Albion, a club he had so much time for – but even when that didn't quite work out, our relationship stayed strong. He went to the Football Association, has been a trustee of our charity and I'm very fortunate to have called him a colleague, a confidante and, most of all, a good friend. It's also worth mentioning that I approached Brendon. He didn't approach me. That's how much faith I had in him.

Gordon Taylor OBE, Professional Footballers Association chief executive (1981-2021)

CHAPTER EIGHT
Back to The Hawthorns

"...There were too many jockeys on the same horse..."

By the turn of the 21st century I was starting to think about new challenges. We had just concluded a new Collective Bargaining Agreement (CBA) for 10 years with the Premier League and the other football bodies in respect of the domestic TV broadcasting rights so the financial future of the PFA was secure. I had no ambitions to be the next chief executive having worked closely with Gordon for nearly 20 years the association would need a fresh face with new ideas at the helm.

I had a couple of offers to move away from the PFA, including one from West Brom when I met then-chairman Tony Hale in the late 1990s. It wasn't a very serious conversation.

I knew I'd eventually want to return to a club environment, and I always thought West Brom would be that ideal club for me. I felt I wouldn't be able to resist had they come in for me, but that period of the late 1990s with the PFA was a very exciting time. There were rumours that an Albion shareholder had been interested in me back in 1992, but they were only rumours.

It was third time lucky in 2002. There had been some manoeuvring behind the scenes as West Brom were trying to get promotion to the Premier League. Jeremy Peace was hoping to wrestle control of the club once it got promotion, knowing that the then owner Paul Thompson and the manager Gary Megson weren't getting on. Jeremy told me to sit tight because once he got hold of the chair and control of the club then he'd give me the green light.

Jeremy had been to see me in Broad Street when I was chairman of PFA financial management. I'd never met him, I knew nothing about him – I knew he was a West Brom director but I didn't know why he wanted to speak to me. It was only later that I realised that he was sizing me up. I thought he was only trying to get information about player contracts.

He then showed his hand when he made it clear that if things went as he hoped then he would be taking over the club and, also, that it hinged on promotion. This is when Paul Thompson was still owner. It wasn't something that played on my mind. I obviously wasn't privy to what went on behind the scenes during that period, but it was fairly clear that Jeremy Peace was going to get his wish to replace Paul Thompson, who by now had a very toxic relationship with his own manager.

It wasn't unanimously approved by the other Board members but it eased pressure on the future of manager Gary Megson, who said he would be willing to work with Peace and nobody else. That effectively handed the chairmanship and ownership to Jeremy Peace.

Cecily wasn't sure about me moving back to a club. She knew West Brom, having just been promoted, might end up getting relegated after only one season. I knew that, but I also needed a new challenge. The PFA is a great organisation, but it felt right moving on. Was it a risk? Yes, absolutely, but I knew what I was getting into.

I told Jeremy I wanted to be involved with the football side. He set out a vision where he would be at arm's length and would leave the running of the club to the executives. The other thing that swayed me is that I'd been at the PFA for nearly 20 years by this point. We'd had three threatened strike actions, we'd not long concluded a brilliant 10-year deal for the players through the PFA, thanks to the efforts of Gordon. I thought it was as good a time as any to move to a club and obviously West Brom was very close to my heart.

Jeremy told me that if we get promoted to expect a call. And I can tell you where I was when it all began to gather pace: I was at the Manchester Ringway airport hotel – I was flying out the next day to the World Cup in Japan.

There was one issue nagging away. I asked what the situation was with John Wile, who was the chief executive and, more importantly, a former colleague of mine and a friend. He was also a very popular figure at the club. Even though it wasn't like for like - I was going in as Managing Director, and he was Chief Executive - I knew that at some point it might make things awkward. Jeremy made it very clear that he considered John as Paul Thompson's man – in other words, John would be leaving the club.

The first time I met John after that, yes, there was an awkwardness. It wasn't awkward for me, because I had nothing to feel awkward about, but I realised John obviously wasn't comfortable with it and I was mindful that he might be thinking I had played some part in him losing his job. That was certainly not the case. I explained to him that I played no part in that. His fate was sealed the moment Jeremy Peace became owner of the club – it's as simple as that.

There was no honeymoon period, despite the club's promotion. The first thing I have to do is deal with civil unrest between the club and players over their bonus schedule for that season. The players were actually threatening to not play a friendly against Torquay, with further threats that might escalate and interfere with pre-season preparations. Not the ideal way for the club to be starting its first-ever Premier League campaign.

The team were based at Nigel Mansell's hotel in Exeter and I remember driving down with Jeremy wondering what was going on – I had no idea what they'd been promised. But with my PFA hat on I knew the players could be fined two weeks wages if they refused to play. The leader of the pack was Derek McInnes, who was team captain. I spoke to him and the other players and advised them it made no sense for them to act in this way when there was still time to resolve the situation. As long as they signed a new bonus schedule before the first game of the season – and had it lodged with the league – then it would be fine. They also needed to know that for every breach there is a potential maximum fine of two weeks wages.

And what they were talking about was giving up a proportion of their salary to try to get a bonus schedule that in the cold light of day they must have realised was unreal. There is always a compromise when that happens. And they were getting good money to play in the Premier League.

It seems strange that something like this could derail a team who have won promotion to the Premier League and were, just a year earlier, in the second tier. But this was a big deal. What we as a club proposed as a new bonus structure was geared around success in the Premier League. That's what a bonus should be. It is generally tiered but what they had been offered by the previous owner Paul Thompson wasn't feasible. For a first team appearance they had been promised £5,000 per man, with £7,500 for a draw, and £15,000 for a win – crazy figures and totally unrealistic. You have to structure a contract, so you get a premium for being in the Premier League and if you go down, you lose that premium. In the end we effectively said there would be a big bonus for staying up, with the bonuses increasing the higher you are in the league.

Appearance money is usually included in a contract for young players as an incentive as they make their way up the professional ranks. Once a player becomes a regular in the first team and is negotiating a new contract we at the PFA would advise against having appearance money in the contract as it could be easily manipulated by a club who may decide to stop selecting a player for whatever reason to avoid paying that extra money.

That season was a big learning curve. By then I'd had nearly 20 years in football administration but both Mike O'Leary and Jeremy Peace were financially astute and I learned so much in a short space of time. They'd be rattling off figures and numbers and I'd be struggling to keep pace at times.

Anyway, I was trying to calm the players down. They were talking about refusing to play. You simply cannot do that. In the end we got to a place where common sense prevailed. Gary Megson got caught in-between, because he'd just received a new contract, but he also had to be sympathetic to the players' position and get them on-side. He did that but it was a very tetchy time. From a front-facing point of view I was there working for the club, making sure the club did everything appropriately, but I was also trying to chat to the players to ensure it worked out. I actually drafted a very strong letter that would have gone out had the strike happened – which Mike O'Leary said might be too strong – but I was under no illusion the players had to see sense as the figures being talked about just didn't add up. It would have bankrupted the club.

In the end we reached a compromise. We worked out something the players could accept, and Gary Megson was integral to that process. He had enough to deal with given West Bromwich Albion was about to start its first season in what was now the Premier League, some 16 years since it had last been in the top-flight of English football.

Apart from that it was an exciting time – it was a massive challenge to be back in the top-flight. We knew that if we didn't stay up, we'd need to rebuild towards coming back up. Gary was a very dynamic manager, very strongly opinionated, who knew what he wanted. I didn't always agree with him in terms of how we played. My view was that the more you give the ball back to the opposition, the more they can hurt you. But, actually, he nearly got there. We lost a lot of games by the odd goal – fine margins indeed. We didn't have enough goals in the side, we had nobody who got into double figures, but I always felt that this was part of West Brom's journey. I hear supporters saying: "I'd rather be in the Championship because we win more games," but that doesn't help the development of the club. You should always strive to be better, while finding as few bumps in the road as you can. Albion got better and better at dealing with that.

One thing I quickly realised as the 2002/03 season began was that we didn't have enough quality in the squad to really be competitive. Some players knew they would still be playing even if their performance were below par for a couple of games. Behind the scenes Jeremy Peace was acquiring more and more shares towards his own stake so he was becoming more powerful and with that he was assuming more control of the executive side of the club – he was not just acting like an owner, but also like a chairman and chief executive. Ultimately that was having an impact on me. I felt like there were too many jockeys on the same horse.

When I arrived at the club I was insistent that I wasn't given the job title of technical director. This was 2002/03 so that particular role was still viewed with suspicion that you're trying to wrestle control from a manager, but that was the last thing I ever wanted to do. I saw my role as supporting Gary as much as I could but I didn't want to be in a position where we signed a player without his say so. And that was the case while I was there. He might have a first, second and third choice but that's the business. He had Frank Burrows as his assistant, who was very knowledgeable and a good foil. Yes, there were players I wasn't sure about that Gary brought to us, but I supported him in that process because actually if it isn't going to work for a manager then it needs to be down to his decisions, not mine or somebody else's.

That season stirred my managerial juices. There were times when I watched us and wondered why we were playing so long. As a defender I knew that the longer a ball was in the air, the more time the opposition had to adjust, and we were playing a lot of long balls to opposition defenders in that manner. I didn't always enjoy our style of play – yes, we had some good results and near misses, but against the better teams we got picked apart. Gary's mantra was that we needed to be better than three teams. It was all about survival. That kind of football wears you out, it wears players out and it kills enthusiasm. I felt that sometimes the players weren't trusted to pass the ball unopposed. That was Gary's prerogative, but I did wish he had given the players more licence in that respect. But then who am I to argue with the guy who has just taken West Brom up? It was his job to do what he saw best, and I supported him as much as I could.

That summer we signed a few players. Sean Gregan was one. He scored the winner in our first Premier League win. He was strongly-built, a good passer of the ball and a bit of a holding midfield player in the team. We did a deal with Preston and got him. And then we got Jason Koumas, who was a very, very talented player who should have achieved so much more with his ability. He was the best midfielder on the park in so many games. But not often enough. He was our record signing for a day and then we re-signed Lee Hughes from Coventry, just 12 months after he'd moved across the West Midlands in a £5million deal. The deal to bring Lee back came about as there were still outstanding payments from Coventry – he came very late in that window because we were short of a striker. I didn't agree with that signing because I felt he wasn't good enough for the Premier League. He had a relatively poor year in the Championship with Coventry. Jason Roberts, on the other hand, had blistering pace and you needed someone to be a natural foil for him – Lee Hughes wasn't that player. Jason should have scored about 15 goals that season but he scored just three times for us.

Lee was a smashing player for Albion in the second tier but there was a feeling Coventry were desperate for money and needed him off the wage bill because ITV Digital had gone bust. They still owed West Brom instalment payments on the transfer so we did the deal to bring Lee back to The Hawthorns. But it just didn't work out for him in the Premier League.

There was also an issue between Jason Roberts, his uncle Cyrille Regis who was also his agent, and Gary Megson. Jason and Cyrille weren't getting on with Gary, but I tried to keep those relationships on a professional level. There always seemed to be a simmering resentment between them, but I steered well clear of that.

By January we were struggling and we had the first-ever January transfer window. It was the reality that we were fishing in a very small pond. Why would anyone join us? It was almost impossible and certainly myself and Gary had the view that if we cannot improve the team now then we would just have to struggle on with the players we have with an eye to next season in the Championship. We did try for Tim Sherwood, but we had no chance. We became a bargaining tool for players to get better deals elsewhere. We were being used like that. We could only offer a player contract terms which included a clause that they would have to take a cut if we were relegated. It's back to that premium of playing in the Premier League again. You have to pay Championship wages and pay a premium for being in the Premier League. If you go down, that Premier League premium no longer applies. It's a model that many clubs adopted and have stuck by since. You have to protect the club. I used to have a right battle with agents because they work for themselves, then work for their players and the clubs are a distant last. The amounts clubs pay to agents are unbelievable these days. Back in 2002, I knew many were also in it for themselves. We had examples of agents totally acting for themselves, or they would take their fees off a player's gross salary or such like. I hated dealing with agents because I knew there were some bad ones out there. Too many clubs caved into agents. What doesn't help is that many managers just want a player to sign which is understandable. They don't care how or what is needed to sign that player. They just want that player because they want him in the team as soon as possible.

In terms of recruitment, what didn't help is that I was abroad as I had a family holiday planned to Grenada that Christmas when I took the job and I do wonder if that played a part when the club made a decision over me. It's my own personal feeling that particular decision to go on holiday was held against me. My holiday coincided with the January transfer window that had just been introduced and, yes, I was contactable, and people could get hold of me, but I do think that was held against me. With hindsight I shouldn't have gone.

West Brom were staring relegation in the face from very early in the season and it was apparent Jeremy and Gary weren't getting on. I even heard rumours that Jeremy had called in the media to discuss Gary's future, obviously behind his back. One of the issues was around recruitment. Jeremy didn't think it should be left to the manager. I was having to go to Gary and ask him for a list of players and that was cause for the friction. Jeremy wanted to see a list of signings, but Gary was of the view that as we didn't know with any certainty what division we would be playing in nest season or budget available it was too early to address the subject. There was a big difference of opinion, and it was causing friction and tension between chairman and manager.

I remember Gary telling me when the writing was on the wall: "Brendon, people are going to lose their jobs." I don't think Gary felt he was under threat because he had taken the club up just a few months earlier against all odds. The fans loved him, and he was given little to work with in terms of improving the squad in that first Premier League season. The bigger issue was perhaps over the long-term plan. How are we going to build a structure for the future, but then as with any manager you're always thinking about the here and now because that's what is keeping you in a job. What I thought would get him the sack was a full-blown public row. Jeremy was very sensitive to what Gary was saying in the media, but it was just manager-speak most of the time. You see it at all levels of the game, including at the very top – all managers want that extra player because what they've got is never enough.

That season West Brom had the lowest budget in the Premier League so it was no surprise that we got relegated. At the back of my mind, I had concerns of the consequences it might have and you're mindful there might be a reshuffle. Mike O'Leary was chief executive but wasn't taking a salary, then there was myself as MD and Jeremy Peace who was increasingly taking a hands-on approach to running the club, whereas initially the idea was to allow his appointed executives to perform those duties. I almost felt my role was becoming diminished. I didn't think I was making a proper contribution because Jeremy Peace started handling a lot of it. I felt less involved and almost marginalised.

Jeremy would end up appointing a succession of sporting and technical directors, including the very successful Dan Ashworth – but that came after I left. That was still a relatively new concept in English football back then. The game was evolving. I remember the old Brian Clough comment that he knew after 10 minutes of watching a player whether he would sign him or not – and on his head be it. But clubs abroad were starting to use more data and statistical analysis before deciding on the players they would pursue, with recruitment staff going to watch those targets and then reporting back to a head coach. There was more of a considered approach, removing some of the responsibility from coaches and managers but ensuring they were engaged in the process. British football culture was yet to change. I went to a dinner once and a manager told me that if a chairman or director had recommended a player to him his instinct would be to say "no", because he didn't want to have the chairman's choice. One, because he would be under pressure to pick him and, two, because if it didn't work, the manager would pay for it. Jeremy was merely trying to reflect the change – he wanted more say in the players coming in. He wanted to know what Gary was doing, while Gary's view was that he didn't know which division we would be playing in so what's the point in presenting a list of names until we know.

In my case, it was frustrating. I was the only person on the board who had played the game and the only person who had worked in football administration, yet here I was feeling that my portfolio was being eroded.

I also had to manage an increasingly delicate relationship between the manager and the owner. I didn't want to feel like I was intruding into Gary's territory, yet I had to try and be a conduit at times. Jeremy wanted the board to decide everything. I got the feeling he didn't want the manager's input on those matters. That dynamic is always difficult because managers want a player in to do a job, but a chairman or owner will be thinking about the investment on wages, the return on that player, especially if things aren't going well for that particular player. You might have a manager who wants 28-year-olds at their peak, but the owner will know there is little return on a player like that when it comes to him leaving so he might seek a lower age profile. In this particular season we were having our legs run off us. We simply couldn't compete against the younger, faster players during that relegation campaign.

It was Mike O'Leary who gave me the bad news. It was on the Tuesday after our relegation. I had a lot of time and respect for Mike, and still do. He's a polished, knowledgeable man who would be an asset to any board as he has shown at Ipswich Town, where as chairman in 2023, he achieved promotion to the Championship. It wasn't a huge shock to me. The disappointment was that I didn't feel I'd done justice to the role in that short space of time. You have to grow into a position like that and everything was so full on from the moment I came in that I never had a chance to settle.

And that was that.

I didn't say a word to Cecily all week. I was still trying to sort out my contractual affairs with West Brom so I wanted to finalise that. On the Sunday, I took her to a nice restaurant in Sutton Coldfield. We had the starter and Cecily said: "Are you going to tell me what's going on?" She knew. And I felt awful – like I'd let her and the family down. She just replied: "We'll be okay" – just like she had 20 years earlier. For those four days between me being told and then breaking the news to Cecily I agonised on how I was going to tell her and the kids. How was I going to support them when I didn't have a job?

We booked a flight to go to Spain and a day or so later I got a call from David Davies at the FA and Trevor East, who was working for Sky and was a big pal of Mark Palios, who had just been appointed the new CEO of the FA. Mark, who I didn't really know at the time but had played against him when he was at Tranmere Rovers and I was at Cambridge, then called me a few hours later where he said he'd like me to help him out with a disciplinary matter on behalf of the FA. There had been a punch up between David Beckham and Aston Villa's Turkey international Alpay in a European Championship qualifier and UEFA the governing body of football in Europe was asking for a report from the FA. That's how I started acting as a consultant to the FA which lasted for 13 years.

So, from 18 years at the PFA, I went to a 10-month spell at West Brom. Initially it had been an exciting time for me, being part of a new Premier League club. I learned a lot in those 10 months, especially from Mike O'Leary who was a brilliant whizz on the financial aspects of the club.

I was philosophical about my time with West Brom. It was the right time to take the risk in leaving the PFA. People felt it was a failure that after 12 months I had left West Brom, having chosen to end my time in a safe job with the PFA.

There is a poem called The Road not Travelled by Robert Frost. Effectively it wasn't the road I had travelled, but was the one I hadn't travelled – so I look back without any regrets. The PFA had been an exciting time and once Gordon had secured the 10-year deal for the PFA with the football bodies, I felt that I had achieved all I could in my current role and it was time to move on. All these years later I've never regretted it. I've done what I wanted, I've been my own boss and chosen to do what I wanted to do. That wouldn't have been possible had I remained an employee with West Brom or the PFA.

Gary Megson was someone I got on with. I made it clear when I accepted the position that I wouldn't be taking on the role of technical director because at that time it conjured up roles that crossed over with the manager. He had an interesting dynamic with Frank Burrows, who was very much a calming influence. Our main focus was obviously how we could stay up, where we could pick up results and looking at games in batches – as in where we could get points in certain games. Staying up was always going to be a major ask and reality started kicking in very early during that season. We weren't even getting hammerings; we were just missing out on points by the odd goal.

Mentally that started getting to the players because the whole emphasis turned to keeping clean sheets in the knowledge that scoring goals was becoming more and more elusive. You couldn't see us getting a draw in some games. And the biggest problem we had that year is that the squad didn't have enough depth. When you don't have enough competition within a team that becomes a problem because it means you cannot give a player a break when they need one and secondly it doesn't push existing players to keep performing at the level required.

There was a feeling among some – certainly Gary Megson and his coaches – that we weren't getting the major decisions in certain games. Gary and Dr John Evans, the very experienced long-serving secretary of West Bromwich Albion, actually wrote to the Professional Game Board to complain but every newly promoted team always feels hard done by particularly in favour of the bigger clubs. I didn't deter them from writing that letter, but I knew the authorities were used to getting complaints like that on a regular basis. Alex Ferguson used to be brilliant at playing the system. He would say things and put things in the referees' head – he was a master at those mind games.

I had a lot of sympathy for Gary that year. I never sat in a manager's chair and the pressures that brings, especially when you're new to the division as a manager and wondering how you're going to extract every little bit from the players. I remember we beat Manchester City and I thought it might be a turning point, but reality returns within a few days. What I will say is that you're better off being in the Premier League, even if it's just for one season. Get the money and if you go down then you can regroup with greater resources.

My take on Gary was that he put up a big barrier between himself and his players. I actually thought he had a great sense of humour away from that environment, but he was very full on in their company. At times I thought he needed to take his foot off the pedal, and just allow them to breathe more. When I was playing and we were struggling I would look forward to a game to try to correct a situation. But you needed the belief in the manager that he believes in you, but I felt at times there was too much of a hand-around-the-throat in that particular relationship between Gary and the players. He was a hard task master and I think he didn't always carry some of the players with him – those that didn't caused disruption for him.

Bobby Robson once told me that you have to love the game more than the result. I've played in games where we've lost but there are times I've known that for the sake of a poor few minutes we should have got something from the game. We played one game against Stoke where Garth Crooks got a hat-trick within the first 20 minutes before Cyrille pulled a goal back just before halftime. We then battered them in the second half, got another goal back, but try as we might, couldn't get the equaliser. Yes, we lost, but we could take some satisfaction from the spirit and ambition we showed. I used to remind Garth about that game with a: "You're a little shit Crooksie to score three against our defence."

As for Jeremy, I found him to be very socially awkward at times. A few years later, in my role with the WBA Former Players Association, we had an event to celebrate the 80th birthday of the great Ray Barlow, who had won the FA Cup with the club and was an Albion legend. I asked Jeremy to come in and make a presentation to Ray and it was almost like he couldn't wait to get out of the room. As a financier and businessman, he was very skilled, but he was no raconteur.

154

I was 50 at this point so I had a good few years left of work, but all of a sudden I found myself unemployed for the first time since I joined Arsenal as a 16-year-old. I had never had to apply for a job before but there I was having made a bold decision to leave the PFA 12 months or so before. I hadn't really consulted Cecily at the time – I just told her what I was planning to do and she went along with it. I'm sure she still would have agreed but I didn't consult her about leaving the PFA for West Brom and I regretted that. I'm sure she felt disappointed that I made my mind up before talking to her, because it was about our future. I felt embarrassed about what had happened in those 10 or so months at West Brom and that I had let her and the family down. I really had to steel myself to tell her. But she just brushed it aside. We went away on the Sunday and on the Tuesday I got calls that took me onto the next journey in my career.

West Brom didn't work out but it ended up being the best decision I made because once I'd left there it gave me the freedom to be my own boss, brought a diverse range of work and introduced me to new challenges and new scenarios. It was unpredictable but exciting.

The PFA is a fantastic organisation – it gave me 18 brilliant years – but that decision to leave for West Brom ended up being the right one in the long term.

TRIBUTE

Who was this guy Big Ron had bought from Cambridge? I think it's fair to say Brendon's debut wasn't his best game for Albion. But things got better.

He was a family man, but he did allow himself one evening out a week with the boys. Thursday night was the bonding night out when most of the squad descended on Liberty's, on Birmingham's Hagley Road. Ron Atkinson knew, but turned a blind eye as we were riding high in Division One. He left them to it. Little did we know then what an impact Brendon would have on football and life in general.

Our friendship grew through the 1990s and beyond - my wife Jane and Cecily were of similar personalities, and we all lived in Walsall.

Brendon returned to Albion in 2002 as MD, with the Former Players Association formed a year later. He asked me if I would like to be involved as secretary. I was honoured.

Cecily and Jane were very close, and I remember clearly the day Ron Atkinson made that fateful comment. The following day the four of us went out for dinner, the two girls wanted Brendon's views and the evening revolved around racism. I think Bren was glad to get home that evening!

Sadly, I will never forget that day in March 2009 when I received a phone call from Brendon. He was due to be the guest speaker at the Arsenal game the following day, alongside Martin Keown, but he had to step aside as he had to take Cecily to hospital as she was unwell. Three days later she was diagnosed with a brain tumour. It hit us hard, and over the next six months we only saw Cecily once. Jane had many conversations with Brendon throughout this terrible time; she was a shoulder he could lean on. On September 18, as I pulled up at Coxmoor Golf Club, the phone rang. It was Brendon to give me the sad news.

He and I continued to spend time together, whether meeting to discuss FPA business, socialising in Birmingham, or just having a chit-chat over the phone to see how things were. And yet several years later he was at the end of a phone for me when I lost my wife. I can imagine Jane and Cecily are looking down saying: "Will those two ever give up the Former Players Association?" Probably not.

Life is too short. When we do meet, we enjoy those many hours, putting the football world to rights, seeing how we can take the FPA onto the next stage or just talking about anything.

I have learned about the two Brendons. There is Brendon: the professional football man and administrator. And then there is Brendon: a man of warmth, humour, kindness, intelligence and someone you can rely on and trust.

I'm proud to call him a friend.

Geoff Snape, West Bromwich Albion Former Players Association secretary

CHAPTER NINE
Dealing with grief

"...To the outside world I was in a good place, but I'd fall apart as soon as I closed the front door..."

It was March 2, 2009 when everything changed. It was a Monday. Everything from that date onwards, for the next few months, remains etched in my mind.

There were things going on in the change of Cecily's behaviour that I never recognised at the time, but I knew something wasn't quite right. I was so concerned that I took Cecily to see our family doctor who diagnosed depression which apparently is a common misdiagnosis with the symptoms Cecily was presenting.

We'd been away that particular weekend. We returned and Bev Regis was coming around on the Monday. Although her and Cyrille were no longer together by then, she and Cecily remained best of friends. They were going out somewhere in Birmingham, while I said I'd stay at home and sort dinner out. I was in the bedroom when Bev knocked on the door and asked: "How long has Cecily been smiling lopsided?" It was as though everything fell into sharp focus at that point because I had been noticing Cecily rubbing her head quite a lot and she'd start a conversation and stop halfway through.

Anyway, at this point Bev had phoned her aunt Nola, who had been a nurse for 30-odd years. I spoke to her. She told me to ask Cecily to raise her left arm which she did with no problem. I then asked Cecily to raise her right arm – she struggled to do so. The right one was lagging. Nola told us to immediately call an ambulance. As you can imagine Cecily was starting to panic now, not knowing what was happening to her. The ambulance came and everything seemed to hit her at once. She couldn't walk and was struggling for breath. At this point I called her sister Yolande in Grenada and told her we were rushing Cecily to hospital. She immediately booked a flight over from Grenada.

Initially, the doctor who examined her at Birmingham's City Hospital said she might have had a slight stroke, which was almost a relief for us. Bev Regis was an absolute rock - she and I stayed all night with Cecily, who didn't show any signs of improvement until late into the night. In the end we were waiting for tests, and I was getting manic. I stormed into a place where I wasn't meant to be and demanded she undergo whatever tests needed without delay. I was in absolute tears, utterly consumed by frustration at the lack of information about what may be wrong with Cecily. Eventually a consultant saw her on the Thursday but by then she couldn't move around so we had to use a wheelchair.

The consultant had a pen, and he asked Cecily: "What is this?" and she replied: "It's a pen." He then pointed to his watch and asked: "What is this?" Cecily replied: "It's a pen." I just closed my eyes and at that point I knew something was badly wrong. They called us back around 5pm later that day. We were shown into a room. Nurses were there, doctors were there, and I knew it wasn't going to be good news. They gave us the news that Cecily had a grade IV Glioblastoma, which they explained is a fast-growing and aggressive brain tumour. It's the most severe brain tumour. I've never been sure if Cecily understood what we had been told but she started to cry. I started to cry.

She was transferred to Birmingham's Queen Elizabeth Hospital that same evening and I spent the night there sleeping in the room with her. We were now at the mercy of the oncologist – it's their call ultimately whether to go ahead with an operation to remove the tumour. They said they would and the next morning they operated.

At around the same period golfer Seve Ballesteros and the opera singer Russell Watson had both collapsed due to brain tumours – so the doctors were amazed that Cecily hadn't collapsed bearing in mind the size of the tumour in her brain.

Looking back there were things that weren't right. For instance, where we lived in Birmingham, in Centenary Plaza, there was a button that you had to press to open the fire doors leading to the car park. I would press the button and Cecily would be pushing away but didn't have the strength in her right hand to force open the doors. The other thing she'd do was instinctively make me walk on her left so that when we held hands, I was holding her left hand as she knew her right hand wasn't quite right. She was losing strength down her right side, which is why she couldn't press the release button to the car park. At times I'd notice her right hand was swollen, and then the next day that swelling had gone. These were all signs of the tumour having an impact on her but it wasn't evident to me at the time.

Again, I look back on it and try to find the balance. There is a poetry book called A Scattering, by Christopher Reid, which I had bought some time before. His wife had also died from a brain tumour and the poem is about the cancer that is going to kill her. It's about how he deals with the journey that leads from illness to bereavement and grief. His wife was in a hospice and while I couldn't always have a conversation with Cecily, I had her next to me at home. That book still evokes a lot of emotions as it became such a personal thing for me.

Cecily had the operation on March 12. By some coincidence in the same recovery ward was a friend of mine Renato Pagliari, who'd had a massive hit in the early 1980s with Hilary Lester, better known as Renee. He got transferred to Good Hope Hospital in Sutton Coldfield and sadly passed away some time later.

Cecily's surgery was, in medical terms, a straightforward procedure to remove the tumour. Unfortunately, they were unable to remove the entire tumour due to where it was positioned in her brain. Now we had to find out whether she was strong enough, not only for radiotherapy, but also for chemotherapy, as they didn't think she was strong enough to cope with both the treatments. It would hinge on if Cecily could convince the medical team she was strong enough following her surgery. Cecily always had a strong determination about her and she was absolutely adamant she would walk again. When she went in to see the oncologist a few weeks following the surgery she got out of her wheelchair and walked into the room. The nurse looked at me and just went: "wow!" He couldn't believe she'd done it. On that basis they decided to give her a course of chemotherapy as well as radiotherapy and with that came hope.

But that too was soon dashed. At the end of the first course of treatment, you need a period of time for those chemicals to take a hold and do what you're hoping they'll do – which is to treat and get rid of the cancer. I decided to take Cecily away, so we actually spent our 35th anniversary in June that year at our home in Spain. While I had to help her walk, we did as much as we could, and we even managed to do some swimming together. I prayed that Cecily was making a recovery of sorts and we made a further trip to Spain in the July. However, by then, her health was beginning to deteriorate and so we returned to Birmingham. We had an appointment with the medical team and that's when we were told that the treatment wasn't working and that there was nothing further that could be done. I was advised that I should enjoy the time I had left with Cecily. Even then I don't think the reality of the situation had sunk in.

At the time of Cecily's diagnosis, I asked one of the nurses of her medical team what to expect. He said the average life expectancy was six months. Cecily made six-and-a-half months, from the date we knew there was a problem to the date she died.

It was a horrible, and at times soul-destroying, period. I also had our kids and our young grandchildren to consider. Both the kids lived abroad, Jason in Slovenia and Zoe was in Spain, so they were rushing back and forth. I stopped working and became Cecily's carer. Jason spent a lot of time with me at our apartment in Birmingham, helping with caring for his mum. Without his help and company I don't know how I would have coped. He was so calm and composed at what was a very harrowing time. Zoe had had her third child Gio the previous September so he was still a babe-in-arms, but she needed to see her mum and travelled with him leaving the other two kids in Spain. I am immensely proud of both of them.

As the weeks went by, Jason and I realised that we needed help with caring for Cecily. We were put in touch with Birmingham St Mary's Hospice. A lady called Mary McLennan is somebody I'll forever be grateful to. She arranged for nurses to come and assist us within a day of getting in touch and much to my relief two nurses turned up on July 31. They made arrangements for two visits per day, six days a week. Sundays was a day for Cecily and myself, and I would look after her. I was panicking to begin with, given all the tablets I had to administer, but it became a part of life. Looking back, it was never a chore – we even had many laughs at times. When she started radiotherapy, she began to lose her hair, so she had it completely shaved off and bought a wig. Because of the radiotherapy the wig became uncomfortable, as the treatment generated so much heat, so as soon as she got into the car on leaving the hospital, she ripped it off and threw it aside! We always laughed about that.

Cecily hated the idea of hospital so for me the one thing I wanted to do was keep her at home with me for as long as possible. The hospice staff were just wonderful. They sorted out a specialised bed for her in the apartment, and I slept on the floor next to her on an inflated mattress. My sleep pattern went to pot and, as the time drew nearer, Cecily began eating less and less. She then started to suffer with something called Cheyne-Stokes breathing where the heart is working really hard, and you have a period of fast and shallow, breathing followed by slow, heavier breathing and even moments without any breath at all. On her visits to see Cecily, Mary would count the seconds in-between. One day she said: "You need to get your kids over." I was in a bit of denial. I thought this would be our life – that Cecily would be in a wheelchair and we'd carry on. Mary returned the following week and said: "When are the kids arriving?" and I hadn't really told them. She said: "You need to get them over now." So, I told the kids, her sister and brother. Cecily's dad didn't travel over as he simply couldn't face it. I then arranged for the Catholic priest from our local church to come to see us and he gave her the Last Rites. The rest of my family had travelled up to Birmingham and over the course of a few days we all said our goodbyes. The irony is that when Cecily was sleeping I would always listen out for her breathing. On that last night, I fell asleep but awoke just before midnight and checked on her. She was sleeping quite peacefully. I went back to bed, fell asleep and then something woke me up with a start – it was 1.26am in the morning. I jumped up to check on Cecily, but she'd passed away. Mary later told me it was the rhythm of her breathing that helped me to sleep. The moment she took her last breath, that interrupted my sleep and that's why I woke up.

Cecily passed away at home in the early morning of September 18.

I was devastated, and there's a part of me that will never get over losing her.

To be without my soul mate of nearly 40 years was something that still affects me to this day.

That period was chaotic. Arrangements had to be made for Cecily's funeral and all the other related matters. We took her ashes back to Grenada and buried them in the same plot with her mum: a great spot on a hillside overlooking the sea.

What followed was a period that I've never really opened up about before. The trauma, the pain of losing a loved one to such a brutal illness, the notion that the person you wanted to grow old with is no longer there. I'm by no means the first or last person to suffer this. Nor is there anything necessarily unusual about what I went through. But I'm keen to put it down on record as it's such a very important thing for me to talk about.

That thing being grief. And the impact of grief. More so, the impact of dealing with trauma.

It took me a long while to get my life back into any kind of normality. I had one-on-ones, I had group therapy and I thought I was doing okay, but I was in a right state until 2020. At the urging of someone close to me, I eventually phoned up a former colleague Dr Michael Bennett, who is the director of the wellbeing department of the PFA. I had known him for years. When he picked up the phone, I said hello and just burst into tears. Everything just hit me. He pointed me towards a counsellor called Duncan who lived in Sutton Coldfield. Everything was online at the time because of Covid and I was, by then, living in Spain. After about 20 minutes I just felt it was going to be the same-old-same-old and not going to make any difference. And then he asked me a question, then another question, and for the first time he mentioned the word trauma. I had never thought of the loss of Cecily as trauma. At that moment the penny seemed to drop. My interpretation of trauma is if you've been through a life changing accident, or come through a warzone and seen those horrors, but I never realised what I'd been through was on that level. Now I look back and think some of my behaviour was appalling because I didn't care about relationships and a lot of things that I should care about. The only thing I cared about was my immediate family, almost to the exclusion of others. It was like I ring-fenced them away from the realities of life.

I didn't recognise that I was doing anything wrong but everything else just felt unimportant. I was asking people if they thought I was okay, but I wasn't. It was pretence. I put on an act when I was outside, but when I came back to my apartment, I would be a wreck. I was on the 11th floor of the Centenary Plaza in Birmingham and so many times I would look out and think: "Right now I could take a running jump." It was only because I had kids and grandkids I realised it would be a selfish thing to do, but I did feel I was on the edge at times. I couldn't cope. In my work environment I was fine, but in my personal life I was struggling. I was trying to portray that I was okay and was coping.

People talk about getting over it and moving on. Forget that shit – it really doesn't work like that. Men are supposed to be the ones who don't cry, or don't show emotion. My son Jason studied psychology and he told me that one of the problems is that we're supposed to go before our partners, while women are wired to be the one left behind. Suddenly, you lose your life-long partner and you're floundering. And that's what happened to me, and it left me feeling adrift.

I used to have a dream that completely ruined my sleeping pattern. I'd be dreaming that I'd be out swimming in the sea as it's getting dark. I can't see land, but I know I'm going in the right direction. And then I hear this roar behind me in the form of a mountainous wave. At that point I would wake up sweating, completely dishevelled, with the bed sheets all over the place. Because of this recurring dream my sleeping was going to shit, so I went to see my doctor who prescribed some mild sleeping tablets, which did help. And yet this dream still used to get to me. It was part of the trauma that I was experiencing. Even now I'm much more sensitive to certain aspects of life which before I would never have given a second thought.

It might sound glib, but life is what it is. The anticipation was that Cecily and I would build our house in Spain and retire there. Jason was settled in Slovenia, as were Zoe and her kids in Spain, and that we'd have many years ahead of us. And then suddenly all of the things we thought and hoped for were all utterly wrecked in the space of six months. It had all gone. And, after Cecily died, I was fighting and railing against reality. I remember in the early days I'd be walking along, looking at other people and thinking: "What are you smiling at; don't you know I'm in mourning and life is shit?" Another time I was walking along the beach when I saw a couple in front of me. She put her arm around him and just rubbed his hair, something silly like that. But just witnessing that one intimate gesture left me in tears, realising I don't have that somebody to share that kind of moment with. I was fighting this all the time. To the outside world I was in a good place, but I'd fall apart as soon as I closed the front door.

I don't kid myself that I'm totally over it because I'm not. But I'm better. Much better. And I'm certainly happier. It's been a long journey and I'm still on that journey. I have my counsellor Duncan to thank for helping me reach calmer waters, and of course, the love of my family and friends.

My family are everything to me. Their love and support saved me.

TRIBUTE

I've known Brendon for about 45 years, pretty much not long after he joined. I was a designer and I came up with a product called Sportrait, which was effectively pencil drawings of football teams and players. I used to sell it in various club shops around the West Midlands and it even featured in Shoot! magazine. West Brom's commercial director Brian Boundy spotted these and ordered some. I delivered them up to the Hawthorns club shop just as Brendon was signing photos. He asked me who I was, what I was there for and was none too pleased, as the club's union delegate, to find the club had commissioned sketches of the players without their say so. Anyway, to cut a long story short, we managed to calm that somewhat tense moment and Brendon ended up asking me to do a picture of his young daughter Zoe.

From there on we became very good friends.

We've had some memorable moments. I drove the support van when Brendon and a few others did a London to Paris charity bike ride. My job was to drive on ahead and meet the riders at various pre-arranged pit-stops along the route, where I'd provide drink and food. That was a real experience, not least when Brendon and the others arrived at Eiffel Tower, but couldn't find me. Unfortunately, I got horribly lost in Paris and was late by about four hours. Brendon was fearful he'd have to phone my wife and declare me missing. Brendon's face when I finally arrived was one I'll never forget – it was one of relief and anger!

Brendon is godfather to one of my sons and has been my best pal for more than 40 years. If I had a call to say Brendon was stuck in Australia, I'd jump on the next plane to Sydney. That's how much he means to me. Zoe even refers to me as uncle David, which is such a lovely thing. We are close as you can be without being family.

David Garrett, friend

TRIBUTE

I first met Brendon when my company Swan were shirt sponsors under the BSR brand. I used to go into the players' lounge after games and it was then that I was introduced to Brendon as he had just moved to Stourbridge, which was in the same area that I lived in.

He stayed with me for a while when my wife died and after he had lost Cecily. Cecily passed away in 2009 and my wife Ann in 2015. They were very close too.

Whenever I am over in Spain we'll always meet up and I'm very close to Zoe too, who has lived over in Spain for many years. He always said we were brothers, but the joke is that the mother got out one night!

He's a good man. I'm proud to call Brendon a friend and I am delighted he has finally found time to tell us all about his incredible life story.

Garth Wooldridge, friend

CHAPTER TEN
Laurie and Cyrille

"...Laurie, Cyrille and I gravitated towards each other with our shared history...we appreciated what our parents had been through..."

As you will know Laurie and Cyrille were already at West Bromwich Albion when I signed. I'm uneasy sometimes speaking about us as a trio because it was never like that for me. We were part of a team. But we were – rightly or wrongly – packaged together for the very obvious reason.

Laurie was an interesting guy. He was someone I first saw play for Orient when he was making his way through their ranks as a 14 or 15-year-old. Just by chance Clyde Best, the former West Ham player was sat next to me. I remember watching Laurie that day and as I went to leave the ground I said to Clyde: "I think this lad might have a chance" because he was electric. He was like a stick insect. I had finished training at Arsenal that day and there was a real buzz about this young lad at Orient. He was getting publicity and I went to see what the fuss was all about. Little did I know we'd one day be team-mates.

By the time he'd signed for West Brom I hadn't really taken notice of how he had got on, so it fell under my radar, but it was when Cyrille moved there that I got more interested in what was stirring at West Brom. I had remembered seeing him on TV in a cup game and dragging defenders here, there and everywhere. When I got the call from Ron, he said I'd be good for Laurie because he was very introvert off the pitch, but flamboyant on it. Cyrille was five years younger than me, Laurie was three years younger than me, so I was a more seasoned pro having been with Arsenal and Cambridge.

It wasn't in my mind that we had that publicity around us. My take was quite simple: I'd played in the top division for Arsenal without being convincing in my performances and now I had another chance with Albion. But this time I intended staying there.

We had the drama of my first training session, where Laurie took the wrong turning on the M5/M6 junction and instead of heading down south towards Junction 7 we were heading towards Junction 10 and

169

heading for the North West. That was my first training session with Albion and we were late. I was absolutely mortified to be late for my first training session. Laurie? He was calm, measured and didn't panic. That was him all over.

He was shy, had a charming smile and was very quiet. But he came alive on the pitch. He was so elastic, so flexible. He had done ballet as a kid and you could tell. His movements were very fluid.

Cyrille – who I often called 'Reggae', because of his surname - was raw. It was his first football gig in the professional game. He always talked about how tough it was working as an electrician on a building site. And don't forget that his manager at Hayes was Bobby Ross, who I'd played with at Cambridge – along with Alan Harris, brother of Ron 'Chopper' Harris, and Vik Akers, who is still Arsenal's most successful manager as the coach of the women's team.

Apparently, Bobby kept turning down clubs, telling Cyrille to bide his time until the right club came in for him. And that right team happened to be West Brom. People forget Laurie, Cyrille and I only started 38 games together over the course of 15 months. I barely missed a game once I became established, Cyrille missed a few, but Laurie missed the most during that period.

Ignoring my debut game and the one that followed which were both horrendous, the game that really proved to me that I was good enough for this league was against Everton in which Laurie, Cyrille and I started our first game together. We won 3-1 with Cyrille scoring a fantastic goal. At he end of the game Gordon Dimbleby, the commercial manager, came up to me and said: "Welcome to the club – what a great game you've had." Music to my ears!

Laurie played on my side with Lenny Cantello in front of me, and Laurie ahead of us. At full-back were myself and Derek Statham. Derek was a fantastic left-back particularly when running with the ball, while I liked making runs off the ball and running into space. Laurie was one of those wingers who could hold the ball for a period of time and he always wanted the ball which was great for a full-back. Lenny was the big influence in terms of me settling into the team because he appreciated that Laurie and I were developing a good understanding, so he would happily let us go off attacking down the pitch while he would sit behind us, covering. Lenny was a very intelligent player who read the game brilliantly.

China is where we bonded. The football games were a release, mainly because it was such an ambassadorial trip. But it was also the trip where Laurie, Cyrille and I gravitated towards each other with our shared history. We didn't need to talk about it, but we appreciated what our parents had been through. There was a general comfort to the three of us being in that group.

I think Laurie was the one who found barracking the hardest to cope with. You have to remember he met his girlfriend, who was white, when they were teenagers. He was having to confront that, as well as the crap we were getting on the pitch. When I was younger I loved going to Blues Parties, or what Sir Lenny Henry would call Rent Parties – where people would empty their house, get a big sound system in and then charge people for drinks and food, just to make some money. And these parties were popular with white girls because they loved the music. That caused a lot of tensions because you'd see mainly white girls with black lads, rather than the other way around. That was a big challenge for him. He used to get some horrendous mail - horrible, racist abuse.

I actually thought the three of us together would be a positive visible presence, like a signpost to the future. There were Ces Podd and Joe Cooke at Bradford, Viv (Anderson) at Forest, Clyde Best at West Ham and one or two others. Luther Blissett was emerging at Watford, with John Barnes following him some time later. We had been used to receiving racist abuse at schoolboy level. Some time ago I read a book by Mihir Bose, the British Indian journalist who had been BBC Sports editor for many years and he spoke about his experiences. They were all similar stories – the things we had to put up with.

When I joined West Brom it was the volume of the abuse that struck me. That first game for Albion against Birmingham when I ran out of the tunnel and slipped. I looked down and saw I had stepped on a banana. Gradually I found a way of tuning out. Back then you could name the away grounds where you knew the abuse would be loud and hostile: Newcastle, West Ham, Leeds among them. I think Laurie really struggled with it at times and had I been in a position to advise him otherwise, I'd have urged him to stay with us for a couple more years. But then, who can turn down Real Madrid?

171

The Madrid interest came out of the blue. He had two very big games for us. Manchester United away, when he was outstanding, and then the Valencia game. And yet by the end of that 1978/79 season, Laurie was actually struggling a bit with his form. We had the big freeze up just after New Year when we were top of the League and Laurie never recovered his form. As a team we had lost our consistency, but Laurie was especially struggling. We were about to play Everton around May Day, which is when the PFA awards were due to be handed out. Ron called me in as the PFA delegate and said: "I've got a problem Batman...I need to drop either Cyrille or Laurie." He was going to drop Cyrille, but then he got the call to say Cyrille had won the PFA Young Player of the Year so he decided he couldn't drop him – so he dropped Laurie instead. That awards' night was amusing because I was voted into the Third Division side having played for Cambridge earlier that season. Anyway, when it got to the Young Player of the Year nominations they started showing lots of clips of the players involved, including footage of Laurie creating brilliant chances for Cyrille. Back then the vote was counted very early so none of us thought our lads would win and if anyone did win, we assumed it would be Laurie based on the clips they were showing. And then they announced Cyrille had won and the whole room fell momentarily silent – as if to say "What?" Everyone was convinced Laurie had won it.

Like I said earlier, Laurie couldn't turn down Madrid, much like Bryan Robson couldn't turn down Manchester United. And yet Pop flourished at Old Trafford. For Laurie it went the other way and he was probably never the same again. Initially he was the toast of the town. He played one game against Barcelona where he was taking corners with the outside of his foot, which was something I'd seen him do at Albion in training, but he'd never had the nerve to do in a game. But there he was delivering these brilliant set pieces. It was very exciting for Laurie but he got done in training by one of his own teammates. Some of the players over there apparently never took to Laurie. Some did, but some were resentful of him. And it didn't help that it was a big Catholic country – Laurie was living with Nicky, she was white, he was black. Cyrille used to go and see him a lot and his first wife Bev was good friends with Nicky. The other thing to remember is the traffic going out from English football to abroad was very sparse. Denis Law and Jimmy Greaves went to Italy in the early 1960s before they banned foreign players – a rule they lifted in the late 1970s. And then you had

Kevin Keegan. But it wasn't until the 1980s that you would get British footballers going abroad in numbers – players like Liam Brady, Ray Wilkins, Graeme Souness, Mark Hateley and Trevor Francis all tried their luck in Italy. And then it became more commonplace when the Heysel ban kicked in so you had more going to European clubs, just to get into the UEFA competitions. In 1979, when Laurie went to play for Real Madrid, we simply didn't have a culture for players going abroad. Cyrille was wanted by Saint-Etienne a year or so earlier for £750,000 so we could have lost both players.

Laurie I felt wasn't mature enough to go to the Bernabeu. Had he gone with someone else, in the way that Ossie Ardiles was joined by Ricardo Villa at Tottenham, or Frans Thijssen joined Arnold Muhren at Ipswich, then who knows how things might have gone. But I remember hearing how isolated he was. There wasn't a particularly harmonious integration and I'd hear stories of certain Madrid players being resentful of his status. Why would one of his own team-mates injure him in training?

Personally, I lost touch with Laurie during this period. We would occasionally go out when he came back. Although Laurie, Cyrille and I had common backgrounds, I was very much a married man. Cecily had never been one for mixing or socialising in footballing circles. I was of the view that while my team-mates were colleagues and friends, and I enjoyed their company during the week, I didn't want to be going out with them on a Saturday night with my wife.

I actually became better friends with people like Tony Brown, Ally Robertson, Cyrille and co after we all retired because I felt more able to enjoy our time together. We weren't together during our working days. Cecily became very good friends with Bev Regis and remained so even after her and Cyrille split up, and with Irene Brown, Tony's wife.

From afar it was clear that Laurie's career wasn't going well. He became a bit of a journeyman, although he won an FA Cup winner's medal with Wimbledon in 1988 and could have played in the '83 final with Manchester United had he not declared himself unfit.

By summer 1989, he had moved around quite a bit. At the PFA we had a disengaged players' list and he got in touch with me to circulate his name. We had a bit of a chat and a catch up. And then a couple of weeks later I got the call...

Laurie had been killed in a car crash.

Cyrille and Laurie had an accident in 1987 and I didn't know this until sometime afterwards. It was on the same stretch of road that was to claim Laurie. On that occasion they both walked away. Sadly, Laurie's luck ran out on that July day in 1989. By all accounts Laurie had someone in the car with him. He was wearing a seat-belt, Laurie wasn't. His passenger walked away, Laurie didn't.

I heard from Ron Atkinson, who was manager at Sheffield Wednesday at the time. I don't recall my reaction because I was so stunned – I'd only spoken to Laurie a few weeks before. These were different times. Laurie was out of sight. He had played in an FA Cup Final a year before but we didn't have the saturation of pan-European football coverage that we have now. What I do remember: when Laurie left us, I had a photo of myself, Cyrille and Laurie – a photo that isn't in circulation. I asked Laurie for his autograph about a week before he left. Within a week or two of him dying, I desperately searched the house for this photo and when I finally found it I decided to ask Cyrille to sign it, added my signature and get it framed. Years later, during Black History Month, a gallery in Brixton asked to display it for several weeks. About a month later I went to collect it and they couldn't find it. Eventually they found it and I won't let it out of my sight now.

Laurie was like the strike of a match. His career ignited and then before you could blink it felt like it had gone. The Manchester United and Valencia games – both away – stick out. That was Laurie at his peak and if he ever played better then that must have been a sight to behold. He was so quick with the ball, and he had this upright running style, with small steps. He never appeared to be sprinting. Laurie never looked quick, but he was blisteringly fast with the ball at his feet. People talk about Laurie's performance at Old Trafford in that 5-3 win where one of his memorable moments was the build up to Lenny Cantello's goal where he came in from the left-hand side, shifted past a couple of challenges and then knocked it into Cyrille, who just back-heeled it perfectly for Lenny to smash into the roof of the net. Lenny, of course, got the praise for that wonderful goal that won the ITV Big Match Goal of The Season, but credit to Laurie and Cyrille for the part they played in the build-up.

How would I describe Laurie's legacy? He was exciting, he captured the imagination. I used to get cheesed off when I saw references to the Black Pearl with Laurie. Nobody ever talked about Pele being black, or Eusebio being black – they were Brazilian and Portuguese. Yet in England he was referred to as a black footballer. He was one of a kind of that era. A lot of snaps of Laurie were of an exciting, athletic, balletic footballer. People didn't realise how good he was. I only played with him for 15 months and maybe only appreciated him when he'd gone. I joined in February 1978, he left in May 1979. But, yes, he was a special footballer.

Cyrille was a different kind of character. There was an exuberance about him, a raw energy that maybe emanated from his sudden rise from non-league. There are some players who you just want to leave alone and don't want to coach those edgy, raw bits out of them. That's how it felt with Cyrille. For people watching him during those early months it must have been one hell of a shock – a "What on earth have we got here?" type of moment. And I mean that in a good way. These days those runs and goals would have been plastered all over social media. There are so many great pics of him lashing the ball, with both feet suspended high above the ground, where you just see those incredible muscles in his legs. There was game at Palace where we drew 2-2. I put this cross in and all I saw was this giant rising at the back post and him planting the ball in with his head. That was Cyrille – I cannot remember any simple goals. He would either smash balls out of sight or drag half of the opposition defence along as he ran towards the goal, before finishing it off.

He was an effervescent character, but in a quiet way. There was this incredible presence about him, not just his physicality. He had this wonderful smile, with big dimples and a warmth that very few had. He was extremely handsome. And he became a better man after he finished playing. I think he matured a lot more after that. Cyrille admitted himself that he had a lifestyle that he wasn't always proud of when he was younger. Afterwards, after he retired, he did change. I recall him ringing me up when he'd left West Brom during his brief time there as a coach. He called me and said his first engagement as an agent was with a company that I really wasn't sure about. I told him honestly: "Cyrille that isn't going to work out." From there he went to the Stellar Promotions agency, where he went onto blossom. What he did was focus on recruiting younger players. And they saw that he had a real connection, not only with the young footballers but with parents. They trusted him and that's so important for parents.

As a player he was something else – almost like a throwback. I remember seeing people like Ray Kennedy, Frank Stapleton, John Radford. They were all great players, but were all coached and coached and coached. Cyrille, meanwhile, played like he was still at Hayes. He took players by surprise because he had the power and the pace. He was explosive. I remember Martin Jol telling me that he'd tried to get hold of him in training and Cyrille just over-powered him and accelerated away. That was him.

I suspect the death of Laurie had a great impact on Cyrille. Oddly, we never really spoke directly about it. We were all very saddened by Laurie's death but you can almost accept that people can be unlucky and that accidents happen. Laurie will forever be 33-years-old to me – he never grew old. There is now a statue in West Bromwich town centre that depicts the three of us. When I first went to see our statue in its mould, I literally jumped because staring back at me was Laurie just as I remembered him. There was an acceptance that it was a tragic accident, and yet I also felt privileged that I had seen Laurie at the top of his game.

Cyrille's death, however, had a huge impact on me. It still does. I could not believe that Monday morning on January 15, 2018 when I took that call from his brother Dave. I was at St George's Park in Burton upon Trent. Myself, Garth Crooks and Paul Elliott were due to meet with the FA that morning, where we were going to propose a new initiative around diversity in coaching. That was scheduled for the Monday morning. The three of us all stayed over the night before at St George's Park.

It was about 4.45am on the Monday morning when my phone rang. I saw it was Dave, Cyrille's brother, calling me. I answered and Dave just burst into tears. He said: "Brendon...Cyrille's died." My response was: "What do you mean he's died?" which looking back is the most ridiculous thing to ask. You're not yet processing it, it's just words. I cannot even remember what followed as I went into disbelief. I do remember "Cyrille's died" just echoing around my head.

I didn't actually know the details until I got it from Julia, Cyrille's wife.

My phone then started to go like mad because the press were getting wind of it and looking to get confirmation – they didn't want to print anything without it being verified. I phoned Garth and Paul Elliott – they couldn't believe it either. We ended up having a meeting with Dan Ashworth, who was the Football Association's Technical Director at the time, along with Martin Glenn, who was CEO. We just seemed to carry on with the meeting, which feels utterly surreal looking back. And yet there are things I'd clearly forgotten. For instance, I found out some years later that I'd actually been on BBC Radio WM that morning, crying my eyes out. I have no recollection of that. Whether it was the shock I don't know. I only remember that meeting because it seemed to take our minds off the dreadful news for a brief while.

In the afternoon, myself, Garth and Paul came back to Birmingham because they were heading off to London. We ended up going to a restaurant in the Mailbox where we just sat and toasted Cyrille and exchanged stories about him. They were due to go back on the train to Euston at 3pm, but they wouldn't go. They wouldn't leave me or let me go back to my apartment. We just sat there in a sense of disbelief.

I had actually seen Cyrille a few days before. He used to pick me up to go to the West Brom games because I hated driving. He lived nearby in Edgbaston and if we were doing events together he would come and pick me up. I was due to see him at The Hawthorns on the Wednesday but sadly he died the previous Sunday night.

I wasn't aware of him being ill or unwell. You hear stories afterwards but not at the time. I knew Cyrille had an operation on his ankle a few months before due to a build up of calcification on the joint as a result of all the kicks from behind that he took. I'm not sure if in some way that may have been a contributory factor in his death.

I've since found out that he was due to have a test on the Tuesday as he hadn't been feeling great. He and Julia were members of Edgbaston Golf club and used to play with some of the surgeons. He had an appointment with one of the consultants a few days later. Someone I knew had been with him at the training ground watching a youth team game on the Saturday and he wasn't feeling the best then, he was out of breath and felt cold.

Julia told me the story that she was going to visit her sister in

Nottingham. Cyrille had a meeting in London the next morning so he was leaving that evening also. He convinced her to carry on to Nottingham, while he stayed at home. Julia rang him several times from her car but with no reply. She got to her sister's house and rang again but still there was no reply. So, she turned around and drove back home only to find that Cyrille had already died. It was a cardiac arrest.

What really hit me was that I'd lost two of my good mates. Suddenly I was on my own. And it does register with your own mortality. Both were younger than me. But equally I struggled with the perception of other people treating us like a three-man team. I still do. Even to this day I have people coming up to me saying: "Look after yourself Brendon, you're the last one" or "Crikey, it's only you left now." You don't want to be rude, but surely people could say something better than that? But equally it was always about the Three Degrees: Laurie, Cyrille and myself. Now it was just me.

Cyrille's death brought back everything I'd been through with Cecily. It shocked me. Cyrille wasn't ill, he didn't look ill, and there was nothing I saw to make me think something would happen to him. He was a few weeks away from his 60th birthday. It's still tough to this day. I have funny days when I'm up and down with Cecily. Even now I struggle with the loss of those close to me. I couldn't speak Cecily's name for ages – I'd burst into tears - and now I'd lost one of my mates.

With Cyrille it still haunts me. It made me look at myself. It made me somewhat reflective particularly when I was at Cyrille's funeral and saw his children and grandchildren. They all looked so vulnerable, and although he and Bev hadn't been together for many years I appreciated that she would be the one dealing with their grief. Suddenly, I'm thinking did I do enough for my family when Cecily died? Was I so consumed with grief that I didn't do enough for them?

Cyrille touched football. You only had to see the outpouring of grief when he died to see how loved he was. He was not only a champion of West Midlands football, but there was so much respect for how he conducted himself. I think he became a better man after he retired from football. His legacy was so much more than just football. Kids wanted to be Cyrille Regis. It didn't matter if they were black or white, they wanted to be him. The way he brushed people aside, the way he knocked people out of the way. I recall him dragging Dave Watson and Mike Doyle at

Manchester City – they couldn't cope with him. That picture at Old Trafford, when he scored the fifth goal, is just wonderful. Big muscles, big dimples and a shirt that looked three sizes too small.

When they first spoke about a statue, Cyrille and I travelled down together to London. He insisted on driving and while we were heading down he was giving me all of this advice on what I should eat, how I should use a Nutribullet blender and make smoothies. He would eat the right things, he took pride in his appearance and kept himself fit. He was loved. We have the Regis Suite at The Hawthorns and there were times I would go in and I would instinctively know he was there without seeing him. He had this presence.

The Celebration Statue in West Bromwich town centre depicts myself, Laurie and Cyrille. I'll be honest, it wasn't something I was particularly keen on at first. I especially felt uneasy with the fundraising of it, but the way Jim Cadman sold it to us was impressive. We met the then leader of the council, Darren Cooper, and the concept of it was interesting. I see it as a statue of what black people contributed to football in a similar way to the Windrush statue at Waterloo Station. I spoke to one or two people who said it was a great idea, which is why I gave my approval to it. It was clear it wasn't going to be at The Hawthorns because there were tensions between Jeremy Peace and Jim Cadman, who was the organiser of the statue. In a way I'm glad it's in West Bromwich because it's for the community. We didn't realise the impact we made because as footballers we were in a bubble. At the end of the football season, we'd disappear on holidays and then be back to training for a new season. I now feel that I should have maybe contributed more to the black community back then, but I suppose I was very much wrapped up with playing and raising a young family. I guess footballers at that time weren't as socially switched on as the likes of Marcus Rashford and others are these days. Having that statue in the town is for the impact we made to the community. I take a lot of pride in it.

It takes me back to a dinner I went to at Northampton for the 10th anniversary of the National Association of Black Police Officers. Some of them were on the frontline with the Metropolitan Police and getting not only grief for serving as officers, but also for being black. They had it both barrels. I had one tell me that they weren't West Brom supporters but whenever we were in town they'd come and see us

– we generally had a good record in London – and if we won, they'd be walking into work for their duties the next day or on the Monday with their chests puffed out saying: "The lads did it again." That's the impact we had. We were the standard bearers for a generation. You think about Arthur Wharton, who was considered to be the first black professional footballer in the world. He was a fantastic footballer and cricketer, but he died a pauper and whilst we talk about what we put up with I can hardly imagine what he would have had to endure. Then there was Walter Tull, who was killed in action at the first Battle of Bapaume, during the Spring Offensive in March 1918. Or Jack Leslie, the Plymouth footballer of the 1920s, who had his England call-up revoked when selectors realised he was a black man. He too has been recognised by the people of Plymouth. These were people whose legacies live on. I'm proud to have been part of that movement and, I hope, made a difference to some people's lives.

Laurie and Cyrille will live on in the memory of many. I was proud and privileged to have played alongside them and considered them more than just friends.

I guess it's a big reason why this book is called The Third Degree.

TRIBUTE

Every journalist admires Brendon Batson as a legend of the game for his work on and off the pitch.

As a talented, nimble full-back, Batson stood up to some of the most skilful wingers in the 70s and 80s. As a man of great courage and dignity, Batson stood up to the racists. As a highly regarded union official, Batson represented the players powerfully and eloquently. As a spokesman and ambassador for football, Batson has always been a trusted voice and wise counsel for the media to turn to for guidance.

I have often contacted Brendon for an informed, measured view on the issues within the game. His opinions carry great weight. As a reporter, I could build a piece around Brendon's views because he is so respected.

His name is a byword for truth and authority.

I was always surprised the Football Association did not appoint him to their board. I know the FA used Batson as a special advisor, but his experiences and expertise should have been better used by the governing body.

Batson has been an important figure in Show Racism The Red Card campaigning but such a natural statesman - through word, deed and bearing - should have been placed at the heart of English football, at the FA, not only leading the fight against racism but drawing on his deep knowledge and love of the game.

Henry Winter, The Times chief football writer

CHAPTER ELEVEN
The struggle against racism

"On April 20, 2004, everything changed between Ron and I..."

Ron Atkinson was an important person in my playing career.

Cambridge United was his first professional club as a football manager. He'd been player-manager with Kettering Town and such was his profile that when Cambridge sacked the manager some of the boys were running a book of who our next manager would be. Ron's name didn't once come up.

I knew nothing about Ron but it was clear he was an absolute whirlwind, with a personality to match. He wasn't just a manager or a coach – he did both of those. He was hands-on from the start, he was very loud and the one thing we all noticed as players straight away was the ambition he so clearly had.

We would be doing our warm-ups in the cold, wearing our tracksuit bottoms tucked into long socks. He made us take those off and put shorts on – pointing out we don't play like that, so we don't train like that either. He stopped us gambling on away trips, he made us more professional. It was all about bettering ourselves. We quickly appreciated that he would take us onto better places if we bought into what he wanted to do.

And then there was the car. He must have been the only manager outside the top division who owned a white Jaguar, when most other managers and coaches in the lower leagues were driving more modest cars. On a personal basis I always felt I could play at a higher level and Ron was able to tap into that, even though we had our differences for a long time at Cambridge. Eventually I realised that falling out with my manager wasn't going to end well for me, so Cecily told me to prove to him I was a better player than he thought I was. It was around that time that Cecily miscarried and because I opted to play-on – perhaps unwisely on reflection – Ron treated me just the same as anyone else. I shouldn't have played because my head was all over the place, but it had

183

been my decision to play on so I could have no complaints. There were times we didn't speak for weeks, but my respect for him was immense.

The one thing he'd do is watch from the stand and if things weren't going right, he'd stand up, and march down with his long leather coat flailing. It was all for effect and to gee up the supporters. It worked too. "If I'm bored, the crowd will be bored" – so he'd make a massive scene to get the crowd going, marching down stridently from his seat in the stand and down to the touchline.

The other thing he never did was treat me differently. Ron could poke fun about anything and within a football environment he was part of that banter that you get around football clubs. I remember one example at West Brom where we had a dinner for John Wile's testimonial at a hotel in Birmingham.

As is often the case a group of the lads were stood around, with Ron in among us. We were making jokes, chatting to each other, making fun of Tony Godden's shirt or Ally Robertson's hair, that kind of thing as you do after a few drinks. The next thing we know this guy has walked in and started asking for autographs, which was fine. But while he was doing this some of the jokes continued. At this point this guy made a comment that Cyrille clearly took exception to – I have no idea what it was. With that Ron grabbed this bloke and practically threw him out of the room.

And yet, when Ron made me captain at Cambridge and signed me for West Brom, little did I know how much my feeling of warmth, immense respect and genuine affection was to be challenged.

On April 20, 2004, everything changed between Ron and I.

It was during his ITV commentary of the Monaco versus Chelsea Champions League match that Ron made an unforgivable comment about Chelsea player Marcel Desailly. Believing the microphone to be switched off, he said: "...he (Desailly) is what is known in some schools as a fucking lazy, thick nigger."

It was a comment that was picked up on overseas' feeds. Viewers in the UK were, I'm told, unaware of what he'd said until it leaked out.

Cecily and I were on our way back from Grenada with a stop-off in

Barbados. We were in a restaurant watching Monaco play Chelsea. A good friend of mine used to work for British Airways and would look after my car while I was away. When I saw him the next morning as I picked my car up the first thing I asked him was how that particular game had finished. And he immediately said: "Have you heard about Ron's comments?" I had no idea what he was talking about. I drove home and within 20 minutes of me getting back to Walsall I had a call from the Daily Mirror, asking me if I wanted to make any comments about Ron. At this point I still wasn't sure what Ron had actually said, other than been told something anecdotally. The one that really set me off was a call from John Goodbody of The Times. He gave me a phone number and asked me to call the PR people of ITV to find out exactly what had happened and then to get back to him, which I did.

I was shocked when I heard the transcript. I immediately rang Ron but didn't get a response, so I called John Goodbody back and told him of my shock, hurt, disappointment and surprise. Those are feelings I still have to this day.

I actually managed to get hold of him the next day.

What Ron then said has stuck with me since. He said: "To be fair Batman, I thought the microphone was off."

I don't swear often, but I can recall my reply: "Ron that's even fucking worse. Are you telling me you'd have said that if the microphone was off – so the impression you're giving me is that you'd have used that kind of language anyway?"

I was furious.

The problem with Ron is that he thought he could make a joke about anything and get away with it. You also have to remember that by 2004 Ron was known to a wider audience more for his brilliant analysis as a TV pundit, than he was as a football manager as he had been during the 1970s through to the early 1990s. I think Ron became somewhat blasé and got carried away with his celebrity status.

The other thing he mentioned in that call was how much it would cost him because he was forced to quit ITV but then that was down to his own making. It still hurts me now when I think about it. I cannot quite understand what made Ron say what he did and one of the worst things is that he never apologised for the comments.

People could draw their own conclusions based on what they heard but the hurtful aspects of Ron's comments was his excuse that he got caught with the microphone switched on, and the lack of apology. That's what really upset me.

You have deeds, you have actions, and you can say you have words. I'm not saying Ron was supportive of black footballers exclusively, more so he was supportive of good footballers. He didn't sign me because I was a black player, he signed me because he felt I could bring value to his team. The fact that his West Brom side, a bloody good and flamboyant team, just so happened to be represented by three black footballers was purely a matter of recruitment. Myself, Cyrille and Laurie hadn't been signed because we were black, nor was it a conscious decision to sign three non-white footballers – we were brought in because the managers, coaches and scouts actually rated us. Laurie was signed by John Giles, Cyrille came in on Giles' watch but on Ronnie Allen's recommendation and I was signed by Ron. It was hardly joined-up thinking. That we were pitched together was coincidental, almost accidental. But, whether Ron appreciated this or not, it did enhance his reputation. He was as part of the narrative as Laurie, Cyrille and I were.

That Desailly comment was also against the grain of some of his other work. Ron was extremely supportive of Kick It Out, the campaign set-up to combat racism within football. Ron also jumped in to manage the black team in Lenny Cantello's Blacks vs Whites testimonial game. He didn't have to do those things, he didn't have to attend those dinners supporting anti-racism campaigns and yet he did.

A few days after that Chelsea game I went to a dinner, attended by ex-Arsenal man Paul Davis and Terry Venables, the former England manager. They wanted to talk about what had been said, others were approaching me wanting to talk about it, and in the end I wish I hadn't gone because all people wanted to chat about was what Ron had said. I recall Paul actually saying: "Bloody hell Bren, as black players we all thought the world of Ron. We never played for him, but we saw what he did with you, Laurie and Cyrille and others – so how must you feel?" And I was upset. I was hurt.

You have to also remember that by 2004 there were people who wouldn't have known about his relationship with myself, Cyrille and Laurie and so it wouldn't have registered with them – they would have just seen him as Ron Atkinson, the football pundit.

I honestly think Ron got ahead of himself and put himself in a position where he felt he could say what he wanted…and finally he got caught out by that bravado. He could back up that bravado because he was a brilliant analyst, he was good with his words and was liked by the watching public. He had gone from being a football manager to being a TV celebrity, yet to this day I will never understand that episode. It cost him dearly.

We were part of a documentary a couple of years later – myself and Cyrille – which was instigated by a West Brom director Jeff Farmer, who was formerly of ITV Sport and good mates with Ron. It was presented by broadcaster and Albion supporter Adrian Chiles, with Ron going to Alabama on some kind of redemption expedition. But on reflection I don't think we should have taken part in the programme as it didn't really help his cause in any shape nor form. The whole thing felt very shambolic and disingenuous.

Some people might level the whole notion that it's a generational thing, but I disagree with that. My own personal view is that we've all had to become more aware about language and how we conduct ourselves. We no longer use the term BAME to describe people from ethnically diverse communities, but the LGBTQ+ deem it acceptable to use the word "queer". All of this can cause understandable blurring of what is and isn't acceptable. But what Ron said on TV that night could not be interpreted in any other way, nor is it an excuse to say he was of an older generation for whom such language was once acceptable. We all have to evolve and modify our behaviour to fit in with change around us. I remember having to apologise to a Muslim girl once because I just forgot myself at an event and went to kiss her goodbye as I was leaving, completely forgetting that you're not allowed to do that. I was horrified but she was absolutely fine about it. Nevertheless, I was apologising like mad because I knew I'd nearly done something socially unacceptable in certain communities.

When you know you've made a cock-up, you should apologise. I'll tell you this now: if anyone ever called me a Nigger I would hit them. If Desailly has had a bad game, he's had a bad game. But once you bring skin colour and a lazy cliché around colour into it, you've crossed the line. Ron had been part of people like myself overcoming that. Laurie, Cyrille and I held our places in the team because we were good footballers, not because he was making a PR gesture.

I wouldn't say we kissed and made up, but we let bygones be bygones due to some circumstances that brought us together when Cecily was at the QE hospital. Ron was good friends with the Italian tenor Renato Pagliari, who was on the same recovery ward as my wife following her operation. I didn't know Renato's wife but she spotted me and must have told Bobbo (Ron's driver) that she saw me and that Cecily was unwell.

A day or so later I received a call from Ron and he said: "Batman, I've just heard; I'm phoning to see how things are and can I do anything?" I think at that point everything just fell away from me in terms of any anger that I had towards Ron. We'd had words, we'd not spoken for a while, so he didn't have to call me, but I appreciated that he did reach out to me.

Since then, we've done a few events together, I've seen him at various lunches or dinners – we travelled together to Jim Smith's funeral. We don't go out socially, but then that's not unusual, although we did speak a lot during Covid as I did with other people. We're on good terms now.

I guess this takes us back to the late 1970s and the whole publicity stunt of the Three Degrees. It was an obvious monicker in many respects. We were three black guys. They, the actual Three Degrees, were young black female singers. I never thought it was particularly crass, but I knew the other lads were getting pissed off with the focus being on us three black lads. The spotlight fell on us because we were a good team. If we had been bottom, or mid-table, nobody would have bothered with us. We just so happened to have two brilliant attacking players who were black, an outstanding full-back in Derek Statham and one of the best midfielders to emerge of his generation in Bryan Robson. We also had Tony Brown, still playing like a 16-year-old in his 30s, with Ally Brown up front and some great defenders. Ron saw myself, Cyrille and Laurie as a great opportunity to showcase the club, give us some publicity – and himself, no doubt – at a point where we were one of the best teams in the country. We knew Ron was going places. I knew at Cambridge that he wouldn't stay long. And I knew at West Brom that he wouldn't stay long when it became clear that he was getting us noticed.

The Three Degrees publicity thing went on too long. I felt extremely uneasy about it all given I was happily married and there was always a lot of innuendo about who was paired up with which girl. That wasn't for me. To this day the stories and questions have never stopped.

And then we had the whispering campaign that black players couldn't play in the winter - where you'd need white men because the blacks couldn't handle the cold or the wet weather. What a load of rubbish.

I was very much aware of this: "They're quick, stick them out on the wing, they can't defend, they're lazy, they have no bottle." You knew you'd be singled out. If there was a black player on the team, you'd be identified as having these so-called weaknesses. Yet ironically, myself, Viv Anderson, Cec Podd and others played in defence. People were struggling to cope with three black footballers joining one team and smashing every single cliché and stereotype. We didn't conform to the image of black footballers, because we were bloody good at not only playing football but doing all the things that we were being accused of not being able to do.

I don't remember Cyrille, Laurie nor I really speaking about the social issues around racism. We just felt loved by those around us. Laurie used to get some pretty horrible hate mail because of his relationship with Nikki, but actually we always felt that our own fans had our back. I recall not long after I had joined West Brom receiving some abuse from a supporter following a game against Aston Villa, when I had won us a penalty. The next day I was having lunch with some friends at the Europa Lodge Hotel when a Villa fan came over and called me a "cheat". In the end I had to threaten him with being thrown out, because I knew the staff there, but that was a robust conversation about football. That's all it was. Perhaps I was living in a bubble where if we were recognised, we were embraced.

Ron's comment about Desailly was a one-off remark, which I've spoken about and don't wish to dwell on anymore. But we do need to touch upon how society has changed in recent years. There is a sinister racial edge that has been fuelled by extremism on social media but, also and certainly in the UK, has been given some further momentum by Brexit.

I actually think this country's decision to vote to leave the EU in June

2016 was a defining moment for all of us.

I knew the vote was going to be close, but I was really surprised when it came through as Leave. Boris Johnson had a big part to play in this because he switched from Remain to Leave and, obviously, he has been the Prime Minister in recent memory. I didn't see it coming. I didn't think the British people would vote for it given all the many benefits we had from inclusion of the European Union. I saw at first hand the benefits of being part of Europe, as did my children. It allowed Jason to move to Slovenia, find work, find love and find a home there. It allowed my daughter Zoe to move to Spain and find a new happy home there after leaving the UK in 2005. And, of course, I built a house there, where Cecily and I had planned to spend much of our time. So, the privileges of being part of this community were important to our family's life. We've all been used to being able to move around freely and I just cannot fathom why people would vote for something that effectively ends this free movement.

Since then, it has emboldened people to express previously-suppressed racist and bigoted views. It has given people the licence to be less fearful of reproach and more strident with extreme comments. I know of Muslim friends who have had hijabs being pulled, or who have been spat at – all of that had gone away, only for it to return post June 2016. We had this narrative that I could never understand around controlling our own borders. I never understood the logic of this. Some of the biggest benefits we've had were as members of the EU, such as the European Court of Justice, Human Rights' issues and yet they were thrown away. The thing that shocked me most was that Birmingham opted to leave. How can it be that a city as culturally and racially diverse as Birmingham would vote for something like this? I was actually going to Barcelona on the Friday, with the vote taking place on the Thursday. I voted in Birmingham, then went down to Gatwick and spent the night in a hotel. Whenever I have an early-morning flight I never seem to sleep well, so I woke up around 4am, put the TV on and saw Leave was winning. It was close enough that it could be overtaken, but David Dimbleby was saying that the one they were looking for was the Birmingham result. When that came through as Leave I felt physically sick. I couldn't believe it. At Gatwick I got on the Monorail that took us to our departure gate and I could see people in the carriage in utter disbelief, just shaking their heads. I couldn't believe what people had voted to do.

Whenever I go into the centre of Barcelona there is a little café I always go to, yet on this day I felt utterly out of sorts – I bought a coffee and a croissant, and I just felt utterly despondent and sick. To this day I cannot believe we did it. The younger generation, especially those who were too young to vote, were badly let down by those of us who could. I must admit Brexit made me feel even more politically conscious. The one day there was a rally in Birmingham led by Tony Robinson, who played Baldrick in Blackadder. He was a staunch anti-racism campaigner, while at the opposite end of town there was an English Defence League (EDL) rally led by Tommy Robinson. The two are certainly not to be confused. I was actually in my apartment at the time and came out to see loads of police. I bumped into one police officer who knew me, and he tipped me off that the EDL were trying to march to Centenary Square. Groups like the EDL and others grew in importance and attracted more members because Brexit empowered and normalised this anti-immigrant rhetoric, that not only had an impact on EU nationals living and working in this country, but anyone who fitted the non-British profile. This is a vote that split families and friends. I spoke to one former work colleague who just started spouting nonsense about taking back control, controlling our borders and all of these meaningless clichés that, when you break them down, the EU never actually prevented us from doing. Take the European Court of Justice – that is about individual rights and making sure the little person can have their day in court against the state. It's an avenue available to everyone who feels hard done by. When you have people like Priti Patel and such like doing what they like, the European Court of Justice was there to rein them in. Theresa May introduced her Windrush policy and, as I write this book, the government have only just started paying compensation to those affected by this policy and sadly several victims have died before receiving any compensation.

The Windrush scandal began to surface in 2017 when it became apparent that hundreds of Commonwealth citizens, many of whom were from the Windrush generation much like myself, had been wrongly detained, denied legal rights or simply deported. All of this was part of the Government's Hostile Environment policy, which had been introduced in 2012 and tasked landlords and employers with enforcing immigration controls. The aim of it was to force people to leave. The

Windrush scandal was not an accident, but a result of policies designed to make life as hard as possible for those without the appropriate papers. It was solely aimed at reducing non-white immigration and it had a profound effect on the non-white immigration from the Commonwealth. Again, much like Brexit, it destroyed communities and it heightened intolerance. People died, people were deported…and many of them had every right to stay in the UK.

Then there was the George Floyd killing in the US. He was an Afro-American man murdered by police – the very people who are there to protect civilians and make them feel safe. I remember attending a march for George Floyd in Centenary Square in Birmingham and feeling like it was a seminal moment. What was great was seeing such a young crowd of different colours. It felt like this was a real moment because it was not just black people but Indian, Chinese, white people all marching to the same beat, to support a cause for the good.

Around the same time, I was watching on TV and listening to Star Wars actor George Boyega talking about his experiences as a young student and some of the hostilities he had encountered. And a lot of what he was saying was pretty much what I was saying at his age. So, what has changed? I never got stopped and searched like some of these black youngsters, but other than that much of the discrimination remains. Actually, I tell a lie - the police did stop me once. I was heading back from an event in Birmingham city centre and driving along the Aston Expressway towards Spaghetti Junction, heading home towards Walsall. I saw blue flashing lights, so I pulled over. I had removed my bow tie, I had not long changed my car and was hopeless with registration numbers – I'm not a motoring fanatic, I've always hated driving. It's 1am in the morning and the one officer started questioning where I'd been, persistently asking whether I'd had a drink. I'd only had a few orange-and-tonics, so I was fine in that respect. The other officer was just staring at me. He asked if I owned the car and then asked me the registration. I had to admit that it was a new car and I couldn't remember. While I was doing this, his colleague was getting the car checked out. The second officer then approached me and said: "That's a nice car isn't it?" So, I asked him whether it was a statement or a question. He came back aggressively and said: "Are you trying to be funny?" He made a move towards me, so I asked to see his number. At this point his colleague stepped in and said: "It's okay, you can leave now." I felt extremely intimidated by that and had the other office not been there, I dread to think how that would have unfolded.

Things have improved in many ways, but we still have many inequalities in society that still exist. Think about sport and football in particular. Look at how many black footballers we have in the Premier League and Football League. And now look at how many non-white people we have on the touchline or in the boardrooms across the country? Not many. Les Ferdinand stood out at Queens Park Rangers, but he has since left. I was obviously a director at West Brom for a time, but there aren't many. Boardrooms across the football landscape are still very white, still very male. And there are still not enough black managers in the game. Coaches perhaps, but how many black men are given the job to lead a team as manager or head coach? Again, not many. We now have more than a third of the Premier League made up of non-white footballers, yet that isn't reflected elsewhere.

Ricky Hill, the former Luton and England midfielder, was the main campaigner behind the Rooney Rule in England. The Rooney Rule was pioneered by American Football chairman Dan Rooney in 2003 to help increase the number of ethnic minority coaches in senior operational positions. Under Ricky's interpretation of the rule he wanted all 72 EFL clubs to sign up to a scheme requiring them to interview at least one qualified Black, Asian or Minority Ethnic candidate for every managerial position. The PFA pushed for this, as did Sir Trevor Brooking and FA chairman Greg Dyke, who had previously spoken about the BBC being "hideously white." We'd had meetings in London about addressing this, which is something I took on when I was working as a consultant for the FA. Myself, Garth Crooks, Paul Elliott and, with support from Les Ferdinand, we went to see the FA in 2017 when Martin Glenn was the CEO. We called it the Elite Coach Placement Programme to begin with – where we have a black coach with every England squad, from the 15s to the seniors. We spoke about visibility. So recently you'd have seen Chris Powell, Paul Nevin and others on the bench as part of Gareth Southgate's coaching team. We extended this to the women's team, although that game is in a different place to the men's. I introduced a bursary scheme funded by the football stakeholders, whereby 90% of the course fees were paid for any ethnically diverse coaches to get enhanced qualifications so that when opportunities came along, they could throw their hats into the ring. Now we're starting to see more black coaches but it's still not enough. Why is it being done for black and ethnically diverse coaches? Because there is massive underrepresentation in the game from those communities. People might confuse this with positive discrimination, but it's not that - it's positive action. Positive discrimination is illegal in the UK. You simply cannot do that. But you can take positive action where there is underrepresentation. I would dearly love that we didn't need to do this, but we have to because it's still necessary, it's still needed. Much like the Black Lives Matter or Gay Pride movement – we shouldn't need to be continually highlighting these issues, but we have to because of the discrimination and hate that people from those communities still face. It's about fairness and being presented with equal opportunities in society in all that we do.

Regarding the Black Lives Matter, I agree with the principle of it. It's not a political statement but a narrative that highlights inequality. My one caveat is that I feel the actual gesture of taking a knee has lost its impact somewhat. When Colin Kaepernick, the San Francisco 49ers NFL player, did it for the first time there was a real symbolism and meaning behind it. But the question is what else can we do? When are we going to see diversity in action because, right now, we're not seeing it enough? We had Jake Daniels come out as the country's first gay professional footballer since Justin Fashanu but what has anyone's sexual orientation got to do with anyone else? Nobody should care about your sexual orientation. What I want to know is can he play. If I give him the ball, can he hold onto it, pass it back to me or one of our team.

Racism was engrained in our culture growing up – if not explicitly, then certainly sub-consciously. Growing up as a young man in England, there were programmes like Love Thy Neighbour, Til Death Us Do Part and The Black and White Minstrel Show. Instinctively, I hated those programmes. They were just awful, even if in some of those shows the black characters were depicted to actually be winning at the end. Then at the opposite end of the scale was Desmond's, which was a comedy about a black barbershop community where there was a token white character, who was the butt of the jokes at times – effectively switching the emphasis around.

When John Barnes went to Liverpool as a player, I said to him: "John, whatever you do, don't fail." This was in 1987 and the reason I said that was because Howard Gayle had been there before him and got abuse from some of his own team-mates, supposedly dressed up as banter. I remember going to an anti-racism meeting in Manchester, listening to a few black and Asian Liverpool supporters. One fan stood up and said that I didn't understand what it was like to be a supporter trying to go to a game because as a player I'd been on a coach and in a privileged position to not have to worry about tickets. They were scared to wear their own colours – not only because of the rival fans, but also because of their own supporters. They would sneak in late, just before kick-off, and leave early so they wouldn't have to interact with the crowd.

There was one story I heard during this meeting that really shocked me. The aggressors used to carry golf balls that they'd knock nails in and then snap off the head of the nails so there would be just the sharp bits exposed. The mentality to actually go to the trouble of doing that just because you don't like a black person or an Asian person supporting the same club as you are just chilling. I was absolutely horrified. I didn't realise it was that bad and that supporters would turn on their own in such a brutal way. It was shocking and maybe I was naïve to think differently but it was a lesson to me.

To this day Arsenal have always had a very diverse supporter base, in many ways because of their players of the late 80s – people like Paul Davis, David 'Rocky' Rocastle and Michael Thomas. That drew a lot of black supporters to the club but if you look up and down the country that wasn't replicated elsewhere. Yet as more and more black players came into the professional game, that should have been the blue touch paper for more black supporters to come into grounds. In fact, it was a missed opportunity, not only because of the well-documented hooliganism, but, more so, the racial intimidation.

The authorities dealt with the hooligan problem. Sir Bert Millichip was the main driver for removing our clubs from Europe – and rightly so. But the problem of racism on the pitch and on the terraces was never addressed. I recall one game when a black player got spat at as he came off the pitch and went down the tunnel. He ended up spitting back in retaliation. I absolutely despise spitting and do not condone his actions, but I can totally understand why he reacted and lashed out in the heat of the moment. He did what they did to him. As a result, the FA banned him for a number of games.

When I got sent off for Cambridge for retaliating to racist abuse, I got away with it the first time because the referee spoke on my behalf. But for the second and third time I knew I couldn't use that defence again.

It was only when Kick It Out started in 1993 that something big happened in terms of addressing the issue of racism within the game. The Football Association didn't come on board straight away – although they swiftly did when David Davies, who was the Executive Director of the FA at the time, realised they needed to be involved – while the Football League were a bit quicker to realise its importance.

This was around the period of Stephen Lawrence's death. Stephen was a black teenager who was killed in a racially motivated attack in south east London. That became a defining moment in attitudes around racism and the intolerance towards black people. That's why Lord Herman Ouseley, who was then CEO of the Commission for Racial Equality (CRE) – now the Equality and Human Rights Commission (EHRC) – knew that football and society as a whole needed to address this issue. Louise Ansari, who was campaigns manager for the CRE, came up to my office in Manchester to see me and as soon as she outlined what the campaign was about – it was a Eureka! moment for me. I popped into Gordon Taylor's office gave him a summary and said we needed to be involved with this initiative not just as a black issue but a white issue also. Without hesitation he agreed.

I knew it couldn't be a six month, or a one-year campaign, it had to be a long-term vision, and right away I was totally on board with that in my position with the PFA. We had people like Gary Mabbutt, Ian Wright, Pat Nevin, Paul Elliott, Garth Crooks at the launch a few months later so we could show a united front from the entire footballing community, not just black players. I remember the very first slogan we used to launch the campaign said: "It's only the colour of the shirt that counts," against a backdrop of football jerseys.

And then there was Show Racism The Red Card. It was Shaka Hislop who donated the first £50 to that charity in 1995. He was outside St James' Park after a Newcastle training session when he got racially abused by some school kids. Then they realised it was Shaka Hislop and asked for his autograph! That's when he realised something needed to be done.

When I was at Cambridge, we played a game at Bradford when there was actually a National Front rally going on during the same weekend. It was absolutely horrendous. During that game we got a throw-in. I went to retrieve the ball and some guy grabbed hold of it and threw it straight at me. As he did so he started giving me racist abuse, so I was ready to snap at this point.

He came running down the terracing and as I braced to launch myself back at him, I felt someone grab me and yell: "Get on with the game Batman." It was John Docherty, our assistant manager. It seems ironic now that it took a white Frenchman, Eric Cantona, to confront racist chants, when he launched himself at a Crystal Palace fan after being sent-off during a game for Manchester United. That happened in 1995, while my incident would have been a good 20 years earlier. For all that time we had to put up with whatever was thrown at us – literally in some cases – during our 90 minutes of work. And let's not forget, that's what we were doing. We were just a group of people trying to do our job and yet hundreds, sometimes thousands, would deem it acceptable to give us abuse of the worst kind.

When I got to West Brom the volume increased hugely. When we arrived at away grounds you would see the NF there in what I would describe as their uniform: a union jack tee-shirt, boots, jeans and braces. That was their outfit. You would see them handing out leaflets, encouraging football fans to join their cause, but the authorities did nothing.

We would be getting off the coach before away games being spat at, getting abuse, having things thrown at us and nobody would defend us or try to stop the aggressors. There was no such thing as a safe zone for players arriving at a ground until 1986 when Manchester United players and staff were sprayed with ammonia by Liverpool fans as they got off the coach outside Anfield. I'd retired by then, but I remember reading about it wishing they'd been that concerned when black players were getting missiles and spittle aimed at them.

And the media didn't always help matters. While there were some who wrote things in good faith, there were obviously some newspapers who were less than receptive to inclusivity and racial tolerance. There was one comment from a journalist called Peter Batt, who described Laurie as a "George Best with charcoal make-up and a Cockney accent." I used to get really upset with comments like that.

I look back now and wonder how the hell did an editor allow Peter to write that? Why not just say: "He reminds me of George Best…and has a cockney accent." Once you interject colour into anything, depending on context, it can become offensive. It was insulting, yet this was the era we lived in.

Music was the one culture that perhaps reacted to this better than football. We had the Two-tone label in Coventry, which emerged during the late 1970s championing the likes of The Specials and The Selecter. In Birmingham we had The Beat and another Brummie band UB40, who had white guys singing reggae, which was unheard of at the time. That was fantastic. Their music was catchy, they bought into the genre, and all of a sudden there was a social awareness in the popular culture that we could relate to. These were bands that weren't afraid to challenge political narratives, social decay or discrimination. UB40 sang about the inner-city riots of the time, while the other bands I mentioned were represented by black musicians playing alongside white artists – people like Terry Hall, from The Specials, who was hugely influential back then, alongside Jerry Dammers, Neville Staple and Lynval Golding. It was white guys, performing alongside black guys, for a mixed audience.

Ska music was something I knew as a young lad, before being introduced to reggae. And to see white musicians like Terry Hall, Dave Wakeling of The Beat and the Campbells from UB40 producing music that transcended communities was wonderful and such an important cultural landmark for the time. Before that I recall being drawn to Tamla, which was a big form of music in the US and ended up becoming known more commonly as the Motown sound. Authorities were trying to ban the dancing from universities back in the 1960s, so it was quite interesting as a black man to see the transition of the enjoyment of music that was traditionally the domain of black people. Likewise, this was the era of Cassius Clay, who later became Muhammad Ali – the brilliant boxer who was idolised by white kids in my school. He wasn't the black boxer, he was the greatest boxer.

Football was still catching up in that respect. The media didn't always help, despite the best efforts of people like Gerald Sinstadt and those willing to challenge racism. I didn't even keep a scrapbook when I was a player. My mum did – but I didn't know about that until much later. I wasn't keen on the media. There was that reporter who absolutely nailed me following a game at Queens Park Rangers – I was booked, I was at fault for the goal and I had a disaster. I thought I don't need people to tell me how well or how badly I played.

I never took much notice what journalists wrote about me, more so when I was written about as being a black footballer. I felt singled out, I felt impacted by what was being written about black footballers and didn't like the tone of it. At Arsenal I was singled out as the "black player" – I was very aware of that. I wanted to be a player, a footballer, preferably a good footballer...not a black footballer.

I grew up with people thinking we – we, being black footballers – were lazy, lacked bottle, didn't like the cold. It's what I was told; it's what I read. I was fortunate that Arsenal protected me from such bullshit, and I had a family who appeared not to be bothered by such ignorant views. But I was aware of the stigma attached to us and I know it influenced the parents of some of those black footballers who might have made it – they were diverted away from going into professional football, told to look at other careers.

Many years later the one-time Crystal Palace owner Ron Noades spoke out that you needed a "white hard-man" for games in the winter and he got pilloried for it. I knew Ron well and said: "Ron, how can you even say that?" I wanted to get away from that. I hated Laurie or Cyrille being referred to as the "Black Pearl" or "Black Flash". It was horribly naff and cliched. I knew some managers still had that thinking.

I remember people saying: "Play the white man." So, basically, forget your own culture and background, be like us, the white people. It's a phrase that is inspired by stereotype and almost urges you to suppress your own culture and conform to somebody else's standards and values. That was an insult and I hated it.

I knew I couldn't fight it. Maybe I could win nine out of 10 fights, but what if I lose the 10th fight? This wasn't something I could continue with. I had to deal with it, not fight it.

The Nigger word conjures up something so abhorrent to a black person that you just cannot swallow it, no matter what. There are other terms and words you may reluctantly have to live with, otherwise you end up fighting people all the time. They became part of human interaction. I remember being jarred by Roots – a 1970s' drama series about the

US slave trade. It was just awful. Watching that and then hearing comments from people, including team-mates, made me feel uneasy. You had to deal with those situations and words as to what you could tolerate. Incredible as it is to say, there were words that I thought were better than others. And there were words that were a high bar then, that are now a very low bar. Things were said which were irritating – some bordering insulting, insensitive, cruel, vindictive. Once too many of those boxes are ticked you know you have to tackle it. It becomes unacceptable, and yet that was my journey of integration.

I read comments from the Black Players' Forum some time ago. It's a well-known statistic that we have a lack of black managers. While I was writing this book Crystal Palace sacked Patrick Vieira, who was the only black manager in England's Premier League at the time of his dismissal. He was replaced by Roy Hodgson. I have absolutely nothing against Roy – I know him very well, he's a great man and a gentleman – but it is symbolic of where football is. What does that say to aspiring black coaches who want an opportunity in the top-flight? We seem to be making very little progress on that front. I would like to think that Patrick Vieira will get another opportunity to continue his coaching journey in the not-too-distant future.

Jermain Defoe said black players might not want to go into coaching, because they may not see any opportunities. This is something I've been saying since I was playing. You ask yourself what has changed? How has it improved? What's going to change? I hope the next generation have a more forceful approach to the lack of representation. I despair that the authorities at the top don't do anything to change the narrative or the status quo. The Football Association are culpable in this.

Footballers are now moving in different circles. As somebody said to me, they've gone from beer, to Champagne, to drugs. And I have never understood this obsession to out footballers who are gay. It is a personal choice. It is nobody else's business. However, the more people do come out the easier it becomes for the next person to do so. I've never known anyone from my playing career who I knew to be gay. And had they been it wouldn't have bothered me. The big problem is the crowd and social media. Some of the stuff out there is just vile. Look at the way Bukayo Saka, Marcus Rashford and Raheem Sterling have been treated over the years – some of the abuse they've had has been completely horrific. When Rashford, Jadon Sancho and Saka walked up to take their penalties in the Euros final against Italy I was praying for them each to score, not just because I wanted England to win, but because I knew what would be coming if they didn't. Ironically, neither Sancho or Saka missed because the keeper saved it – nobody ever talks about Gianluigi Donnarumma's saves – but sure enough those young players were singled out and given racist abuse by a small but vocal minority and it disgusted me.

There has been what feels like an undercurrent within football for a while that looks ready to kick off. We saw it with some so-called England fans in that final and we saw incidents during the play-off games the following year. I know police have reservations about safe standing being introduced because it is more difficult to control standing supporters than those who are seated. I hope I'm wrong, but it feels like we're going back to a more unpleasant time and an undercurrent of a right-wing movement, not helped by what a lot of people call the nasty party governing the country. I don't like this Conservative party. On the whole the UK is a very tolerant and inclusive country, especially compared to others, but there is a whole group of people who seem to ignore the fact that inclusivity and migration has been the bedrock of this country for so long. And let's not forget the Windrush generation were invited to this country - we were invited to help build the post-war infrastructure. We helped build roads, buildings, we provided nurses, other care workers. This notion now – peddled by right-wing extremists - that immigrants get first dibs on housing or medical care, for instance, is just utter rubbish. There is a distorted view being pushed out by certain people and by the media, especially the Daily Mail. That's a big reason there is this undercurrent of anger and simmering resentment.

I am very grateful for what this country has done for me and my family, but we must never lose sight of the fact that we have a long way to go to achieve equality. That there might be countries and regions that have bigger societal problems around racism and discrimination shouldn't be a get out for us.

We can do better. We must do better.

TRIBUTE

When Ron Atkinson signed Brendon from Cambridge United it was no great surprise that he wanted to join up again with his Fourth Division championship winning captain.

What we all wondered was whether a full back from the lower divisions would hack it in a team which Big Ron was assembling to become a force in the topflight. We did not need to have any such worries. Brendon immediately fitted in as a cultured defender, capable of performing his duties alongside John Wile, Ally Robertson and Derek Statham. What the Baggies also got was an articulate, forthright dressing room personality whose opinions were highly valued.

Those qualities were evident when he became a prominent figure in the Kick Out Racism campaign as a leading PFA spokesman.

His relationship with Big Ron was an intriguing one. Their careers were intertwined but they also had their differences, notably when the former boss came out with his infamous off air racist remarks about Chelsea defender Marcel Desailly which were picked up by microphone.

Cyrille Regis immediately came to Ron's defence saying the remarks were racist, but his former manager was not a racist. Brendon was less forgiving – initially – but eventually they resumed their friendship.

I remember Ron once telling me that when Brendon's wife Cecily died, so tragically and prematurely, he was one of the first people to ring to offer his condolences. Thereafter, the bond between them was secured for ever.

I was fortunate to go on Albion's historic trip to China in 1978. For most of the players it was not the ideal one at the end of a gruelling season.

But the Three Degrees, Brendon, Cyrille and Laurie Cunningham embraced it for all they were worth. Their thinking was that they grew up originally in different cultures and were keen to discover what this mysterious country was all about. Brendon was an outstanding ambassador for the Baggies and football in general. His contribution on and off the field was immeasurable.

David Harrison, journalist (covered WBA from 1977-82)

TRIBUTE

I first knew Brendon when he emerged as a player with a lot of potential at Arsenal. Subsequently he went onto Cambridge and went onto become one of the Three Degrees at West Bromwich Albion. It was there that he gained a lot of publicity and became someone who was recognised instantly by white fans and black fans. He became a recognised face of diversity.

Brendon used to work in an unassuming way behind the scenes when others wouldn't put their heads ahead the parapet. I had tried to change things myself as a fan having also endured abuse as a player but, when I became the chairman of the Commission for Racial Equality in 1993, I knew that we had some power and legislative authority to do something more prominent. Brendon was extremely helpful in that respect. I tried to pull together alliances within football to try to get things moving and Brendon, along with people like Garth Crooks, Paul Elliott and John Fashanu, were very supportive.

Brendon used his influence within the PFA to bring the issue to prominence. He was always constructive, but also in asserting himself with authorities.

What I like about Brendon is that he's always had a charm and robustness about him. He was always continuously working away at bringing alliances together to push things on. We still have problems today, but rest assured that Brendon was instrumental in bringing about change in the first place.

Lord Herman Ouseley *founding member of Let's Kick Racism Out of Football (which later became Kick It Out).*

CHAPTER TWELVE
I'm honoured

"...I'm grateful to have played alongside, and against, some of the best footballers of that era..."

I enjoyed a good, fulfilling career both on and off the field.

I would love to have had a longer playing career but I'm mindful that my first serious injury at Arsenal could easily have finished me off when I was still young. With that in mind I'm grateful to have played on for another decade, alongside, and against, some of the best footballers of that era.

I'm also very grateful to have been on the frontline of major change of the English national game during the 1990s, when we helped to safeguard the future of the Professional Footballers Association and its members.

It's also been an honour helping to raise money for some charities close to my heart. Birmingham St Mary's Hospice provided fantastic care for Cecily when she needed it. I rode from the church we got married in at Chingford, back to The Hawthorns – that wasn't for charity, but more so just to mark the first anniversary of Cecily's passing. I did that on a hybrid bike and all these road bikes were whizzing past me. I then decided to give something back to the wonderful people at Birmingham St Mary's Hospice. I got a team together including a couple of my colleagues from the FA and we did the London-to-Paris ride. There were five of us riding with my great friend Dave Garrett driving the support van. We had great fun and also raised about £17,000. We started off at Wembley, went to Newhaven and got the ferry from there to Dieppe, then onto Paris. It was about 170-odd miles.

Among the most privileged highlights of my career was being fortunate enough to be honoured for services to football and anti-racism campaigning. I was awarded the MBE in 2001. I got notice of it a few months earlier, in around September 2000. A brown envelope arrived in the post. I assumed it was something to do with tax, so I put it aside.

When I finally opened it, I noticed it was from the Government. It was extremely nicely written, and I had to reply whether I would accept it. I just assumed it was somebody taking the piss.

The announcement was embargoed until New Year's Eve. I then had to go to Buckingham Palace to receive the honour. Of course, I took Cecily, Zoe and Jason for what was a fabulous day out, including a Champagne reception at the Palace. I received my MBE from the Queen, which was just an amazing experience.

It was all very grand. You get a briefing beforehand where you're told how to greet the Queen as part of the protocol. I was told that she may speak to me, but she may not. But I was informed that if she did speak to me then she would shake my hand and push me away when she was ready to move on. The guy briefing us said: "You will know when it happens." And he was right. She was only a tiny lady but, my goodness, she did it with some force. If you're not braced for it, then you would stumble backwards. To meet the Queen was an incredible honour and privilege, as you can imagine.

Funnily enough, Ted Bates – who was effectively Mr Southampton FC – was just ahead of me, also receiving an honour. When he got called out the usher said "Mr Bates?" And he suddenly responded with a shout of "What? Eh? I cannot hear you." He'd forgotten to turn his hearing aid up! Then there was Audley Harrison, who was absolutely huge. We also had some of the bomb disposal guys there receiving awards, presumably for their immense bravery. When they were telling me about their jobs, I just couldn't believe what they went through to try to keep others safe. It was a very humbling experience. I felt like a fraud getting an honour for kicking a ball around and anti-racism campaigning alongside people who literally risk their lives in their working environment.

I recall when I got my MBE, the late and lovely Jimmy Armfield, who was a great guy, coming up to me and saying: "Congratulations Brendon... but it's only an MBE isn't it?" He'd already received his OBE. A few years later I took great pleasure in reminding him of our earlier chat when I finally received the same honour as him. By then of course he had received a further gong – the CBE!

That happened in 2015. On that occasion it was Prince William handing it over. As I was approaching, I could see an equerry whispering in his ear, presumably something along the lines of: "Brendon Batson, PFA... anti-racism work; footballer." As I walked forward to shake his hand he said: "Well done Brendon, you're doing fantastic work." It was brilliant and clearly you could see his appreciation for football, a sport he quite obviously loves. He's a lot taller than you expect him to be too.

You do feel humble because you see what some people have received their awards for. They're the ones you don't really hear about, but there were some wonderful people there being recognised.

They were two very proud moments in my life.

TRIBUTE

My father has always been many things to many people.

To some an icon, to some a pioneer, to some, particularly footballers, a progressive force in football, who not only tried to tackle the issues of inequality in the sport but supported players of all backgrounds in whatever they wished to do.

However, my father was only ever one thing to me: put simply, a father. A father who tried to guide me as best as he could. A father with strengths, with weaknesses, but significantly a father with one goal in mind, for his children to have more options available to them than were available to him.

My father taught me, through his actions within and outside of the footballing world, the importance of perseverance, of turning the other cheek, of proving yourself in the arena that counts, in his case the football pitch.

My father taught me the importance of knowing that every person is of equal value, no matter your place in society and everyone can have an impact on others.

I recall working at Halfords in my teens, in the bike section, helping one gentleman buy a bike. After he paid for it, he told me that my father helped him so much to complete his dream of becoming a priest after his football career had ended. It was in that moment that I realised that this perfectly epitomised the lessons of my father.

You can simply be helping someone buy a bike, you could be helping someone fulfil a dream, you could be showing a whole generation of future footballers that regardless of your ethnicity, religion, sexuality or socioeconomic background, if you can dream a dream, if you can persevere and stay true to your calling no matter the obstacles and adversities that may be in your path, you can succeed and inspire others, sons, daughters, strangers, spectators and future athletes to do the same.

My life has been filled with lessons of those who my father has inspired and helped, but it is important to say the help and inspiration he gave so effortlessly and selflessly to the world was a byproduct of my father's central purpose in life, to play football, to be involved in football, to live the game and love the game. Passion is contagious and those who are passionate naturally become inspirational.

My father's ultimate lesson, find your passion, love what you do, inspire and help others to do the same. Directly or indirectly we all have the capacity to change the world, simply by doing what we love.

Jason Batson

TRIBUTE

I wanted my dad to write a book for so long now as I want to know it all! Whenever we are together, I hear another story. Whenever I meet someone who knew my dad throughout his career, I hear something new and more remarkable.

As kids growing up, we knew my dad played football but myself and my brother never remember him playing. So, I personally absolutely love to see photos, videos and hear all these amazing stories.

The one thing we never experienced growing up was racism. I'm not even sure I was aware that really existed. I now look back and know we were under that protective "Brendon Batson" bubble. At primary and secondary everyone knew who we were (again this was completely normal for us). It is only when I went to London to study at university, I discovered racism existed. But by then my dad's job was done. I was incredibly confident and was able to make friends and speak to anyone. Nothing was too challenging, and I was not afraid to try anything. I now know as an adult with three children of my own that my dad did so much more than give us the best life, best education and a safe and loving home together with my mum.

He gave me a fierceness and power that he had throughout his career the thing that has made him one of the most incredible people I know. He was wise enough to choose my mum as his partner in crime throughout his journey and together well...the proof is in the pudding. I have all I need and it's not just because my dad was successful, it's because he gave me those tools to do just that.

I wanted him to write his book because his story can never be repeated – it's so unique. It will stick in my head forever and say it to people all the time. My dad came across to England at nine-years-old, never having kicked a football in his life, and became the first black football player for Arsenal and went on to have a professional football career....WOW! That's my dad. And even after the game his career just continued to excel. There's nothing my daddy can't do!

I love you dad, my hero.

Zoe Batson

CHAPTER THIRTEEN
My family and I

"...God bless you all..."

Cecily and I had two children: Zoe and Jason.

Zoe was born in August 1977 at Addenbrooke's Hospital in Cambridge at about 11.30 in the evening. She was the youngest of her peer group, being born on the final day of August. Within a few months of her birth, I joined West Brom and we were kindly put up in a lovely suite in a hotel in West Bromwich. Zoe was obviously a babe-in-arms and she just wouldn't settle, no matter what we did. One day I came back from training – Cecily and Zoe had only been there a couple of nights – and I saw a row of suitcases packed up. I panicked and wondered what was going on. It turns out Cecily just wanted to take Zoe home as she couldn't settle in the hotel. My routine was play a game on the Saturday and by the time I got home to Cambridge Zoe would be asleep. I would then leave on the following evening for training on the Monday. I thought well, that's okay, because the season will finish in May. Oh no. They decided to send us to China for three weeks, so I had even more time away from Zoe. I came back from China, and brought back some lovely silk pyjamas for her. Anyway, Zoe was so used to being with Cecily and nobody else that she would turn away from me and didn't want to bond. Cecily's aunt – who we affectionately called Grandma Maysie – had nicknamed Zoe as "Cecily's shoulder broach." It literally took Zoe about a week for her to bond with me. The first time I took her to an Albion function, there was a right frown on her as she clearly wasn't keen on people coming up to me asking for autographs.

And then in February 1979, along came Jason, born in Mary Stevens Maternity Hospital in Stourbridge. By then we'd moved to that part of the world. We bought a house from an estate agent called Jack Downing, who was a charismatic chap who wore a big eye patch. He was an auctioneer, who also happened to be an estate agent. He had this incredible booming voice and he used to tell the story of when he got really excited at Albion games, somebody would pat him on the back and his glass eye would pop out.

Anyway, when Jason was due to be born it was during the big freeze-up of that 1978/79 season. Jim Smith was manager of Birmingham and big mates with Ron Atkinson. They decided that the best thing to do would be to take both teams away for a friendly in Guernsey as it was the only part of the UK that didn't seem to be affected by the bad weather. I told Cecily about this and she said it would be typical that I wouldn't be here for the birth. Anyway, that morning I was about to leave to join the lads for the flight across the Channel. As I was getting my stuff together, Cecily came out of the shower saying that she thought she'd wet herself, which I found bizarre. "What? You've wet yourself?" And then it dawned on us that her waters had broken, so I called Ron up and told him what was happening. There was a pause and Ron just said: "Don't you want to come to Guernsey then Batman?" And with that I put the phone down.

Jason was born on February 16, 1979, and I spent the next few days running up and down a snow-laden road trying to keep fit.

It was a pleasure and privilege to be present at both births. Both my children are very close. Zoe is hustle and bustle. She's very dynamic, especially when she wants to go shopping – she's like a train and I don't even bother trying to keep up with her. Jason is much more laid back, with a great sense of humour.

When I retired as a player, we all moved to Cheshire for a year, which was a terrible decision. We didn't stay there long. We sold, bought, sold, bought, all in the space of 12 months, between 1984 and 1985. I lived around the corner on the Park Hall estate from Ally Robertson and Tony Brown, who still lives in that area of Walsall now.

Both my children went to the Queen Mary's Grammar school in Walsall. Both ended up at the same university, in Kingston – Zoe did computer science and Jason did psychology. Zoe did her training and ended up with Virgin, which was fantastic grounding. She always wanted to move to Spain. After moving to London, neither came home. She got married, had two children and unfortunately her marriage didn't work. I recall she called me when that happened. She came back to Walsall. We remodelled the house to accommodate Zoe and the two grandkids. We all went off to Spain so the workmen could do their work, but having spent some time there she decided to make Spain her home. She met someone else and had another child and all of them are fluent in Spanish.

Zoe is now a website designer, she set up her own business and, then just before Covid hit, decided to buy a gym in Calpe. She loves all of that. She also teaches IT at one of the international schools. She's very full-on, very dynamic. Her eldest son Lui celebrated his 21st birthday with me in Grenada. He's the eldest of my five grandchildren. Eva was 19 in October 2022. She is in her second year studying law at a university in Madrid. And then there's Gio, who's 14 at the time of writing this and very much a teenager.

Jason, meanwhile, decided he was moving to Slovenia. He was a year ahead of Zoe in that respect and said Slovenia suited his personality – tranquil, beautiful and quiet. He had qualified as a teacher and was teaching maths at a school in London but always wanted to travel. He and his uni mate were on their way to see a friend who lived in Vienna. They happened to be sharing a carriage with a lot of girls and one was from Slovenia – the lucky sods. He struck up a friendship with the girl from Slovenia ended up in the capital Ljubljana and fell in love with the place. He ended up becoming a teacher at an international school in the city and has remained since. He's now the deputy principal. His partner is Slovene and they have two non-identical twins Angellina and Mikela, who are 11, and share the same birthday with grandma Maysie, the person who first introduced me to Cecily.

Jason wasn't tempted to go down the football route, although he did play for Walsall borough. When he had an interview for Queen Mary's Grammar School, he told them he played football. I just remember the headmaster looked back at him and shook his head. Football was frowned upon as it was a rugby school.

When he told me he was going to live in Slovenia I was quite worried as there aren't many black people there and concerned about how he would settle and of course not being able to speak the language. I needn't have worried as one of Jason's qualities is his personality and he finds it very easy to meet and get along with people. I have met many of his friends and colleagues over the years and they all refer to Jason as "a good Slovene boy"! I love spending time over there with him.

Despite the distance Zoe and Jason are very close. We've also done quite a lot of skiing in Slovenia. We love a road trip from Spain to Slovenia, with a stop-off in France and Italy. All the kids are really good skiers and Lui is an excellent snowboarder.

The first Christmas after Cecily died, I suggested we all get together and have a family holiday in Grenada. Jason said: "We don't need another beach holiday...let's go skiing instead." I'd not been skiing since I was 14 and Arsenal stopped me doing that as they didn't want me to break my leg. Anyway, so I went skiing for the first time in over 40 years. I went from a nursery slope onto a steeper one. Then my ski instructor took me up another slope got off the ski lift and buggered off leaving me to get down this slope by myself. Thankfully I got better and better. Mind you, I did have one drama. Jason and I came down one run, and I was becoming more and more confident. On the final one, I thought the ski lift was going a bit high... I looked down and my stomach just turned. All I could see was this sheer drop and, in the distance, an ambulance picking someone up on a stretcher. I thought there's no way I can get down there. Anyway, somehow I managed it – it was the first black run I've done. Thankfully I didn't require that ambulance and I've yet to break anything, touch wood.

Oddly, skiing probably isn't the most dangerous pursuit I've enjoyed. I've also been a keen flyer and scuba diver. When I first came to England, I became good friends with a lad who was an air scout. He asked me to come and play football for his team so to do that I had to join the air scouts and, as part of that, we used to go gliding at Biggin Hill, down in Bromley. I must have been about 14-years-old at the time, and when Arsenal found out they asked: "What the hell are you doing?" We had a few flights and I had ambitions to do some more gliding, but I realised my football career would put a stop to that. But many years later I got the bug again. Cecily initially bought me a flight at Coventry airfield. I loved that so much that I then ended up doing my training at Ha'penny Green airfield which, ironically, had been owned by the Silk family who were directors at West Brom. In order to do that you needed to see the ground, so you needed visibility of no less than 1000 feet. Many a time I'd set off from my home in Walsall only to find the British weather had let me down by the time I got to Ha'penny Green. After a number of flights, I remember going up with my instructor. I went up for my lesson, did whatever I was instructed to do by my instructor and landed. At that point the instructor turned and said: "Right then, off you go...do a solo flight." And with that he jumped out and left me to it. I ended up doing about 12 hours of solo flying. It was brilliant. One of the joys of doing my flying was that I would always ring my mum as soon as I landed – because she was always worried about me – and I'd then go off and have brunch with her. Sadly, when she passed I lost my enthusiasm for flying because it had become such a routine for me to go flying, then ring my mum and then head over to see her for a late breakfast. Even so, it was great fun while it lasted. Oddly, I have always hated driving, but I never had a problem with flying.

I also fancied scuba diving. I did a course with BSAC, the British Sub Aqua Club, where I would go down to 50 metres. You had to be 14-years-old so I waited until my son Jason was old enough so we could do it together. My window-cleaner was a diving instructor where we lived in Walsall, and he was the one who got me scuba diving. We did our training in Tamworth and eventually we got our diving licence, which we've gone onto use many times in Grenada. You can be 40 or 50 metres down over there and it's still 20c. It's such an unreal, amazing experience.

The death of Cecily hit us all very hard. When she fell ill, Jason was fantastic. He came across in the June and he stayed practically all the way through, helping me to nurse Cecily. Zoe came over immediately, bringing Gio with her who had only been born a few months earlier. My sister-in-law "Cutie" arrived after we had given her the news. All of the family rallied around. Her dad was in bits, as you can imagine. Lui was only seven at the time and extremely close to Cecily. To this day I always feel that maybe I didn't do enough for Lui after his Ma, as he called her, died. I found it very difficult to talk about Cecily with the kids and although it's very hard, that has become somewhat easier. I do sometimes wonder what life would be like if she was still here.

I didn't know what it was like to have grandparents. My mum was the centre of my universe, so I've tried to be as close as I can to all of my children and grandchildren. She was a wonderful mother to Zoe and Jason. Zoe had a sister-like relationship with Cecily. They were extremely close and even now Zoe I feel is still somewhat fragile. I used to hear Cecily asking: "Zoe, have you got my blouse?" or "Zoe have you got my perfume?" Now Zoe gets the same from her own daughter Eva-Lynn, as I call her. My mum was Evelynn, so I refer to Eva as Eva-Lynn.

215

One day when she was growing up – when she was about five or six – somebody called her Eva-Lynn and she told them off: "Only my Pa calls me that." I also have Lui taking my clothes – I once saw him walking off for a night out wearing one my shirts.

I think Jason was a bit more pragmatic in dealing with the loss of Cecily. While he, of course, misses her he has often said to me that his mother had prepared him well for his adult life and done as much as she could to make him the man he is today.

It was so tough for us all.

My mum died just after the Millennium. She had moved to Walsall, just a couple of miles from me, and was very close to Zoe and Jason. She used to give me such good advice on certain matters when the kids were young. The influences and sacrifices she made will never be forgotten.

She had been suffering with angina. She was a dynamic woman but at around 63 she decided to open a retirement home. She got so involved with the community and it was a fantastic support for her. Ultimately, she was in and out of hospital and it was her heart that gave up in the end. I used to love going to her house, where she'd cook me a steak and kidney pie or liver and bacon – things that Cecily hated cooking. I remember on the final night, Cecily and I went to see her in hospital and the nurses let us stay longer. We got home and just after 12 we got a call from the hospital. Cecily said we had to get straight back to the hospital and sadly she already knew that mum was at the door, so to speak. I didn't realise – I couldn't accept it. I think my mum had wanted me to go home before she passed. It was a real shock to me but I think my brother and sister were more accepting of the situation. I struggled with it.

My mum had been everything to me – in many ways she was mum and dad. She was very brave. She was so bold and not afraid to make big decisions. She used to say that the little mistakes didn't matter, but make sure you get the big decisions more right than wrong. Everything started with my mum. She brought us up not to be afraid – that was reflected by myself, my brother, my sister and my kids. Both Zoe and Jason made big decisions to up-sticks and move abroad. Jason now speaks Slovene, Zoe is fluent in Spanish. Both had to work at that. Mum was the centre of my universe. I don't think any child accepts when a parent is at death's door – I couldn't accept it at all. I miss her to this day.

With my background – which isn't unique to a West Indian family – we came to this country in 1962. My mum was a single parent. When she was having me, my mum went back to Grenada. We lived on the corner of Green Street and Tyrell Street. My memory is that my sister lived with my aunt in St George's, while my brother lived with my uncle in Antigua. I only found out recently that he lived there for two years so I didn't see him for that period. I recall we were often split up during my early years. When my mum moved us all back to Trinidad we lived in and around Port of Spain before finally moving to Diego Martin which was a slightly bigger suburb.

My brother and I then moved to England, which is where we formed a strong bond. I don't remember him being involved in sport, but it was he who recognised there was something going on between football and me. He also knew how to keep me in my place. There was a confrontation just after I'd signed as an apprentice with Arsenal because he felt I was too big for my boots. He'd always had the upper hand over me despite being shorter than me. This time I thought "right I'm going to sort him out now." I didn't. The last thing I saw was a fist coming towards my eye – and the next thing was seeing my brother looking back at me with horror. What I really should have done was hit him back, but I was more concerned with my eye, which was now closing up very quickly. It taught me a lesson that my brother recognised that I was getting too big headed. My stepfather had asked me to get him some cigarettes and I'd refused. This was my brother's way of telling me I'd overstepped the mark and was being disrespectful to my stepfather.

When I was having my problems at Arsenal, I remember speaking to him about leaving. I always felt he gave me good advice. He became an electrician, but he didn't share much with me. I know he had to put up with a lot on building sites. I got the easy end growing up when it came to dealing with racist issues. He had to put up with a lot of crap. In my day-to-day job at Arsenal, Cambridge and West Brom I never had to deal with anything like what my brother would have faced.

He was a great influence on me, as was my uncle Dennis and Auntie Cybil – they were like a mum and dad for me at times.

217

When my mum was seconded to be a housekeeper at the Hilton in Jamaica, I was already over in England freezing my whatsits off, as I experienced snow for the first time in my life. Meanwhile, we had a photo sent to us of my sister, in a swimsuit, diving into a swimming pool at this Hilton in Jamaica, against a backdrop of brilliant sunshine.

We all went to the same school – the McEntee Tech. My sister went onto become a laboratory technician, while my brother ended up owning his own installation company. My sister came to the country in 1964. My mum had a vision of something better for us. And England has been very good for us.

My sister lives in Derbyshire. She has two boys Mark and Paul, with her husband Graham who sadly passed away just after his 70th birthday. My brother has two daughters (Marisa and Anne-Marie) and a son Michael. They've also been blessed with grandchildren.

My mother married an Englishman called Desmond. He was a sous chef at the Hilton Hotel in London. I was a bit put out when he popped up on the scene as I didn't like the idea of sharing my mother with him, after all I hadn't seen her for two years. I just remember my sister and my brother telling me not to dare make a fuss. I bit my tongue and never said a word, but actually he was a good man and I'm sad to say he died when Zoe was just a toddler.

I spent my 70th birthday in Grenada, with my grandson Lui who turned 21 the month before. He took his first steps in Grenada, and he celebrated his landmark birthday with me there. It feels like my children and grandchildren now know their heritage. They've all been to that part of the world and I feel pleased for myself and Cecily that our family know their background and heritage.

This has been a period of discovery for me and something that I've wanted to do for some time.

Cecily has been gone since September 2009 and when I'm in Grenada I feel so much closer to her. Her ashes are here, with those of her mother's, and I feel like it's part of my healing process. I can go to the cemetery where her ashes are buried. Her resting place overlooks the sea and I sometimes go up there just to spend some time with her. She is always in my thoughts and I'm glad I'm able to do this. This is home. I can recall my time running up and down Grand Anse Beach. It's the most beautiful beach in the world. It's a utopia for me.

I have been very fortunate in that I've been blessed to meet good people. My mum's vision to want something better for us, her strength of conviction in seeing that through as a single mother with three children, is something that I can never forget.

Being friends with Dennis Sheridan, the boy who introduced me to football, was pivotal to making me interested in the game that was going to shape my entire career.

Going onto Arsenal as a 13-year-old was key to my development – there was no better place to learn at the time – not least under the great Bertie Mee. It wasn't just about developing boys as footballers, but nurturing young men.

I've been fortunate in my career. I've had to work at it because talent is never enough. I've had challenges, like all black footballers of my generation, but we prevailed. There was something in me – a competitive edge – that drove me on. I was almost embarrassed when I played badly because I felt it reflected poorly on my community as well. There is no hiding place when you're the only black player on the team.

Meeting Cecily as a 17-year-old, getting married four years later, was to shape my life. She was the best thing to happen to me. One of the biggest compliments I can pay her is that I fully believe all my best decisions were made when I spoke about it with Cecily. And all my bad decisions were made when I didn't confer with her. She gave me the best bits of advice – when I fell out with Ron Atkinson at Cambridge, for instance. When I had to retire from the game early, she just said: "Brendon...it'll be okay." When I took the plunge to join West Brom and it didn't work out well, again, she was there for me.

Cecily always told me that I didn't realise my standing in the game. Perhaps I didn't. Perhaps I was just fortunate that people gave me opportunities. I've been able to raise a family, travel back to Grenada when I want and blessed to have wonderful grandchildren.

My family is everything. They sustained me when Cecily died. Even now I struggle with it all and often ask myself whether I did enough for my kids. But they're the ones who sustained me during those dark times. From the bottom of my heart, I thank them for those periods when they lifted me.

When I'm here in Grenada I do struggle with it. I'm always asking: "What if Cecily was still here?" Life is full of If onlys or What ifs? But then I'm not unique in that sense. I feel close to her when I'm here, but also I feel that life isn't fair. Why should my family have to go through that?

I will always come back to Grenada, for as long as is humanly possible. I can always get assistance in getting on and off the plane from the airline, if I need to! Although I'm not yet at that stage, I hasten to add.

At this point, I wish to pay tribute to my mother for having the strength to open up a life of opportunity. And I also pay tribute to my family. I'm so wonderfully blessed to have them in my life. I am now resident in Spain and live permanently in the town of Calpe which is in the province of Alicante. Zoe and the grandchildren also live in Calpe, so we see each other all the time. With Jason and his family living in Slovenia it gives me the opportunity to travel there to visit them which is a real pleasure. Knowing I have them around me is a joy and has sustained me. That's Cecily's legacy. I'm so proud of my two children for making new lives in Spain and Slovenia.

And finally, a big thank you to everyone who joined me on this wonderful journey – whether you've been part of my life in some way, or simply by reading this book.

God bless you all.

CHRIS LEPKOWSKI
The Third Degree, Ghost Writer

Chris Lepkowski is an experienced sports journalist, with more than 25 years of experience working for a host of national and local media titles. This is his third book, following In Pastures Green and From Buzaglo to Balis.

Chris is currently the course director for sports journalism at Birmingham City University, while contributing to the BBC, The Blizzard, These Football Times and FourFourTwo, taking a particular interest in football's complex relationship with the media.

Despite having a face more suited to radio, and a voice more suited to written media, Chris continues to podcast on a regular basis.

Something that didn't happen too often - me scoring a goal. Coventry City were the victims in this 1979 FA Cup game.

My daughter Zoe and I at the unveiling of the Celebration Statue in West Bromwich, May 2019

One of the best days of my life. June 15, 1974. The day Cecily said "I do".

Cecily and I in 1972. Sadly, I no longer have that shirt...

Zoe, Cecily and Jason join me on the proud day I received my MBE in 2001.

Confirmation of my MBE in November 2000. I initially thought somebody was winding me up.

My mum with her husband Desmond Moore.

Can you feel the love tonight? Elton John joins my brother Godfrey and I for a quick snap.

My mum and her husband Desmond, alongside Cecily's Aunt Maysie and dad Cecil Kenrick Sylvester on our wedding day.

Pele and I stand proudly beside PFA Young Player of the Year Robbie Fowler and Les Ferdinand, the PFA Player of the Year, 1996.

Enjoying holiday time with Zoe and Jason on Grenada's Grand Anse beach, 1987.

We've got the style: Cecily and I in our young and carefree days, back in 1972.

On your marks, get set... Jason joins me for a run during my ultimate unsuccessful rehab from a serious knee injury in 1983.

Young Guns: Neil Freeman, Jimmy de Garis, Terry Burton and Graham Horn join me following an Arsenal training session.

Monday the League championship . . . Wednesday the F A Youth Cup . . . tomorrow the F A Cup?

Cup winners: Myself, Jim De Garis and Terry Burton celebrate the 1971 FA Youth Cup win. And, yes, the senior team won the FA Cup the following day....

"I'm going to marry that girl." And I did. Cecily was very much my better half in every way.

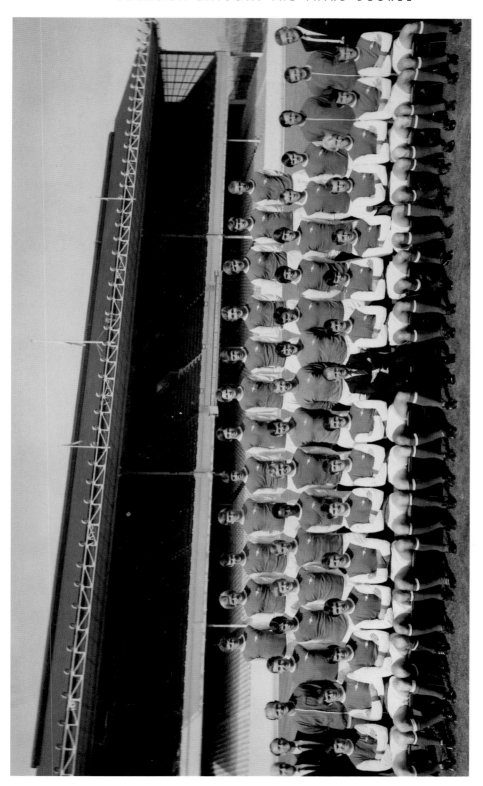

The calm before the storm. The Arsenal first team and youth side line up for the annual photo-shoot in summer 1969. Two years later we won the League and FA Cup double, along with the FA Youth Cup

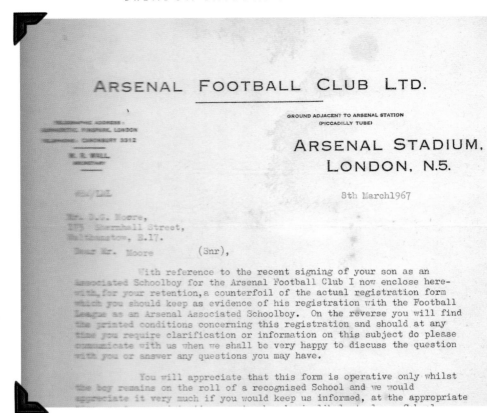

Signing for Arsenal: The confirmation letter that changed my life.

Winners. From left-to-right: Peter Simpson, John Woodward, myself, Bobby Harding, Charlie George and Jackie Carmichael.

If it's any consolation: Me, in action against Wolves in the 1973 FA Cup third-place play-off at Highbury. We lost 3-1 and only 21,000 bothered to turn up. The play-off match was scrapped two years later.

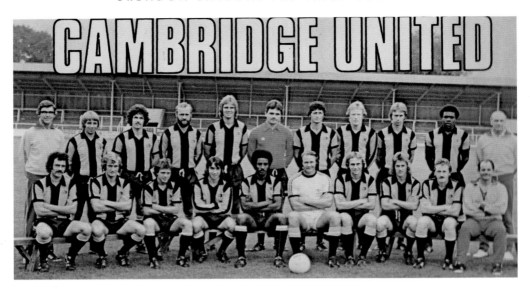

Cambridge United, summer 1977. Within a few months both Ron Atkinson and I would be leaving for West Bromwich Albion.

European nights: A memorable UEFA Cup night in Valencia during the 1978/79 season. Our inexperience of continental club football was to cost us in the quarter-finals against Red Star Belgrade.

Daily Express — January 25 1979

★★★

INTRODUCING A NEW ENGLAND TEAM

ALAN THOMPSON reveals plans for a match which will capture the imagination of every football fan in the country . . . an all-white team against an all-black team.

True to form, the idea came from West Bromwich whose enterprising and imaginative play has swept them to the top of Division One.

SOCCER'S ALL BLACKS

By Alan Thompson

STAND by to welcome an exciting new Soccer team—the England All Blacks.

They are being lined up to play against the white members of West Brom's League leaders —plus three white guests—in the most intriguing match of the season.

The match, brain-child of Albion manager Ron Atkinson, will be for long-serving Len Cantello's testimonial on a date to be fixed.

The possibilities are endless. I confess that when I first heard of this suggestion I expressed concern over the possibility of creating further race relations problems. But the deeper I dug into the idea the more exciting it became.

Atkinson told me: "Laurie Cunningham and Cyrille Regis are tremendously enthusiastic about it—they've even picked their team."

Belly-laugh

And the bulky, muscular frame of Regis quivers like jelly as he belly-laughs: "We have a ready-made manager. Enoch would be my choice."

The Cunningham-Regis partnership has come up with a team strong enough to test any in the First Division.

The line-up : RICHARDSON (Q.P.R.); ANDERSON (Nottingham Forest), BERRY (Wolves), HAZELL (Wolves), BATSON (West Brom); HILL (Luton), HILAIRE (Crystal Palace), CROOKS (Stoke City); CUNNINGHAM (West Brom), REGIS (West Brom), THOMPSON (Coventry City).

There are other black players good enough for inclusion if they had England qualifications—for example, Jamaican-born Luther Blissett (Watford) and Nigerian-born John Chiedozie (Orient).

And but for a shortage of goalkeepers they could almost pick two teams from men like Roger Palmer (Manchester City), "Pedro" Richards (Notts County), Joe Cooke (Peterborough), Bobby Fisher (Orient).

I recently received some crank letters from National Frontists after referring to

And my choice for manager would be Enoch, jokes selector Cyrille

Cyrille Regis . . . enthusia[stic]

Forest International Viv Anderson as a first-generation Englishman—but that's what he is. And so are the other members of the England All Blacks.

Furthermore, they are increasingly adding a new and exciting dimension to both the League and international structure.

It is my conviction that sport should know no boundaries and I have never met finer men than the late Sir Learie Constantine, Sir Garfield Sobers or Muhammad Ali.

The West Brom match promises to be as exciting as it is revolutionary.

Indeed, I would like to see the idea taken further.

Why not an "England All Blacks" against the present England national team? That would be a match to set the pulse rate soaring.

DEREK RICHARDSON

VIV ANDERSON

GEORGE BERRY

BOB HAZELL

BRENDAN BATSON

RICKY HILL

VINCE HILAIRE

GARTH C[...]

LAURIE CU[...]

Blacks versus Whites: Imagine that now? It became a reality in 1979, for Len Cantello's testimonial. Unfortunately, Enoch Powell was unavailable to take charge of our side...

58 THE VOICE June 9, 1987

SPORT

BRENDON'S STILL REACHING FOR A GOAL

Martin Bashir on an ex-footballer aiming to cross the great divide

Brendon getting involved during his playing days.

"Hello Terry, how are things ... So you've got problems with your wages over the summer ... OK ... I'll see you tomorrow, before the appeal, and we can talk about it then ... OK? ... See you tomorrow, then".

Another player, another problem and Brendon Batson is behaving impeccably as Assistant Secretary of the Professional Footballers' Association (PFA). His job is one of mediation, and his skills of diplomacy are always in evidence; even when interviewed.

It is surprising, perhaps, that a footballer who twice played under Ron Atkinson, should appear so subtle and diplomatic. But skills of negotiation did not come easily to Batson. After two years at Arsenal, and ten appearances in the first team, this Grenadian born full-back decided that he wanted to be the No 1 at No 2.

"I wanted to play in someone's first team, but I was behind Pat Rice and Peter Storey at the Arsenal. Bertie Mee said I was being rash and impatient, but I was simply ambitious and wanted to get on".

So although Cambridge United were relegated to the sediment of the Football League in 1976, Batson was bought for £8,000 and fulfilled his ambition for first team (if fourth division) football. Ron Atkinson arrived after ten games and the move north of London began to make sense.

"When Ron arrived, we just knew that the club would go places. He was confident, and it was a tremendous combination. We went 22 games unbeaten, and in 1977 were promoted to the third division".

But the following year, the Batson-Atkinson rapport went further north, when both ended up at West Bromwich Albion, in 1978. It was here, in the soccer-mad Midlands, that Batson's career enjoyed its heyday. He established himself as a first division defender and won five England 'B' caps.

"The the age of 26," said Brendon, "I had risen from the fourth division to a high standard of football. We had an exciting side with Laurie Cunningham, Cyrille Regis, Bryan Robson and Remi Moses. It was a joy to play in that side".

But joy came to an end, when he was forced to undergo a second cartilage operation in October, 1982. It was the same right knee which had been operated upon when Batson was a 17 year old at Highbury.

"The injury caught up with me," he explained, "and it soon became obvious that I'd never be able to play at that level again. Football was all I had known, and my whole working life had been spent within the game".

Football had been dealt a double blow. Whilst Batson's knee was certified in Birmingham, Steve Coppell, of Manchester United and England, was hearing the terminal case against his footballing career. Both were forced to retire. And both found themselves at the PFA. After absorbing the shock of early retirement, Coppell was made chairman of the PFA. But Batson had other ideas.

"As soon as I knew that I'd never be able to play again, I wanted to go into management. Although I was young (31), I just hoped that an opportunity might arise. It had always been my intention, as I got older, to leave West Brom and join a club in a lower division, as player-manager. However, the injury stopped that, so I applied for management jobs all over the place".

But no opportunity arose. He managed one interview, back at Cambridge United, but was rejected on the grounds of inexperience. Having already acquired his full Coaching Badge at Lilleshall, Gordon Taylor invited Batson to assist him in the work of the PFA. It was a move further north, to Manchester, but one which the Assistant Secretary acknowledges as extremely valuable, and relevant to his greatest ambition.

"For the past three years I've been learning all about the administrative side of football. Working alongside Gordon Taylor is excellent, because he is so good at his job. But the ambition to be a manager is still burning brightly within me. That is still what I want to do".

Without wishing to upset his plans, Batson ducks away from questions about the rumoured disputes with Ron Atkinson, and avoids the suggestion that there is no black manager in the football league, and never will be. He prefers to remain silent on such issues. "I don't want to be renowned as one obsessed with racism or anything. I want a chance in football management".

Until that chance arises, Brendon Batson will remain the polite diplomat that he has become, aiming to win over the football prejudice which bars him from his most coveted position. He deserves his chance.

"The ambition to be a manager is still burning brightly within me. That is still what I want to do."

BREAKING NEW GROUND: *Brendon at work.*

By Martin Bashir

Part of the Union: During my early days with the Professional Footballers' Association - an organisation I was proud to serve for the best part of 20 years.

Making history: Arsenal's first-ever black player.

The treble: Bob Wilson, John Radford, myself and Frank McLintock join Arsenal team-mates on the top deck of the open-top bus tour following our League, FA Cup and FA Youth Cup successes of 1970/71.

The first chapter: Peter Storrie watches on as I enjoy my early days as an Arsenal first-team player.